THE STRUCTURES OF LAW AND LITERATURE

The Structures of Law and Literature

Duty, Justice, and Evil in the Cultural Imagination

JEFFREY MILLER

McGill-Queen's University Press
Montreal & Kingston • London • Ithaca

ISBN 978-0-7735-4162-7 (cloth)
ISBN 978-0-7735-4163-4 (paper)
ISBN 978-0-7735-8898-1 (EPDF)
ISBN 978-0-7735-8899-8 (EPUB)

Legal deposit second quarter 2013
Bibliothèque nationale du Québec

Printed in Canada on acid-free paper that is 100% ancient forest free (100% post-consumer recycled), processed chlorine free.

This book has been published with the help of a grant from the Canadian Federation for the Humanities and Social Sciences, through the Awards to Scholarly Publications Program, using funds provided by the Social Sciences and Humanities Research Council of Canada.

McGill-Queen's University Press acknowledges the support of the Canada Council for the Arts for our publishing program. We also acknowledge the financial support of the Government of Canada through the Canada Book Fund for our publishing activities.

Library and Archives Canada Cataloguing in Publication

Miller, Jeffrey, 1950–
    The structures of law and literature : duty, justice, and evil in the cultural imagination / Jeffrey Miller.

Includes bibliographical references and index.
ISBN 978-0-7735-4162-7 (bound).–ISBN 978-0-7735-4163-4 (pbk.)
ISBN 978-0-7735-8898-1 (PDF).–ISBN 978-0-7735-8899-8 (EPUB)

    1. Law and literature. 2. Law in literature. 3. Legal literature –
History. 4. Sociological jurisprudence. I. Title.

PN56.L33M55 2013   809'.933554   C2013-900058-5

This book was typeset by True to Type in 10.5/13 Sabon

For Joan Fotherghill,
former secretary at the St. George Graduate Residence,
who queue-jumped the author into Suite B310 in September, 1973,
just as I had resolved to leave Toronto and Canada for good,
about a week into my graduate English studies
at the city's university.

Contents

Acknowledgments

This book has been published with the help of a grant from the Canadian Federation for the Humanities and Social Sciences, through the Awards to Scholarly Publication Program, using funds provided by the Social Sciences and Humanities Research Council of Canada. I am gratified and deeply grateful for their support.

The work owes much of its creative impetus to Ian Holloway and Michael Lynk, formerly dean and associate dean, respectively, of the law faculty at the University of Western Ontario, for their early and generous interest in my idiosyncratic approach to the field of law and humanities. Their invitation to teach a course on law and literature finally impelled me to organize my disparate thoughts on the subject and set them out in a systematic way.

Philip Cercone, of McGill-Queen's University Press, Daniel Quinlan of the University of Toronto Press, and my wife Phyllis Miller have been unfailingly supportive, patiently faithful to the project, while Professors Julie Desrosiers (Laval Law) and Peter Goodrich (Cardozo Law School) – along with the board at *Law and Literature*, the journal Peter edits – have been more than encouraging regarding the discussions of Marcel Aymé and the Sirens. Thanks are due, as well, to Gary Watt and Paul Raffield (University of Warwick) for their comments on my comparisons of sin and crime (at the conceptual stage of this book), and to Professors Goodrich, Watt, James Boyd-White (Michigan), Guyora Binder (SUNY Law), and Ian Ward (Newcastle) for their correspondence with me about teaching law and literature, or law and humanities, at their own faculties.

Cynthia Ozick has been an inspiration throughout my reading and writing career. As usual, she was generous, warm, and witty in answering my questions about Ruth Puttermesser in Paradise, as well as in raising interesting quibbles about the central paradigm in the methodology here proposed.

The "cases in point" (Chapter Six) treating Marcel Aymé and what the Sirens sang appeared, in somewhat different forms, in the autumn 2012 editions of *Cahiers de droit* and *Law and Literature*, respectively. Small parts of some of the commentary about Moses and Job appeared, in much different forms, in *The Lawyers Weekly*, and I thank my editors there for publishing material that is not "trade talk" of the limited moment and geography. Some of the discussion about "French fries are meat" in Chapter Five appears, in a different form, in my *Naked Promises* (Random House, 1991), now out of print. In Chapter Five's addendum, regarding "judicial philology," I include (more soberly, perhaps) some examples I first covered in my *Where There's Life, There's Lawsuits* (ECW Press, 2003), and I originally wrote about the "parking lot is a bawdy house case" in *Ardor in the Court: Sex and the Law* (ECW, 2002) as well as in the aforementioned *Naked Promises*.

Working with managing editor Ryan Van Huijstee, the editorial, production, and marketing professionals at McGill-Queen's have proved to be refreshingly attentive and conscientious. Joan Harcourt's deft, light hand has made this a better book, while Katie Heffring, Jacqueline Davis, and Filomena Falocco have been indispensible in letting the world know about it.

It can sound smarmy to thank one's students (I always think, when somebody else does it), but it is nonetheless true that – sometimes inadvertently – they can get you to look at certain nooks and crannies of what you're proposing in a different light. I sincerely hope my students at Western Law, present and past, will not take that as a backhanded compliment. Working with them, or at least for them, has driven everything I say here. And those who take my course in the spirit it's intended inhabit a treasured place in my affections.

Clearly my biggest, and certainly the most evident, intellectual debt, here and regarding the humanities generally, is to H. Northrop Frye. As a callow "Amurrican" graduate student at the University of Toronto in 1973, I enrolled in Frye's course in literary symbolism. This was a breathtaking bit of ingenuous fortune, during a year that altogether changed my life and renovated my way of thinking. (It was also at U of T that I met my wife, not to mention the English literary critic and poet William Empson. Through his work and by correspondence, Empson became another inadvertent mentor as to reading and writing, and figures here and there in these pages. In concert with the writings and teaching of Professor Frye, his criticism remains the best evidence that the profoundest thoughts are expressed plainly, and by extension that we are most high-falutin' when we have nothing much to say.) Frye was one of the great wit-geniuses in the history of ideas, and also a dedicated, plain-speaking, and compassionate teacher. His *Anatomy of Criticism* stands with the central works of Freud, Jung, Lévi-Strauss, and J.G. Fraser as twentieth-century monuments in the history of ideas.

THE STRUCTURES OF LAW AND LITERATURE

And there's a curious symbolic contrast between the fact that the successful and prosperous empires of Egypt and Babylon and Assyria produced the great temples, whereas the Israelites, who were never lucky at the game of empire, produced a book. To the people who wanted the kind of success that Assyria, Persia, and Babylon had, production of a book must have seemed a good deal like a booby prize. But if you think of the relative durability of a book and a monument, you'll see that the facts are very different.

Northrop Frye, in Northrop Frye and Jay Macpherson,
*Biblical and Classical Myths: The Mythological Framework
of Western Culture*, 2004, 149.

I

First Principles and Controversies: Is Law and Literature More Than a Distraction for Bored Law Professors?

I had the core idea for this book thirty-two years ago when I was a first-year law student obliged to write a paper for a jurisprudence course. I had come to law a few years after graduate study with Northrop Frye, who had convinced me (awed me, more exactly) that it was possible to understand literature in a systematic way – as cultural narrative – while accepting, ecumenically, that the student could supplement this with all sorts of other analytical approaches to the enterprise. In fact, it became obvious that the other methods of literary analysis in many ways assumed this "anatomy of literature" without necessarily accepting it – in some cases even rejecting it violently for reasons that now strike me as rooted more in territorial anxiety than analytical rigour. As a law student it seemed to me that, although "law and literature" was not a discipline in itself then, the two disciplines were tied culturally, inextricably. It seemed fundamental, and not just because I had to produce a paper for my grade, that the notions informing law and justice in western culture share patterns and assumptions that inform every other way we express ourselves culturally.

As I have written elsewhere, from the first day of first year I was ignoring my property law instructor's advice not to read the cases "as though they're crime novels, to see how they come out at the end." To me, it was all about the human drama. The legal principles were secondary, while the cases were novelistic, carefully shaped narratives (those shapes sometimes clashing depending on which judge told the story, a state of affairs that paralleled Faulknerian narrative), cutting out the mundane and getting down to the crises that really show what we're made of. And so for Jurisprudence I wrote a paper called "Case

Law as Narrative," in which I described the basic scheme I outline in the next chapter of this book. It was thin and unfledged at the time; it looked only at law AS literature, as it hadn't yet occurred to me that the same principles applied, vigorously, to law IN literature. The opportunity for fleshing and feathering came twenty-eight years later, when Ian Holloway, then dean of law at the University of Western Ontario, asked if I'd like to teach a course in his faculty on law and literature.

I enthusiastically said yes, though my thinking about the subject hadn't progressed much in the years between law school and Dean Holloway's invitation. I had been reading the law-and-literature critics, all right, avidly seeking an inter-disciplinary connection that I couldn't find outside law AS literature. The law-in-literature connections seemed ephemeral, coincidental, strained; I found myself agreeing with Judge Posner – anxiously, given that I don't agree with him on much else – that the two disciplines didn't have a great deal to say to each other.[1] Putting together a syllabus, I felt a bit of a fraud, thinking I would spend the term confessing to students duped into signing up that the course was basically a sham because there was no necessary connection between the two disciplines in the course title. Then I pulled out my old paper, with a few notes to file made after I'd actually become a lawyer, and felt surprised, then thrilled, that though my ideas in 1980 were sketchy, they still seemed analytically sound, and altogether applicable to the entire law-and-lit project. I felt they solved something.

Whether this was delusional is for the community of my readers to decide – that cohort so beloved of law-and-literature critics these days, who generally don't seem to have a lot of time for the archetypal approach I propose here. Then again, it seems likely that many of these critics, particularly the younger ones, just don't know much about it. If there's no buzz about it, it must be irrelevant; if it's "old," it must be old hat. But of course no one would say that about the theory of relativity or Darwin. And I imagine that what has always made some critics nervous or dismissive about myth criticism is its ambition to be scientific, particularly where it attempts to present a theory of narrative as schematic and more or less timeless, such that we can apply patterns and imagery from the Bible and classical mythology to John Updike or Superman comics or the latest 3-D sci-fi movie. The nay-sayers seem anxious that, insofar as this method relates to those of structural anthropology, group psychology, and psychoanalysis (particularly theories of the collective unconscious), it somehow destroys the variable of individual expression – presumably their own more than the expression of the authors studied. It is so simple in design, they seem to believe (confounding simple with simplistic), that it will make them redundant as scholars. Perish the thought!

While it is true that Northrop Frye in particular rejects originality as unattainable by the poet,[2] he of course embraces the individualized expression that "trademarks" a Shakespeare versus a Milton versus a G.B. Shaw. Presumably the nay-sayers would accept without question my high-school music teacher's observation that, given the physical limitations of the twelve-tone scale, "there are no new tunes, just new ways of expressing them." Why, then, is it so hard to accept that other persistent patterns related to the natural world pervade how we make sense of life (or at least did so before we hid from that world in air-conditioned homes, offices, and vehicles), and that they found the stories we tell ourselves about ourselves as a group, in the western world but also as *Homo sapiens*?

Like everything else, literary criticism is faddish, with new generations of scholars rejecting perfectly good, and thereby shopworn, tools so as to make their mark, show their own "originality" of thought, even if in the last fifty years that thought has depended heavily on the sibylline (priestly?) pronouncements – by now rather shopworn themselves – of four or five professional obscurantists in France.[3] And of course a lot of what has always defined the academy is disputatious ego – which description I mean, in all sincerity, in a non-disputatious, ecumenically embracing manner!

Again, the larger point, which Frye makes persistently in *Anatomy of Criticism*, is that archetypal criticism does not contemplate invalidating other critical approaches. (Here, particularly, the nay-sayers' defensiveness persistently surprises and dismays me.) It simply means to describe narrative impulses and structures, the anthropology or physiology, if you will, of literature, at least from the occidental point of view, but often universally. This anthropology does not oust the critic's other investigative tools, be they structuralist, deconstructionist, semiotic, reader response, narratologist, post-colonial or what-not. As in other human endeavour, there is, instead, cross-pollination, one hopes, cooperative enterprise that helps us dig and unearth better than we might have done with just one tool. For that reason, I tell my students that the sort of archetypal approach that I propose here is an umbrella, really, more than it is foundational. But "Umbrellas of Law and Literature" seemed a better title for an art installation than for a book of literary criticism.

Speaking of which, the book's title gave me as much trouble as anything in it. I played with "Foundations of Law and Literature" before rejecting it as both inexact and arrogant. "Structures of...," without the definite article, would have had the advantage of mimicking Frye's *Anatomy of*, but I've added the empyrean "The" not to signify that I describe the only structures possible (I assume that Frye used no definite article for a similar, modest reason – that he was proposing *an* anatomy*), but only because "The Structures of..." just sounds better (less arty, if somewhat more arrogant) than "Structures of ..." Though "Anatomy of.." would have acknowledged my debt to Frye, I felt it was equally important to signal that this work is a distinct undertaking, specific to literature's legal tributary, that cherry-picks from Frye's theory and frequently expands on it or departs widely from it where doing so seems appropriate.[4] In any event, no doubt my reading of Frye is too idiosyncratic, and maybe even wrong-headed, to constitute anything like an addendum. The method proposed is, for better or worse, original at least in the Fryegian sense of idiosyncracy.

In other words, the method here comes from an ecumenical impulse. I don't doubt that a given text is different every time it is read, or that there is a "community of meaning" independent of authorial intention, or that "meaning," whatever it means, is idiosyncratic, fickle, culturally biased. Indeed, I'm resolutely certain of this last characteristic – that every reader brings to the text shared cultural, psychological, and sociological tendencies that provide the infrastructure to any interpretation. This book is about such points of departure, built on archetypes and symbology that form the cultural basis of western society. Otherwise, dialogue itself is immaterial. In what we have come to call the global village, this cultural basis is evolving, of course, but the basic structures inform that evolution. They might be old hat, but, really, that's the point.

*   *   *

---

*Only after this book was in editing did I recall that Frye's original title for *Anatomy* was *Structural Poetics: Four Essays*. His publisher, Princeton University Press, was worried that "poetics" would mislead potential readers into thinking that the book was about poetic form and that "essays" would suggest the work was not a coherent whole. So Frye dispensed holus bolus with the title. See John Ayre's *Northrop Frye: A Biography* (Toronto: Random House, 1989), 252–3.

Though having lost their early exuberance and law-and-literature studies are no longer called a movement, the enterprise struggles on, never mind that many of those teaching and writing in it long since decided that it doesn't exist – that its "inter-disciplinarity" is impossible or at best mythic (which is why I just used the word "enterprise" instead of discipline, which I might have used instead of movement).[5] As I've mentioned, I agreed with such nay-sayers for a long time, while at least a little bitter that this imaginary world afforded them impressive university appointments and a very congenial lifestyle. Those seemed pretty concrete to me. But I couldn't help noticing that a great deal of the writing, at least during the 1980s and '90s, was adversarial, falling into the academic pattern of building a career on squabbling, fleshing out the publications section of one's résumé not on one's ideas, but on deriding those of others.[6] The objective reader had to think that the field was dominated by law professors with barrister envy, to put it euphemistically. (I am aware that in saying this, I engage in what I pretend to abjure, and there are other parts of this book that are adversarial more directly. Reactive response is an occupational hazard; the trick is limiting it.) There was something uncomfortably Oedipal about it, and also redolent of the nastiness of litigation practice. To prove they could go one better, some writers crammed their essays with jargon and migraine-inducing syntax that made barristers' legalese sound like pillow talk. Worse, and maybe sometimes causing this defensiveness, law-and-literature courses frequently have been offered by those who apparently like to take a break from law with a good novel, but who have little or no training in literary theory. I asked several law-professor friends about this, before I taught at a law faculty myself, and depending upon how well the professor knew me, he either gawked or squinted at me like I'd gone simple. But each replied, "Well, yeah, but if they've got tenure, they can teach whatever they want. That's how it works."[7]

If you have little or no academic experience in literary studies, you are going to miss the central fact that, without some sort of general theory showing a necessary connection between law and literature culturally, the connection is always strained if not meaningless. The fact that a certain literature might centre on a crime or a trial or racism or lawyers no more qualifies it for inter-disciplinary study than the fact that books with doctors and sick people in them constitutes a distinct discipline of medicine and literature. By such reasoning, the fact that Gregor Samsa wakes up one morning to find himself an insect means we should feature "The Metamorphosis" on the syllabus for Entomology and Literature. Then again, just as all non-legal writing is not narrative, and therefore not fruitful for analysis as imaginative expression, neither is all legal writing of literary interest. As purely pragmatic, statutes, for example, are of anthropological and maybe some rhetorical interest, but case law provides more fertile digging for the law-and-literature scholar.

Then too, without any organizing principle as to inter-disciplinarity, you will not understand that law in and law as literature are distinct, all right, but only as to category. As I try to show here, each should attract the same basic method of analysis. Related to this, I think we must remember that while law and literature might comprise a sort of jurisprudence (as Richard Weisberg proposes),[8] it must keep its own focus. The approach discussed here, for example, concentrates on justice in the philosophical and social contexts of reasonableness and duty. We are not concerned with reasonableness and duty as legal principles in themselves, but their place in the imaginative universe of law – the human narrative we call law.

Even some law professors with PhDs in English seem to forget that political analysis is not by itself literary criticism. Yes, there are Marxist literary criticism, feminist literary criticism, post-colonialism, etc., but if we are even just playing at inter-disciplinarity, as literary critics we cannot focus on plot and theme to the exclusion of language and metaphor, philology and syntax. Otherwise, we should stick to treatises and propaganda.

Harvard University Press recently published Oscar Wilde's earliest manuscript for *The Picture of Dorian Gray*. The publication led Alex Ross to speculate in *The New Yorker* about Wilde's legacy in a legal ethos of increasing individual rights:

> In many major cities, at least, gays and lesbians no longer seem to
> need a safe place in the form of a store [here, the closed Oscar
> Wilde Memorial Bookshop in New York City]. And they no
> longer seem to need the tragi-comic Oscar; the young gays of
> today can revel in the wit and wisdom of [television actor] Neil
> Patrick Harris. All of which leaves Wilde in an interesting limbo.
> What will he mean in a perhaps not too distant time when homo-
> sexuality has ceased to be a conversation stopper?[9]

This is a legitimate question for law-and-literature studies. But if the answer is really to advance our understanding, it must begin at the structural level, encompassing our cultural development from canon-moral law and legalism to equity and so on to our current enthusiasm for individual rights, sometimes over those of the community. It must see that the increasing liberality toward sexual matters, and the expanding influence of popular culture, are part of a broader trend to multiculturalism amid an aesthetic preference for empiricism and irony. It must consider whether such developments are inevitable in human history, or at least that they are in the nature of cultural cycles. Delineating such structures and trends is what I seek to do in the pages that follow.

Indeed, if we are going to bring the politics of law and law faculties into the mix – as with, say, the law-and-economics crowd and the critical-legal theorists – where are the live brown girls, so to say? I have little patience with the moral relativists who insist that Donne or Milton or Orwell have had his day, or that we should fault Shakespeare for, as one critic memorably put it, ignoring the suffering of oppressed Guatemalan women. If I want to be educated about jazz, I must listen to Louis Armstrong, Duke Ellington, and Thelonious Monk, even if I was attracted to the genre by Ornette Coleman, Don Ellis, and Rahsaan Roland Kirk. If I want to understand literature in English, I have to make my way through the work of a lot of dead white guys from "ethnocentric, patriarchal societies." It is a matter of history and of context, not politics. But even where it purports to move beyond the "dead white guys canon" (*Bleak House, The Trial, Billy Budd, Crime and Punishment* ...), the "law-and-literature movement" too often fails to consider contemporary writing. In other words, even those who profess a more political approach do not always practise it. To remain vibrant, not to mention valid, the discipline must be more catholic and open-minded.

To get more directly to the point, it seems to me that if law and literature have anything to say to one another directly, it is through discourse whose focus is, first, law as an anthropological construct reflecting culture, including imaginative culture; axiomatically, law as narrative, or the vehicle of this cultural expression; and finally, justice in human society as the narrative's core subject. From this point of view, nearly all of literature worthy of the name has legal, or jurisprudential, relevance. The law-and-literature scholar studies law as an imaginative quest to understand the chasm between law and justice, and of course certain works lend themselves more readily than others to this task. The discipline's raison d'être is explaining the cultural basis and operation – the human meaning – of justice systems.

Pedagogically this is important insofar as you can go through law school, licensing courses, clerkships, and even an entire career at the bar without having considered what justice actually is. This was true when I went to law school and it is true today, principally because law schools are more than ever trade schools instead of professional schools. In an age of holistic physicians and even accountants, we remain very practical, task-oriented, slow to consider the whole law student, a citizen and a thinking, feeling being who happens to be a lawyer. We mostly ignore that in the real, post-law-school world, our "fallen world," there is always a gap, sometimes huge, sometimes smaller, between law and justice – that the arts, and particularly literature, reunite law and justice, demonstrating the human urge to do, a sort of nostalgia for lost paradise.

The discipline's most thoroughgoing and productive "way in" is anthropological or mythopoetical, and – to the extent that it involves anthropology and mythopoesy – psychological (whether that entails psychoanalytic theory, behaviourism, physiological psychology, etc.). When approaching a text, then, the student should always consider, What really is the intersection here with law? The answer must of necessity be a matter of "humanities," of anthropological linkage. But that is never specific enough. The fact that the setting of *Bleak House* is interminable estate litigation, or that John Updike's Maples stories depict the breakdown of a marriage, does not mean these works are wholly or even largely relevant to the discipline. It is a matter of degree. To read *Bleak House* because its backdrop is estate litigation stays above the surface of law and literature; it doesn't even skim it. What is more relevant, and a better starting point, is that all of Dickens concerns the gap between law and justice, and between law and morality, *in a fallen world, where justice is never perfect and always relative, a matter of nostalgia*. To read *Bleak House* as an instance of this is a good start.

In Francine Prose's *Blue Angel* we find many intersections between law and life, but some of them lead to cul-de-sacs when we consider our "destination," human rights claims in the university environment. For example, a classroom discussion in the novel about appropriation of voice (a white girl writes about the life of an Hispanic girl) has no interest from a law-and-literature view except insofar as it is a byway off the broader road of contemporary human rights claims – or clamour – (including claims of power imbalance) and their effects on free expression, education, and sexual relationships between consenting adults. Unless one's interest is more political than literary, the voice-appropriation discussion is a matter of undertone. Similarly, for our purposes here, probably the only really germane Maples story is "Here Come the Maples," which concerns itself with the subjective heart-break of divorce *set against* the cold objectivity of legal language and process: "Now come Richard F. and Joan R. Maple," its first paragraph quotes, from the spouses' amicably drafted joint affidavit, "and swear under the penalties of perjury that an irretrievable breakdown of the marriage exists." The student of law and literature finds here the inter-section of individual experience with the formalities of culture, a jour-ney from Romance to division of net family assets. Updike does every-thing but shout that he is writing a parody of the Adam and Eve narrative. The soon-to-be ex-wife sums this up brilliantly, and heart-breakingly, when she observes that the relevant phrase should be "there go the Maples." In the secularized law court, evidence of the ways of the heart is admissible only to the extent that it is relevant to bloodless rule and principle. Cain might strike Abel or commit adul-tery in the heat of passion, but by the time the matter gets to court it is mere happenstance, drained of emotion. Cain "assaulted" his broth-er or broke a solemn agreement of fidelity only if legal principle says he did. And to the extent that the matter is reduced to a written judg-ment, entering the realm of case law *as* literature, the document becomes the phenomenon. It is what the event represents, immutably, and lawyers and students will depend on that. Event has become nar-rative, without which it would be meaningless gossip.

In one sense this is merely to restate the truism that our legal system, like other aspects of our culture, is founded in the "Judaeo-Christian ethic," evolving though it might be with increasing multiculturalism. As in other forms of narrative, the world-view reflected in our case law is founded in sacred and myth literature. This is the analytic basis for everything else in this book.

The very fact that we can say, foundationally, that "law is part of our imaginative culture" means this is the main intersection, the round-about. Views of justice comprise the feeder roads in and out of that roundabout. The byways in and out of these primary roads are many, of course, and can include rhetoric, ambiguity, semiotics, and other theories of language as well as psychoanalysis, political theory, and so on. That is, I feel compelled to repeat that, while I view a reworked

"Fryegian" critical methodology as the most productive in revealing the anatomy of law and literature, it would be foolhardy to do so to the exclusion of other schools of literary theory. As any good barrister will tell you (John Mortimer's Rumpole of the Bailey, say, or Sarah Caudwell's Basil Ptarmigan), you use what works. But too often scholarship in the field goes merrily off down one of these byways only to lose its way, precisely because it has failed to consult the map – to ask itself that first basic question: Not "Where down this road can I cleverly apply literary or political theory?" but "What is the real intersection with legal discourse?"

Unlike literature, law is meant primarily to be concrete and practical, to serve a material purpose and to be practised as part of human existence if not experience. Literature is perhaps "practised" by writers, and as a writer I would like to think it has practical (if not immediately concrete) effect – that, among other things, it comforts, provokes, advocates, and broadens our minds by allowing us to live vicariously what we would not otherwise experience, and thereby perhaps helps us to accept the validity of what others live. But literature would exist (at least orally) without writers. People would otherwise express themselves (and have done so) imaginatively, looking for meaning in metaphor. Positive law in modern, so-called developed societies does not exist without practising lawyers or at least lawmakers. Marrying literature to law does not make either more practical, or either more "cultural."[10]

Insofar as "law and literature" primarily concerns justice, it does so presuming or questing for civil – or civilized – order. In this sense, even Kafka's *The Trial* is quest literature: as a citizen of a more or less democratic state, Joseph K is entitled to assume government by rule of law. Within the bounds of this government, he expects justice. When the rule of law becomes indiscernible, no amount of argument will tilt the scales of justice to the defendant's side. Its mechanical governor, reasonableness, breaks down, and leaves the citizen baffled as to his legal duty. On the more bluntly comic side, we have Don Quixote, a reasonable man who looks unreasonable because he believes in an ideal world of perfect justice, formalized as chivalry and courtesy. Like most literary fools, he is a utopian.

The reader will note that, as with my teaching, I have used mostly novels in this analysis. I do this not because other literary genres are less accessible to the method, but because today novels are the predominant literary form, having largely displaced poetry and drama as our favourite fictions. Whether film or some other media will displace the novel remains to be seen, given that such other media work in the same universe as literature, albeit sometimes with different tropes.

Finally I am not concerned here with what is sometimes called the law OF literature – is *Lady Chatterley's Lover* legally obscene, what are the copyright implications of revised versions of *Ulysses*,[11] is Janet Malcolm's *In the Freud Archives* defamatory (never mind how interesting that discussion becomes in light of her later *The Journalist and the Murderer*)? These (it seems to me) are properly the province of media, constitutional, criminal, or intellectual property law – or, in the law-and-humanities context, sociology, history, and politics; the literary aspects are primarily a matter of rhetoric. Consider this, from David Markson's *Reader's Block*:

> When W.H. Auden died, his future royalties were left to Chester Kallman. When Kallman died only sixteen months later, they went to the latter's father, a dentist.
> Then the dentist died and everything went to his second wife.

The irony here is a matter of succession law. The literary context is incidental, never mind that it might raise an interesting discussion about irony. Sometimes the coincidence of the two disciplines is heavier. One could argue persuasively, for example, that whether a certain age considers a work criminally obscene, seditious, or blasphemous (as some did, all at once, with *Dorian Gray*) involves inextricable connections between law and literature. Certainly such questions engage the cultural interplay of law and justice in a literary context. But my premise here is that alleged criminal publication and so on are studied more fruitfully at the frontier of law and morals than at the intersection of law and literature, which as its own discipline must have a deeper, persistent cultural context – one that transcends politics and social trends.

Towards a Typology, Iconography, and Symbology of Law and Literature

I. BASIC STRUCTURE: MOSES, JOB, JESUS, AND THE PROBLEM OF JUSTICE

And Moses went up from the plains of Moab unto Mount Nebo, to the top of Pisgah, that is over against Jericho. And the Lord shewed him all the land..., saying, "I have caused thee to see it with thine eyes, but thou shalt not go over thither." So Moses the servant of the Lord died there in the land of Moab, according to the word of the Lord.

> Deuteronomy, Book XXXIV, the end of the Five Books of Moses

The story of Moses recounts the birth of western culture. It is about the establishment of monotheism and the making of a nation under the rule of law. It concerns personal heroism and the rewards of piety – fidelity to the Law. But it also seems to say that nice guys finish last. In that sense, it appears to be an affront to justice.

The story's most interesting human detail is its most neglected. All the hugely mythic business – the shepherd's rods becoming serpents, the Passover, the parting of the Red Sea, the Ten Commandments, the desert march, the golden calf – makes for thrilling cultural or "national" moments. Cecil B. DeMille and Charlton Heston couldn't miss. But what gets sympathetic readers where they live are the moments just before Moses dies.

It is telling that despite the poignancy of those moments – an episode made all the more poignant in its sparse telling – commentators generally gloss over them as minor detail. In one of his lesser-known poems Rilke seems to *hint* that he sees some injustice there: no angel, only Satan, dares to assert a claim on Moses's soul. Perhaps he has in mind some commentary on Jude 9, where the angel Michael "disputes" with the devil over the body, a last desperate attempt at temptation, as though Moses hadn't already failed such a test (as we shall see). But then, Rilke has the soul accompany God to Heaven, uncomplainingly, for a chat about the good old days, before eternal sleep in an unmarked grave:

> Therefore the Lord, tearing out half of heaven,
> forced his way down to earth and bedded the mountain.
> Laid the old grey-beard on it; summoned the soul
> out of her ordered dwelling: up she sped, and recounted
> countless things in common, untellable friendship.
>
> But at last she was satisfied, completed; admitted
> that was enough. Then slowly the aged
> God bowed down his aged face to the aged
> mortal.[1]

Interestingly, the soul is female, super-rational, beyond positive law. Speaking of which, Freud thought that Moses had been murdered long before the Israelites neared Canaan, and that much of Exodus was an attempt to cover up the murder: there was no Pisgah at all.[2] Is the inference that the glimpse of unattained paradise is psychologically unbearable? Does it signal that justice[3] is unattainable on God's Earth? In recasting Moses, the Moshiach (Messiah), as it were, as the coming of Jesus, Christianity seems to have thought so, and we soon will see the implications in this for law and literature. If we dig down to the collective unconscious and accept Theodor Reik's psychoanalytic view that the Exodus is the recounting of a puberty festival,[4] Moses's death leaves us with no consummation, no entrance into the enclosed garden[5] – the restored, pre-law Eden in the Promised Land, which in Christianity becomes the body of the Virgin Mary and the afterlife and, in profane writing, Muse love-objects, etc.[6] Even Martin Buber, in his profound and sensitive biography of the Lawgiver, dismisses this central dilemma of the Exodus with one sentence: "The wonder-working staff in his hand does not transform him into a possessor of superhuman powers; when once he uses that staff unbidden he is subject to judgement."

Of course, the unmarked grave business is meant to emphasize the point: Moses is not a god or the son of God. Yet Buber was too careful and thoughtful a scholar to believe that this explained the enormity of Yahweh's "judgement," which in fact was a heart-breaking punishment without trial. Any humane view would allow for the inevitability of hope, would at least speculate that Moses must have persevered for forty years in the desert in the belief that God would not really deny him entry. But it is not surprising that Buber would not know what to make of Moses's death, or that others should gloss over it as a cultural embarrassment. It is, after all, THE END of an exhausting, and exhaustive, story. Compared to the *mythos* that precedes it, the death is *apocrypha*, legend, facetiae, local colour. For Yahweh is the protagonist of the Five Books; Moses is merely the prophet-author, the Law's draftsman and, as we shall see, an archetypal judge.

But such an end is incapable of dismissal. Justice, at least in the material or human sense, not to mention the lawyer's sense, does not seem to prevail. In literary terms, we *seem* to have tragedy. I italicize *seem* because in that monosyllable rests the fulcrum of my argument. We are not talking about the end of just any man. We are talking about the end of a hero, the Lawgiver. And in any case, as with even the humblest of us, in his beginning – a child entrusted to God's hands in a basket on the Nile – is his end.

After being spared mandatory death as an infant and having been raised by the Pharaoh's own (unwitting) daughter, Moses "backpacks" forty years in the desert with a band of freed slaves, nomads hardened by the whip and sun, a brutalized underclass who might slit each other's throats to drink the blood were there not safety in tribal numbers. Wrestling every imaginable obstacle, not the least of which is his own modesty and sense of unworthiness, his *self-conscious humanity* and therefore unlikeness to a wonder-working god, Moses hauls this band of gypsies, these *habiru*, kicking and screaming ("murmuring" is the King James euphemism) to the brink of a just and orderly society under the rule of capital L Law. Against all odds, against the call of nature herself, he converts them to a stern monotheism that takes from them their animal, and only, pleasures – unregulated sex and violence, violence and sex. Somehow he convinces a starving, hard-headed, "stiff-necked" people just out of their chains to eschew instant gratification, as if they were American Yuppies. Using narrative, he has imposed the super-ego of civilization on the quasi-savage. He has achieved a sort of communism, as George Steiner described it while the dust rose from the fall of the Berlin Wall:

Marxism brought intolerable bestiality, suffering and practical failure to hundreds of millions of men and women. The lifting of that yoke is cause for utter gratitude and relief. But the source of the hideous misprision is not ignoble (as was that of Nazi racism): it lies in terrible overestimate of man's capacities for altruism, for purity, for intellectual sustenance.

The theatres in East Berlin performed the classics when heavy metal and American musicals were wanted. The bookstores displayed Lessing and Goethe and Tolstoy, but Jeffrey Archer and Jackie Collins were dreamed of. The present collapse of Marxist Leninist despotisms marks the vengeful termination of a compliment to man – probably illusory – but positively none the less.[8]

And because Moses gets shirty on one occasion during all that time and through all that woe, or because for the blink of a sand-blasted eyelash he seems merely as human as the rest of the sun-blistered, broken-backed, foot-weary crowd, God forbids him to enter the Promised Land: "Because ye trespassed against me among the children of Israel at the waters of Meribah-Kadesh, in the wilderness of Zin; because ye sanctified me not in the midst of the children of Israel ... thou shalt not go thither unto the land which I give the children of Israel" (Deuteronomy 32:51). He is sacrificed to the good of the community. Technically, he is punished – as in all tragedy – for hubris, or *hamartia*, a tragic flaw arising from extraordinary stress, and of course the business with the "wonder-working staff" is metaphorical, symptomatic of that flaw: the pride that goeth before a fall. Yet his behaviour is so human, so understandable, it is hardly worth that criticism. Even Job has choices and chances that poor Moses is never permitted. Job rages against "the just" God (what exactly is this "patience of Job" business?), who by way of apology and gratitude repays him double (at least materially) what he has lost. Yahweh gives Job a second chance where he has permitted Moses the Lawgiver, "the servant of the Lord," only one. From both the legal and literary or metaphorical point of view, where is the justice?[9]

There are, of course, good sociological, psychological, and literary reasons for Job's deliverance, along with the sticky issue of how "double recovery," however generous it might seem, is supposed to compensate Job for the death of his children. But those matters push us ahead of ourselves.

Contemporary shepherd-prophets – our own lawmakers – have suffered similar humiliation. Jimmy Carter attempted to lead America out of a moral wasteland by a return to a rule of law with Judaeo-Christian foundations. As under Moses, community was to be paramount: the best for the greatest number with the least cost to individual freedom and rights. This was to be accomplished by individual good works, a sort of Christian utilitarianism, or something between utilitarianism and justice as fairness as espoused by John Rawls. In the early, heady days of this narrative, it seemed that this refreshingly no-nonsense, simple plan, President Carter's just-folks politics, really could have succeeded in a capitalist society where the same idealism had become totalitarianism in supposedly Marxist countries. Populist President Carter and his wife Rosalynn walked in his inauguration parade instead of riding in a limousine. The president held fireside chats on the radio. Having amassed his fortune as a southern plantationist, he made a special point of personally asking Dizzy Gillespie, an African-American who had briefly taken a "Black Muslim" name, to play "Salt Peanuts" for him at a White House concert. He made his good ol' boy brother an advisor.

But simple piety faltered against modern political reality. Religious ecumenism and tolerance were steamrolled by fundamentalism, religious and political. The last days of the Carter administration had a Pisgah feel, which was to be thrown into high relief when Iran began surrendering American hostages soon after Ronald Reagan assumed power and a joke spread like a toxic gas: *What's flat, black, and radioactive? Iran, the day after Ronald Reagan's inauguration.* Alone and disillusioned, brutalized in the final moments of his presidency, Jimmy Carter must have felt abandoned by God – or at least he must have felt that God was berating him that this was an irretrievably fallen world and Carter had a lot of damn nerve to try to reshape it in his mortal hands. We no longer lived in a cosmos that respected good acts, let alone rewarded them. The godhead no longer spoke through him, as it once was deemed to do with the British sovereign.

So the ultimate questions behind the theology in the whole Moses story, the central story of our civilization – along with the Christ story derived from it – seem to come down to this: in a post-Eden world, is earthly justice impossible? Is there a personal Promised Land, a new Eden? Are we doomed, nonetheless, to wear out our days searching for happiness, or trying to understand why we cannot find it? Is the gap between law and justice unbridgeable? Summarily: do nice guys finish last?

These questions, this Pisgah Perplex, are central human questions, ones that have become pointed again in these days when theocracy is a reality in much of the world, and casts a shadow within our own democracies, like something worrying in an X-ray. And it is the death of Moses, not the story of the Exodus, the story of the man *within* the community, that poses these anxieties. From the point of view of justice in law as literature, it is the Exodus which becomes backdrop, local colour, concerned as it is with the community rather than individual perplexity and suffering. In this sense, it is the Exodus that tells the story of Moses. It inculcates an archetypal pattern, beginning with Adam and Eve and resolving with Jesus Christ, in which individual narrative is meant to be universal, demonstrating what justice persistently means in human (or at least western) civilization.

To unearth the archeology of this in the law-and-literature sense – to do the law-and-literature anthropology on it and analyze its persisting reverberations – the most productive tool is archetypal or myth criticism. Axiomatic to this is that it is not necessarily pertinent whether a given ancient text has come down to us in some altered form – that, in the case of the Hebrew Bible, for example, it has been wrongly translated or "sauced" by later writers. In fact, a mistranslation or biased reading is more telling, because what is of particular interest to the myth critic is how the myth develops, how the subscribing society views the particular myth, in whatever form it sees the myth. It is relevant to the archetypal critic that received wisdom (or at least Luke 2:7) says Jesus was born in a stable after Joseph and Mary were turned away from the inn, never mind that a newer translation contends the child was born in a cave, as commonly happened in the day.

As we live in a time of assertive personal sensitivity, I feel compelled to add·a disclaimer here: in discussing sacred texts, I am not talking about religion but narrative, texts that are foundational to our society and therefore key to the way we view our life experience. I use "myth" as a term of art – a narrative not provable but sometimes accepted as true – and not as a value judgment or an insult to believers. The truth or not of a given narrative is irrelevant here. Its truth resides in the fact that it is essential to the broader – some would say universal – narrative we tell ourselves about our earthly experience. At the same time, we can understand why Jewish theologians would be uncomfortable with us calling the story of Moses a tragedy. For them, the beating of the rock unbidden in the Zin desert (his "unlawful" behaviour, as we shall see) hardly signifies tragic hubris, and the Pentateuch's narrative of his life is certainly not personal; rather, it is the opening act in a human drama that yearns for the return of Paradise, on Earth or in Heaven – a success story, in the sense that the Israelites achieved earthly paradise, albeit without the Lawgiver *in personam*. Inherent in this "comedic" resolution is perhaps Moses's greatest tragedy – that he is disallowed heroism because of "Mosaic" prescriptions against idolatry or hero-worship. The law keeps him a mortal cog. The method proposed here treats the Moses narrative as tragic precisely *because* it encapsulates a nostalgia for Paradise, a yearning for perfect justice that is Edenic, pre-law.

When Northrop Frye taught his graduate literary symbolism course thirty-odd years ago at the University of Toronto, he would often sketch this chart on the blackboard, whether he was discussing Homer, the Bible, *Finnegan's Wake*, or the modern French novel:

I   Heaven
II   Earthly Paradise
III World of Experience
IV   Underworld[10]

This paradigm (which Frye calls "apocalyptic")[11] describes the world-view underlying all of our narrative in western cultures, our imaginative life, from the beginning of civilization. It schematizes the structural anthropology of literature, from pre-literate times to the present day. Sometimes Frye expressed the same schema otherwise, as with a typology by representative "being":

I   God/Logos
II   Adam and Eve/Epiphany
III Man (in the Fallen World)
IV   Satan/Evil[12]

The life of Christ, redemptively and as pre-figured by Moses's, encompasses and unifies the four levels. Christ and Moses interact with the godhead, glimpse Paradise from on high, are tempted or fall, live through or harrow a form of hell. The paradigm changes nominally, that is, with a given era or person. In the hands of a Satanist, or in William Blake and the fully realized dystopia of George Orwell's *1984*, it may invert itself entirely.[13] In Wordsworth's Romantic poetry it is expressed as:

I   Nature
II Innocence/Childhood
III Adulthood
IV Urbanity/Industrialization[14]

In modern literature, this four-part world-view in Frye's "theory of myths"[15] can be expressed ironically, with a black twist. A vivid example suggests itself from John Updike's *The Coup*, in which starving African villagers set fire to a mountain of snack foods (an anti- or ironic paradise) sent by the US government, incinerating a State Department official who is atop the pile extolling the virtues of such foreign aid. The blinkered if well-meaning Americans have sent powdered milk to a land that has no water.

In sacred legal narrative, we find Moses negotiating between levels II and III, the paradisal, mountain-top worlds of Sinai and Pisgah, whence God descends to address man, and the (fallen) world of experience. The fact that the Logos meets man in a "raised" geography will be significant for the legal archetypology. Adam started here, in a mountain garden, until the supreme being drove him down and out, into the world where we live and encounter Job, valiantly making the struggle back upwards, only to be kicked down again. In the narrative of Christ's life, there is the Sermon on the Mount, and Frye contrasts the tragedy of Moses on Pisgah with the rebirth of hope in Christ ascendant from the Cross. Discussing Milton's *Paradise Regained*, he writes: "In Milton the temptation corresponds to the Pisgah vision of Moses, except that the gaze is turned in the opposite direction [toward the heavens]. It marks the climax of Jesus' obedience to the law, just before his active redemption of the world begins and the sequence of temptations consolidates the world, flesh, and devil into the single form of Satan."[16]

Implicit in the words, "It marks the climax of Jesus' obedience to the law" is that Jesus resisted temptation, obeying the law, where Moses – only human – failed and was denied entry into earthly paradise. Christ, in other words, is a reiteration of the heroic Moses (Robert Graves goes so far as to speculate that "in the original version [of the myth, presumably] Moses ... had no father, only a virgin

mother"),[17] but this time tragedy is redeemed. The collective unconscious could not bear it. Thus Handel's famously messianic use of "I
know that my redeemer liveth," from the Book of Job (19:25), never
mind that Job is not talking about Christ, or even Moses, but about
someone yet unknown, a *witness*, who eventually will vindicate him
on appeal as a good man who did not deserve the suffering God
imposed on him – as a man who used his life like Moses did, in
the service of God's Law, on the understanding that he would be
admitted to paradise on earth and at the final judgment or end of
days. And thus the Christian concept of *felix culpa* or fortunate fall:
Adam's breach of his covenant with God makes possible the immortality of the human soul through the resurrection of Christ as, archetypally, a messianic "improvement" on Moses. It makes possible, that
is, the ascension by humans to a paradise ineffably higher than the
one from which they fell – a paradise that is the apotheosis of justice: law, morality, and grace perfectly conjoined so that law has
become redundant. This is of course the foundation of Milton's *Paradise Lost*.[18]

   Frye calls the reiteration process "an elementary principle of Biblical typology in which the events of Christ's life repeat those of the history of Israel."[19] If we expressed *this* as a Fryegian chart, it would look
like the following:

MOSES	JESUS
Infancy in Egypt	Infancy in Egypt
Escapes genocide via the sea	Escapes genocide via baptism
40 years in wilderness	40 days in wilderness
Leads 12 tribes	Leads 12 disciples
Receives law on Mt. Sinai	Gives the (received) Sermon on the Mount
Reaches the Promised Land	Is resurrected as the Saviour

   Of course, the evolution of the myth – the boundary between Judaism and Christianity expressed ritually as the evolution of Passover
into Easter – is illustrated most dramatically in its conclusion: Christ
achieves Paradise – a "just" reward – where Moses is shut out, at least
from an earthly version, entombed in that unmarked grave. David
Daiches contrasts the Hebrew biblical resolution with that of Christianity as given in *Paradise Lost*, when Milton has God say of Adam
after he eats of the Tree of Knowledge of Good and Evil:

He with his whole posterity must die,
Die he or Justice must; unless for him
Some other able, and as willing, pay
The rigid satisfaction, death for death.[20]

Christ, of course, is the some other, who dies that man might have returned to him the eternal life Adam gave away, incidentally bringing into the world the need for positive or secular law. Then, too, Moses sacrifices his life that Israel might enter the Promised Land. So the circle completes itself: we die for the disobedience of Adam; Moses dies that we might regain earthly paradise; Christ dies for our sins.

Legal narrative naturally adopts the imaginative paradigms, with the difference that in law the paradigm remains static. The archetypes of the secular legal (law-as-literature) mode would look like this (which are not Frye's formulation, but my own extrapolations from his theory):

I   Legislatures (as godhead, Logos)
II Realm of Legal Fictions (standards of near-perfection/epiphany/priesthood)
III World of Affairs
IV Unlawfulness/Sociopathy (wrongfulness, malice, anarchy)

An interesting way to express this by "being," metaphorically, suggests itself as:

I   Sovereign or legislative-political structure as "God the father"
II Father of the family – the *pater familias* legal fiction which more or less represents the reasonable person in some Scandinavian, European, and South African law
III "Dad" – the more "real," everyday father of the family, as with Willy Loman or the teacher-father in John Updike's *The Centaur*
IV Demonic/absent/abusive/perverse anti-typical father (or son-father), as one finds in Satan in *Paradise Lost* or perhaps in Blake or Nietzsche.[21]

This latter scheme is not definitive, partly because it is based on a patriarchal model that, in modern nation-states, is becoming more inclusive or claims to be less "phallocratic" (or at least more liberal) in principle.

In any event, clearly the legislature is a sort-of-god, a secular reflection of the godhead. What it says goes, as is reflected in such doctrines as parliamentary supremacy, executive (presidential) override or veto, and eminent domain – the pre-emptive right of the government in otherwise private property. Our acceptance of this lies under even our principles of statutory interpretation. When we assume that "laws are remedial" or that legislatures, insofar as they can be said to have intention (like God, they can be inscrutable), do not intend absurd results, we are positing rule by higher wisdom and mercy. We are attributing to Caesar a mind more sophisticated than our own, but nonetheless one that we must assume we can now and then comprehend. These are the same premises we have always made about God: he is scrutable insofar as he wants to be or insofar as we need him to be. While it is legitimate to say that in a democracy it is really the citizen-voter who reigns supreme, the godhead-legislature analogy is unaffected: as believers choose their gods, so do voters choose their rulers.

Then, too, the monarchical precursors to our democratic systems purported, Moses-like, actually to represent the godhead. Bishops anointed British sovereigns, and before the "jury of one's peers" took on the role of trier of fact, we mortals staged trials by ordeal and battle whereby God was to judge right and wrong. (If the burn-wound didn't heal, the subject sank, or his champion lost, God was signalling thumbs down.) Historically, kings were said to rule on earth in the gods' stead. In the Moses narrative, the drive for monotheism breaks this identification, such that mortal Moses is merely God's agent, and he is punished for taking onto himself godlike powers unbidden. His death outside the Promised Land is meant more than anything to emphasize the distinction between him and the Eternal. Christianity restores the direct link between God and sovereign, embodying that link in Christ as the son.[22] Today, North American heads of democratic states purport to act at least Moses-like, "under God" and according to their understanding of "Judaeo-Christian teachings."

Then, too, judges, who "reign" in the world of legal fictions (and rein in such fictions, come to that), are priest-interpreters – nominally like the biblical Aaron, but archetypally like reasonable Moses – mediating between the godhead and mortals. (Although Parliament remains supreme in modern, secular democracies, the sovereign's legal authority is mediated by that of both Parliament and judicial interpretation.) Legal fictions are "epiphanic" or "ideal/paradisal" in the sense that they posit a static state of earthly perfection or near-perfection. The prime example is the "reasonable person," who of course is no person at all but a hero along the lines of his peers in this sphere, including Moses and Job (as well as other quester/adventurers such as Odysseus, Adam, even Superman and Luke Skywalker). He is on the godhead's wavelength (and even converses with gods at some level, if only ironically, sometimes, like Woody Allen getting dating advice from an otherwise deceased Humphrey Bogart in *Play It Again, Sam*), more nearly perfect ("law-abiding") a man than exists in a fallen world. As Justice Holmes puts it in *The Common Law*:

> The law takes no account of the infinite varieties of temperament, intellect, and education which make the internal character of a given act so different in different men. It does not attempt to see men as God sees them. ... If, for instance, a man is born hasty and awkward, is always having accidents and hurting himself or his neighbours, no doubt his congenital defects will be allowed for in the courts of Heaven, but his slips are no less troublesome to his neighbours than if they sprang from guilty neglect. His neighbours accordingly require him, at his peril, to come up to their standard, and the courts which they establish decline to take his personal equation into account.[23]

Secular law is based on the sacred, but there is a paradigmatic shift from the latter, which is perfect, to the former, which is man-made and therefore imperfect. But the paradigmatic modes – of other-worldly perfection – remain the same.

Moses and Job and Christ (and Odysseus, David, Samson, and Superman) are men but not-men: inhabitants of a realm only heroes know. They are legal fictions that mediate the godhead, and as immortal as you can get this side of angelhood. Thus does Eve argue in *Paradise Lost* that in Eden she has no guiding consciousness, innocent as she is of good and evil, an inhabitant of a world that, almost heavenly, needs no body of law:

> What fear I then? Rather, what know to fear
> Under this ignorance of good and evil,
> Of God or Death, of law or penalty?
> Here grows the cure of all, this fruit divine (IX, 775).

She knows that in eating the apple she is breaking a lawful proscription, but not until she has tasted the fruit can she understand the consequences. She is an infant drawn to a pretty fire. (As occupants of an already fallen world, Moses, Job, and Christ are in a different moral and legal position. But the question arises, can "ordinarily reasonable persons" be divinely endowed, "chosen" as leader? Certainly they are chosen by circumstance – being born into caring, community-minded families, perhaps, or experiencing life in a way that gives them a heightened sense for community and justice. Although Moses had been quasi-royalty, in keeping with the saviour/dying god myth, by the time of adulthood he has begun to identify, and be identified with, the slave class. He is by trade a shepherd. Like Christ after him, perhaps muscled with physical labour on the desert pyramids as Michelangelo depicts him, he is a worker and political activist, an Ur-union-man socialist.)

Of course, just as the movement from sacred to secular law causes a paradigm shift in analogies – a sort of genetic mutation by metaphor – the analogies of one to the other are not always perfect. To use a legal metaphor, the antecedent does not altogether mimic the precedent. Sin, for example, is analogous to crime, but the analogy is imprecise. Despair is a mortal sin, the kind of thing Donne writes about in "A Hymne to God the Father" when he says, "I have a sin of fear that when I have spun / My last thred, I shall perish on the shore" – he doubts, that is, the Christian doctrine of eternal life after death. In democracies, it is no crime to doubt or even speak against the rule of law. Anarchism is legal, at least to the extent that you don't act on it.[24]

II. THE INTERACTING TYPOLOGIES OF LAW AND LITERATURE: LAW IS PROSE, JUSTICE IS POETRY

When we unite the otherwise distinct worlds of law and literature, the various myth-poetry paradigms align. As Martin Buber points out, the Ten Commandments Moses brings down from Sinai are themselves not "the fundamentals of religion" but "the fundamentals of community life under the rule of God."[25] They are, in other words, a constitution, the basis for governing a nation under the rule of law in a time when there was no demarcation between sacred and secular. Just as Moses, Job, and Christ experience Hell in the world of experience, so do the inhabitants of Dickens's debtors' prisons, or Kafka's Joseph K, find themselves enmeshed in the non-lawyer's ultimate nightmare about the legal process: every time you think you understand it, the terrain shifts and falls from under your feet. Which soon enough will take us from Moses to Job.

It is no strain, of course, to see Christ's Sermon on the Mount as analogous to a re-interpretation of the Decalogue – as, that is, a broadened or annotated version of the constitution. The sermon is revolutionary in this limited sense. In Matthew's narrative, more lyrical and stirring than Luke's, Jesus himself says, "Think not I am come to destroy the law, or the prophets. I am not come to destroy, but to fulfill" (5:17). This is reverberative. He is hinting, it seems, that he is taking up where Moses left off, not just legally, but narratively, iconographically, imaginatively. His is meant to be a quiet revolution. He as good as says here, "I am the evolving archetype."

And sure enough he cites sundry of the original commandments – the prescriptions against murder, adultery, thievery – and adds not amendments, really, but interpretive glosses that are literally radical, seeking to prevent the sin/crime at its root: don't just avoid murder and extra-marital sex, avoid anger (even the Mosaic convention of *lex talionis* vengeance) and lustful thoughts (the Jimmy Carter, lusting-in-your-heart amendment). Don't love just your neighbour or friend – what's the trick in that? – but love your enemy. The text as a whole seems to say contention is bad for the soul, which is bad for the community – something that is implicit in Moses's struggles with the Israelites, but not in the law he delivers to them from Yahweh. "Just don't go there," Jesus suggests, "not even in your head." Self-interest is the community interest. Beyond the sermon's text, Matthew's narrative contains two signs that we've moved from founding-father constitutional law to an adapted version. Unlike Moses, and reflecting the iconography Frye finds in Milton that distinguishes the Jewish and Christian leaders, Jesus does not come down from the mountain to deliver the law. He remains at this "epiphanic" level. And Matthew concludes on a note that keeps Christ in the Mosaic tradition while perhaps setting him higher, figuratively and otherwise: "And it came to pass, when Jesus had ended these sayings, the people were astonished at his doctrine. For he taught them as one having authority, and not as the scribes" (7:28–9). It remains unclear whether Matthew in fact views Moses as a mere scribe, and Luke's version of the sermon (6:20-49) is of no help here. In Luke, Jesus recalls the Moses narrative insofar as Christ "came down with them and stood in the plain" to speak to his followers and "the multitude." However, Luke makes no

mention of pre-existing Mosaic law, while quoting Jesus to the effect
that his listeners regard him as at least godlike: "Why call ye me Lord,
Lord, and do not the things which I say?" (6:46). This is a "burden"
Moses never carries in the Pentateuch narrative, even if he himself
thoughtlessly, and fatefully, resorts to godlike behaviour in the Zin
desert.

We may now use this constitutional relationship between law and
literature as the point of departure for an expansive, more graphic
comparative narrative. In creating this broader comparison, we will
refer to literary works discussed more fully in later chapters.

Our narrative begins as a person, a protagonist, determines that he
knows the absolute, constitutional truth, the irrefutable law that must
govern all mortal behaviour and set the world to rights. Perhaps he
hears voices telling him this, from a bush that seems to be on holy
fire, on a mountain from a sky father, from a book, from an earth
mother. We can call that person

- Moses, say, or
- Jesus or
- Ruth Puttermesser (the protagonist of Cynthia Ozick's *Puttermesser Papers*, who, before Rudolph Giuliani, becomes mayor of New
  York and creates a golem to rid the streets of crime and filth,
  establishing temporarily in this fallen world a new Eden),[26] or
- Allie Fox (the protagonist of Paul Theroux's *Mosquito Coast*, who,
  in the manner of cult-leader Jim Jones, flees a materialistic, pollut-
  ed America to set up a new, Edenic – pre-law – order or cult in the
  jungles of Honduras),[27] or
- the Robin Hood of "A Gest of Robyn Hode" (a man dedicated to
  the Virgin Mary and the redistribution of wealth),[28] or
- George Orwell's Big Brother of *1984*.

Initially, each of these leaders is a revolutionary, seeking a new
order. The movement is generally from old to new – thus "Old Testament" to "New Testament," old, dogmatic curmudgeon to hopeful,
expectant youth.[29] The leader perceives that, in an imperfect or fallen
world (after Eden), people don't just reflexively do the right thing.
They need more rules than just the one about not trying to be
omniscient like the gods – not eating of the Tree of Knowledge of
Good and Evil. They need to be told exactly how to do their duty, to

love their neighbour. They need positive law. According to the leaders' lights, the world is

LEADER	PERCEPTION OF WORLD
Moses	fallen and irredeemable as such
Christ	in need of redemption
Puttermesser	crime-ridden, visceral
Allie Fox	hopelessly irrational
Robin Hood	infected with a corrupt ruling class
Big Brother	aimless, weak through cheap sentimentality and lack of focus and control.

The leader or a follower reduces this idea to a rulebook, a handbook for repair – doctrine directing where duty is owed by the individual in the society:

LEADER	PERCEPTION OF WORLD	DOCTRINE ESTABLISHED
Moses	fallen	Torah
Jesus	needs redemption/renewal	Gospel
Ruth Puttermesser	crime-ridden	The PLAN*
Allie Fox or Jim Jones	irrational	Revised Owner's Manual*
Robin Hood	corrupt ruling class	manifesto: redistrib'n of wealth
Big Brother	weak, aimless	Goodthink

And what are the *ideals* of the rulebook, the motive force behind each leader's administrative system?

- Moses – earthly paradise/utopia, until end of days
- Jesus – heavenly afterlife
- Puttermesser – earthly paradise, soon to be re-corrupted by mortal failings (after a brief Edenic period, New York City returns, inevitably, to its old, crime-ridden ways)

---

* The PLAN is the blueprint that Puttermesser's golem, Xanthippe, draws for her rehabilitation of New York. (This is discussed in more detail in Chapter Three.) Vacillating between insincere atheism and describing the Hebrew and Christian Bibles as an "owner's manual" for a job God did not finish (the idea of *Deus otiosus*, and then again the Nietzschean view of *Deus absconditus*), Allie Fox sets out to complete and perfect creation – according to his idiosyncratic notions of reasonableness. (See Chapter Four for more detail on this novel.)

- Allie Fox – paradise/state of pure reason (which, in a fallen world, Fox, as self-styled messiah, fails to establish)
- Robin Hood – socialism
- Big Brother – pure totalitarianism

To get his views across, the leader uses a literary process – narrative. He tells cautionary tales. He employs parables. He adapts folk tales and conventional wisdom, he reworks older myths and legends to fit his time, place, and temperament. He uses verbal persuasion – metaphor, literary forms based on what has come before. Everything builds on precedent, or what literary theory calls archetypes. The central idea is to create a legal system informing a certain vision of justice, a means to an end.

At first, the leader has nothing but trouble. He/she is virtually alone, a rebel in the wilderness, subject to temptations of the established systems, going with the flow, of oppressive or demonic forces seeking to use his charisma and good will. But his ideas gather force as he gathers forces, believers, acolytes. Some of his followers elaborate on the body of law. They call it Talmud or wisdom literature or commentary or neo-this, reform that, reconstructed church of the other. Eventually, anyway, there is consensus. Those who disagree are no longer a majority consensus; they are offenders:

LEADER	PERCEPTION OF WORLD	DOCTRINE	IDEAL	OFFENDER
Moses	fallen	Torah	paradise	apostates
Jesus	needs redemption	Gospel	afterlife	heretics/sinners
Putterm.	crime-ridden	PLAN	paradise	criminals
Allie Fox	irrational	Manual	pure reason	"monkeys," savages
R Hood	corrupt ruling class	manifesto	socialism	plutocrats/oligarchs
Big Bro.	weak, aimless	Goodthink	totalitarianism	enemies of people

The doctrine of course establishes *sanctions* for or the *fate of* the outlaws/offenders/ enemies. That is, the point of *law* (the doctrine) is to establish reward (the ideal) and punishment (the sanction; as John Austin tells us, a law is a command with a sanction in the breach),[30] which together make *justice* under the rule of law.

LEADER	PERCEPTION OF WORLD	DOCTRINE	IDEAL	OFFENDER	SANCTION FOR/ FATE OF OFFENCE
Moses	fallen	Torah	paradise	apostates	Hell on Earth/ Gehenna
Jesus	needs redemption	Gospel	afterlife	heretics/sinners	Hell
Putterm.	crime-ridden	PLAN	paradise	criminals	status quo to imper- fect afterlife
Allie Fox	irrational	Manual	pure reason	"monkeys"/savages	Earthly apocalypse
R Hood	corrupt rul'g class	manifesto	socialism	plutocrats/oligarchs	popular revolution
Big Bro.	weak, aimless	Goodthink	totalitarianism	enemies of people	democracy

By the time the system is completely topsy-turvy, as with dystopic visions such as that of *1984* or the colourful advocacy of Milton's Satan, it becomes a parody of what we normally view as appropriate: democracy becomes a sanction; those who seek freedom are, ironically, enemies of the people. The gravitational pull between the doctrinal ideal and the sanctions are meant to enforce a sense of duty. Duty, in other words (in both the tort law and larger, civil sense), mediates or attempts to fill the gap between law and justice:

law (the means – Torah, Gospel, etc.)

|

duty (fidelity to or faith in the doctrine, measured by societal standards such as reasonableness, Goodthink, etc.)

|

justice (the end – Hell, apocalypse, etc., balanced out by paradisal constructs)

The movement of systemic ideals descends (devolving) while, naturally, the description of sanctions ascends toward our own societal idea. There is always this tension between the good and the demonic, mirroring the hero/proponents' struggle between those elements in the movement from deity to hero to mortal to demon. Justice, in its narrative model, is very often the yearning for a return to a pre-law, or at least pre-positive law, condition, the state of humanity before the Fall. Justice in literature is nostalgia for the pre-lapsarian. J.M. Coetzee invokes this nostalgia with great clarity in his 1980 novel, *Waiting for the Barbarians*. The narrator, a colonial magistrate whose rule is usurped by military emissaries from his home country, tries to make sense of the violent oppression of Empire. "All creatures come into the world bringing with them the memory of justice," he remarks, while recalling having passed sentence on a military deserter, a peasant conscript who was homesick. "'But we live in a world of laws,' I said to my poor prisoner, 'a world of the second-best. There is nothing we can do about that. We are fallen creatures. All we can do is to uphold the laws, all of us, without allowing the memory of justice to fade.'"

Our practical, prosaic approach to an imperfect or fallen world is to create a consensus we call the rule of law. If enough people subscribe to the system meant to achieve such rule (the Torah, the Gospel, The PLAN), the system subsists. If not, it is heretical, idiosyncratic, revolutionary, unlawful. In creating a consensus, we seek – as in creating a golem, for instance – to participate in the creative process of the divine, as we do when we write a narrative. But there is no perfect justice under any system we create, because it is a product of an imperfect, fallen, *human* (versus divine) world. (If we all lived in a divine world, it would be perfect and we would not need positive law.) This imperfection upon imperfection presents us with a motive for metaphor, by which we can, in imagination if not reality, create an ideal, paradisal or utopian world. Such a world is one of perfect reason, and perfected humanity – a fictive or poetic realm, a return to Eden where metaphor's cycle began. Law is prose, justice is poetry.

This nostalgia is reflected in rituals associated with sacred law. Jewish practice, for example, methodically makes its way through the law – the Torah or Five Books of Moses – on successive sabbaths throughout the year. Once the synagogue reaches the end of Deuteronomy, describing Moses's glimpse of the Promised Land from Pisgah and his death nearby, it immediately returns to the beginning, the Creation and Eden narratives of Genesis, mirroring the cycles of Earthly nature. The Christ narrative reinvents the cycle, replacing it with a more literal rebirth on high, in immortal Paradise.

III. TOWARDS AN ICONOGRAPHY OF LAW

Western (and some eastern) law courts and justice systems employ an iconography that reflects the legal and literary archetypal scheme we have identified. Again, sacred writing, viewed as a form of law in and as literature, provides the fundaments. In the next chapter of this book, we will see how biblical parables constitute the prototype for law in literature: how, for example, in the parable of the good Samaritan, Jesus uses metaphor – tells a story – to make a central point about the law. Here, then, is an outline of legal-literary iconography. An explication follows the chart.

ARCHETYPE (SACRED/POSITIVE LAW)	SYMBOL	DEFINING TRAIT
Godhead/Parliament/Law	Justitia (an Amazon)	Fairness, objectivity
Earthly paradise/democracy	Reasonable person Also: judge/priest	Innocence/faith, reflexive obeisance to received wisdom or state of grace, pre-law
Material (fallen) world	Officious bystander/ reasonable business-person, trustee, etc.	Duty/enlightened self-interest (act in best interest of stake-holders – devolved duty)
Underworld	Anarchy/criminal rule/ floodgates/prisons	Sociopathy, unmitigated self

The social and literary expression of these archetypes of course evolves with the culture. Pagan mythic archetypes evolve into the "legalistic" or Mosaic archetypes of the Hebrew Bible. The transition into purportedly more "merciful," tempered, or forgiving (less legalistic) and more individualized law in the Christian Bible comes through what biblical scholars call wisdom literature such as Job, Ecclesiastes (and the Talmud, arguably), and sometimes through the prophetic books. This movement from myth through legalism to equity is propelled or paralleled by a narrative movement from polytheistic rule to monotheism to multi-prophetic interpretive monotheism (as with the Jewish Midrash and Talmud) to unified prophecy under Christ:

PAGAN-CLASSICAL LIT.[31]	HEBREW BIBLE	TRANSITIONAL (PASSOVER)	CHRISTIAN BIBLE
"Myth"	Law	"Wisdom"/interpretive	Equity
Polytheism	Monotheism	Multi-prophetic	Mono-prophetic

It is worth restating, however, that Jesus specifically says he is not repealing the Mosaic code, but fulfilling it. Setting up the liberal tradition that law should follow precedent – that it is open to liberal reform but must be predictable and reliable – he offers a broadened interpretation. While his revised covenant is altogether revolution-ary at the sanction/reward level, insofar as it promises redemption through paradisal immortality – justice tempered by a more com-fortable, highly attractive mercy – it largely accepts the existing legal code.[32]

Still, every change is revolutionary in nature, and generally meets resistance in its early stages. (The Exodus story makes this graphic, right away, as, obviously, does the narrative of Jesus the Messiah. Com-pare the politically charged, careerist battles between Lords Coke and Bacon over the bid by the courts of equity to occupy common-law turf.) The subtext of this scheme is the increasing humanization of the godhead/prime lawmaker, through a conception of man in God's image, Christ "the King" as the son of man, etc., and from unsee-able/unknowable and multifarious to unified and knowable or a per-sonal god. Courts move from received law to received wisdom (the Midrash, Christian councils, etc.) to secular or positive law, with an increasing interest in the individual over community ("personal rights and freedoms") over time. Christianity, with its strong cult of the Virgin and the extravagant compassion of Christ, unites the male and female elements of godhead, the female largely having been sup-pressed during the Hebraic and transitional periods.[33] Presumably the female element will assert itself more strongly as we move through this century, with its growing presence of women lawyers, politicians, and business leaders. On at least the imaginative level, the "feminine" is more open and encompassing. (In a sense, this would be restorative or cyclical: in classical literature, Justice is usually female,[34] albeit the supreme power generally lies with the male god.)

Note that these periods in some ways correspond to Frye's literary modes, where the cycle concludes with the "ironic mode."[35] In our context, this mode is perhaps best called "the age of science," the skep-tical period we inhabit now. In that light, the end of our chart would read:

CHRISTIAN BIBLE	SCIENCE
Equity	Empirical findings/logic/forensic evidence/skepticism
Mono-prophetic	Mortal quester/hero/trier of fact

The movement is perpetual, at least so long as human society exists. By this reckoning, the Big Bang Theory is just another creation myth, and will in turn be replaced by yet another when our scientists revise their thinking in years to come. There is also a cyclical movement implicit in this scheme from old to young (sometimes mirrored by the progression of the seasons from birth in spring to death in winter), along with the progression from male to female. Frye limits the rejuvenation movement to comedy, on the basis that comedy begins with an undesirable "old" order – such as where a tyrant imposes harsh laws (as in Shakespeare's *Measure for Measure*) or a hidebound father insists on strict rules (Tevye, for example, with his daughters in Sholem Aleichem's stories) – and strives for a desirable one, usually at the hands of a young hero or heroine. Frye says this progression mirrors such movement in the Christian Bible,[36] but it seems to apply more generally in literature, representing evolution (by revolution) from heavily patriarchal systems to more inclusive ones. In law and literature it appears to be a central motive force. In the *Orestiea*, for instance, tragedy is resolved through restorative justice when younger gods (Apollo and Athene) persuade the Furies, representing the older view of absolute liability for matricide. As Richard Lattimore has put it, the Furies "stand for the childhood of the race before it won Hellenic culture, the barbarian phase of pre-Hellenism, the dark of the race and of the world; they have archaic uprightness and strictness of action ... Apollo stands for everything which the Furies are not: Hellenism, civilization, intellect, and enlightenment. He is male and young."[37]

If we follow our table above from the classical and Hebrew worlds to our world of science and technology, we see a parallel movement of elderly gods and heroes, such as the Yahweh/Moses coalition to the younger, more sentimental Father/Christ pairing, with the female element (moving from the Shekhina to the Virgin and the more "feminine" qualities of Christ) more prominent but still subsidiary. (The rise of mysticism in the prophetic period suggests a mingling of male rationalism and female emotionalism, as they were often stereotyped until our time.) Metaphorically, even the reasonable person gets younger: in Graham Greene's *Our Man in Havana*, for instance, the timid vacuum-cleaner salesman James Wormold immediately strikes the reader as "the man on the Clapham omnibus" transplanted to the tropics. He is in middle age and has been cuckolded, but retrieves his manhood and a restored reasonableness – he rejuvenates – after being tempted away from the duties of solid citizenship ("my madness offends," the refrain from a song, echoes throughout the novel as a *lit-*

erary refrain): he finally stops mourning the wife who has deserted him and his daughter, releases that child to be the grown woman she has become – instead of his substitute, desexualized love object – and establishes new sexual love along with renewed self-respect (as an ironic champion of justice in a particularly Kafkaesque setting of the Cold War) which takes him back to England, the Old World renewed. The reasonable man has no compass – nothing to make him reasonable in an exemplary way – unless he is tested. This, after all, is the lesson of Moses and Christ, who died for our unreasonableness (as it were).

As we have seen, this movement from old to young itself parallels our cultural and juridical evolution from "legalism" to concepts of mercy and equity (a sort of youthful tolerance), until we reach today's world where we seem addicted to constant flux. So, too, does our law seem to be in a parallel flux, sometimes driven by a lust for novelty, panting to keep up not only with the new challenges these emerging technologies (the Internet, cloning, bio-technology generally) impose on everyday order, but with constant new claims to individual rights. The New World itself has come to define the most desirable form of modern democracy, wherein we progressively amend, legislatively or judicially, our charters of rights and freedoms and our human rights legislation.

In other words, in western societies it seems we are in a sort of post-authoritarian age of individualism and reason – beyond comedy, with its happy endings, into terminal irony, rampant individual "realization" amid hair-trigger weapons of mass destruction and global warming. As the earth heats up literally and politically, and theocracies begin to reassert themselves with nuclear bombs, we are also increasingly aware that attempting to conjoin rationality with exclusivity (including the "individualism" of societies taking a neo-tribal view of their exclusive "rightness" against all others) is oxymoronic. Unable to create a true global village, we are in danger of blowing ourselves back into the mythic. Modern literature adopts and elaborates on this anxiety.

The examples are manifold, of course, but one that springs immediately to mind is Don DeLillo's *White Noise*, wherein the "airborne toxic event" serves as a metaphor for the pervasive if mostly invisible toxicity of modern life. In its aftermath, a sort of quiet hysteria overcomes narrator Jack Gladney, who takes the law into his own hands, exercising cathartic revenge that, but for his second thoughts and aid to the victim, would be murder. The "event" breaches civil society's scrim, revealing a veneer-culture that uses consumerism and the propaganda of "self-actualization" to distract it from its weapons of mass destruction, genocide, catastrophic climate change, psychotic global markets, and political terrorism. The inherent anarchy – this vision of a future where law cannot reach – might be our future, but we don't want to think about it.

1. The Godhead or Logos in Metaphor

We noted earlier that, imaginatively, governments, even democratic ones, parallel the godhead, and, indeed, the old argument that free will exists within theocracy suggests at least an urge to personal liberation even in a dictatorship, albeit under imposed rule with consequences not always subject to mercy. Humanity can't help but infuse the mortal view of law even when it is supposed to have divine origin. We are only human, even when we believe we are attending to received wisdom. Here, again, we find the fundamental relationship between law and human creation or art – Creation and creation.

At the iconographic (clearly artistic) level, we have the ideal, Justitia. She shares the imaginative turf with Athena, the Virgin Mary, and the Shekhina, whom Jewish mystics describe as the female aspect of God and also the female side of the spirit he breathed into humans. (In this world, after all, creation involves two sexes.) Some say that when Moses came down from Sinai with the Decalogue, his face was flushed from intercourse with the Shekhina – a sort of muse that conceived the Law.[38] To the extent that this was an "immaculate conception," the vessel was male, the messenger-lawgiver Moses – perhaps fitting symbolism for the concretization of patriarchy.

In secular law Justice is an Amazon with a sword, an iteration of Astraea-Virgo, the daughter of Zeus (the highest god) and Themis, goddess of order and mortal law. She also bears some relation to our first mother, Eve, in her pre-Fall, virginal period: Astraea inhabited earth during the Golden Age, but (in the words of *Bulfinch's Mythology*) "when the wickedness of men increased, she withdrew to heaven and was placed among the stars, under the name of Virgo."[39]

Bulfinch's 1913 description of this time of wickedness sounds a lot like the chiliasmic view we hear constantly today regarding the consequences of what humans have visited on civilization and our planet, the fallen world hitting bottom. He describes a planet where "crime burst in like a flood; modesty, truth, and honor fled." Humans tore apart the earth, dividing it instead of using it "in common," unsatisfied with surface, digging "into its bowels" to withdraw mischievous metals – iron, gold. "War sprang up, using both as weapons; ... Sons wished their fathers dead, that they might come to the inheritance ... The earth was wet with slaughter, and the gods abandoned it, one by one, till Astraea alone was left, and finally she also took her departure." *Deus absconditus.* Justice left the world. In a note, Bulfinch adds, "It was a favorite idea of the old poets that these goddesses [Themis and Astraea] would one day return, and bring back the Golden Age. See Milton's 'Hymn on the Nativity,' xiv, xv."[40] This of course echoes the Jewish idea of the *Moshiach*, the coming of the Messiah, and the Christian apocalyptic vision of Final Judgment.

Such links between sacred and secular law persist symbolically in other fixtures of our legal system, such as the seals, escutcheons, shields, etc. we use in courtrooms and on official stationery, which often include slogans about God and the law. In my own jurisdiction, court walls are decorated with the slogan, "*Dieu et mon droit.*"

2. Justice as Nostalgia: The Earthly "Paradise" as the Beginning and End of Law

Eden – the earthbound utopia – is the beginning and end of law. This is a central premise to the methodology proposed here. At its inception Eden is pre-law because the arrangement with God is a law only in form, and at that, only in dictatorial form. It is, to use Austin's formulation, a rule with a sanction, but until Adam and Eve break it they don't understand what a sanction is, let alone what *the* sanction here really means – its nature. They lack *mens rea*, criminal intent. Imposed on them is something more like a covenant in a lease agreement: you can stay in the garden as long as you leave this particular tree alone. In their innocence, before they fall, they are not equipped to understand this metaphorically, that the condition really means that mortals are not to attempt to appropriate to themselves the powers of the gods, particularly their transcendent knowledge of good and evil. (Although God tells them that they will surely die in the breach – that entropy will enter the world – death does not exist. It is unclear how the first couple are to make sense of this, even under the theological "theory of accommodation," whereby God reveals certain things about his dominion in a manner accessible to human understanding.) In the breach, this arrangement establishes various legal symbols or prototypes. Once the single condition is broken and we fall from the mountaintop, we require an ocean of positive law. In a fallen world, attempts to return to the utopian state of pure reason mark the longing for the end of law. Sociopathy is the dark mirror of this impulse. Like Moses, we never quite succeed at restoring utopia, but we glimpse it.

We find the same idea in the mythology of Yeats' poetry. Yeats envisions the poet in a tower plying his trade in this version of earthly paradise. He personally went beyond metaphor to myth, purchasing a Norman tower and writing poetry in it.[41] In such a "higher" or epiphanic place, the poet is closer to the moon (in Yeats's mythology), whose goddess is his muse. He is different here from Moses on the mountain, as "the Lawgiver" is a man of the light, of rationality instead of sensuality, whose God is a version of pre-existing sun gods. In "The Tower," Yeats contrasts "the brightness of the moon" with the "prosaic light of day" (II, ll. 29–30). The poet succeeds when he can unite these worlds of literalist law and order with transcendent natural beauty: "O may the moon and sunlight seem / One inextricable beam, / For if I triumph I must make men mad" (II, ll. 38–40). But the female reasserts itself, as it must, even in Jewish commentary: again, we have Moses returning "to earth" from Sinai, his face flushed with divine inspiration or intercourse with the Shekhina; later, there is this cult of the earth mother, the Virgin Mary. And as the moon reflects the sun, Yeats perceives Mosaic reflection in the poet; as Frye puts it, "the moon is an achievement the tower doesn't reach."[42] Once you achieve the muse, Paradise, the "motive for metaphor" (in Wallace Stevens's wonderful phrase) evaporates. The tower is earthbound, and perfection is not of this world. Perfect justice never really lives here, at least not as a permanent resident. The lamplight by which the poet works on high is only a very pale version of sun and moon. Wisdom, Yeats writes in "Blood and Moon," "is the property of the dead."[43]

Yeats said the Norman tower was "a permanent symbol of my work" and that "all my art theories depend on just this – rooting of mythology in the earth."[44] Its spiral staircase represented the stages of learning toward longed-for wisdom, as well as the steps on the Platonic ladder which stretch toward the Ideal Form, and the cyclical rise and fall of civilization, or what Yeats called gyres. Thebes becomes Babylon becomes Byzantium, Leda and the Swan become the Virgin and the Dove, and the "rocking cradle" of "The Second Coming" symbolizes Oedipus, Moses, and Christ all at once. In any event, if one actually seduces his muse, he loses inspiration, dying as a poet in his attempts to "know" the godhead. (The Freudian reverberations become quite plain here, of course.) As long as you don't achieve the Muse/Goddess – of which Eve and the deadly Sirens are symbolic reflections[45] – "the sun's / Under eclipse and the day blotted out."[46] You are depressed and perhaps maddened with desire for communion with perfection (especially perfect Justice), but you are also inspired to try to achieve it. You are suspended between the perfect state of Heaven and the fallen world and its corrupted need for positive law. Mortals themselves cannot become one with the Logos/Word/Law, but they can yearn towards it in imagination. Law is prose; justice is poetry.

Creation narratives always describe a new order, a new system of law. They are always more or less revolutionary; more precisely, they are revolutionary or evolutionary. This is true whether they are sacred, secular, or some grafting of the one on the other, as with the creation narratives of colonial America or modern Israel. Each of those stories involves personal sacrifice in a pilgrimage to "conquer" an "untamed" land, in a quest for free expression, culturally, religiously, and individually. They inculcate a nostalgia for natural law – a longing for a prelapsarian utopia where humans lived harmoniously with nature and positive law was unnecessary. Post-colonial criticism, taking account of the aboriginal populations, would reverse these narratives as narratives of destruction or devolution – in America, at least, a movement away from natural or animistic law. Similarly, to polytheistic societies, monotheocratic systems (as under Moses) would have looked degenerative. In any event, we have one legal order being replaced by another – the familiar literary theme of social regeneration.

In the case of more persistently colonial narratives such as in Canada or Ireland, the revolutionary aspect is present but muted.[47] The *evolution* toward full self-expression is slower, the throwing off the old order less violent.

From Paradise to Experience: Adam and Eve as Legal Archetypes

Perhaps the second most interesting law-and-literature point about Adam and Eve (the first being that they personify the beginning and end of law) is that their disobedience, their unwitting "criminality," is what makes them human. Before they give in to temptation, they are

unrecognizable to us as part of our human family, alien in their perfection. As Frye notes, just after the Fall they "remain dramatically in
the position of children baffled by their first contact with an adult situation ... 'Henceforth I learn that to obey is best,' Adam says [in *Paradise Lost*], as he and Eve go hand in hand out to the world before
them."[48] As "children," they are in a pre-law state. As we suggested earlier, they are unaware, even, of what a law is; what they break, to their
understanding, is at most a deal, the first covenant of the Bible, and
possibly even something less, as with a usually flexible rule imposed
by a doting parent: "Here's the deal," God as landlord-parent has told
them: "You don't eat the fruit of this particular tree, you can live here
rent free, no other restrictions. Have all the parties and pets you want.
I won't evict you. Eat from the tree, you're out."

Where adulthood dawns in the world of experience, so does positive
law – or at least the need for it. God, Genesis tells us, created Adam as
his gardener, nothing nobler; but until he breaches the covenant, he is
of another, redemptive world. Temptation, the urges of the ego and id,
we readers understand. At the same time, one could argue that Adam's
sin gives him nobility, not just because he becomes recognizably
human, but insofar as after the Fall he has more to contend with –
what *we* must contend with. And this is how he speaks to us in our
world of positive law, a world of imaginative narrative, or law and literature. In an environment suddenly bristling with dangerous chaos,
he must invent civilization. Before that, he is simply a noble savage.

Also of interest in the Eden story (for our method here) are these
glosses on the Genesis story:

A. EVE AS ADAM'S RIB   "And Adam said," Genesis II, 23–4 tells us,
"'This is now bone of my bones, flesh of my flesh: she shall be called
Woman, because she was taken out of Man. Therefore shall man leave
his father and his mother, and shall cleave unto his wife; and they
shall be one flesh.'"

This of course was part of the rationale in secular law that husband
and wife were one flesh – now repudiated because the one flesh
(under this patriarchal convention and narrative) was the husband's.
In the past, with biblical teachings immanent and conventional thinking more informed by them, woman was "born of" man, who thereby
had a proprietary and protective (and ultimately legal) interest in her
as helpmate, concubine, and "child." (As Genesis II:20 puts it, Adam
names all the animals, who like him are formed "out of the ground,"

but "there was not found an help meet for him." So God anesthetizes Adam, takes "one of his ribs," and "of the rib ... made he a woman and brought her unto the man.")

Earth Mother, with her ties to our Justitia symbology, was conceived "immaculately" of man, presumably all in God's (the Law's) image. Contrast this with Lilith, a succubus whom Jewish folklore conceives as a sort of failed prototype of Eve. Taking the Genesis chronology literally, Jewish mystics considered that the "female" God created in I:27 was distinct from the rib-generated Eve of Chapter II, and the first feminist, to boot. She broke with Adam, the story goes, when he refused to treat her as an equal, and then went off blaspheming Yahweh while attempting to co-opt his creative powers. [49]

B. DEVOLUTION TO *HOMO SAPIENS* AND THE PROTOTYPE OF GUILT
Immediately that Adam and Eve eat the fruit of the Tree of Knowledge, "the eyes of them both were opened, and they knew that they were naked; and they sewed fig leaves together, and made themselves aprons" (III:7). In a breath, the first couple evolves (or, mythologically, devolves) from *Homo ludens* to *Homo sapiens* to *Homo faber.* As we shall see, the interplay of these human states form the landscape of works with utopian themes and parodies, such as Paul Theroux's *Mosquito Coast.*

In shame, Adam and Eve attempt to hide themselves from God, their judge, who pretends to deduce from this that they have eaten the forbidden fruit: "Who told thee thou wast naked? Hast thou eaten of the tree, wherof I commanded thee that thou shouldest not eat?" God as judge here is like the parent who already knows what has happened but stages a trial in any case, as a putatively fair hearing, despite the power imbalance, where judge acts as police and prosecutor. Never mind free will, like the bet between God and Devil in Job it is free will in a circumscribed arena, in which the "justice" of punishing an omnisciently foreseen error has ever founded debate about sacred law. [50] "Didn't I tell you not to do that?" God asks, but purely rhetorically. In this setting, "feeling guilty" shifts personal sensation to community judgment, from "I feel guilty that I did that" to "guilty as charged," the world's innocence having departed with that moment of sensory transcendence, signified by pleasures of earthly flesh, touch, taste, sex.

C. BLAMING THE OTHER GUY

"Hast thou eaten of the tree, whereof I commanded thee that thou

shouldest not eat?" [God asked.]
And the man said, "The woman whom thou gavest to be with me,
she gave me of the tree, and I did eat.
And the Lord God said unto the woman, What is this that thou
hast done? And the woman said, "The serpent beguiled me, and I
did eat." (III:11–13)

Here we have the prototype, times two, of the now shopworn defence dodge where there are co-accused, "Actually, your Honour, she
did it."

D. ADAM AND EVE AS PROMETHEAN PROTOTYPES   Finally, also
prototypically, it is made clear that at heart Adam's breach is a
Promethean power-play, an attempt to be omniscient and therefore
godly, which theme is repeated in the story of Moses and resolved in
the story of Christ:

And the Lord God said, "Behold, the man is become as one of us,
to know good and evil: and now, lest he put forth his hand and
take also of the tree of life, and eat, and live for ever. Therefore the
Lord God sent him forth from the garden of Eden to till the
ground from whence he was taken. (III:22–3)

More metaphorically than but still like his co-conspirator the serpent, Adam is to eat dust "all the days of thy life." (III:14), and now is
doomed to return to that state. (At this point there is no penitentiary
Hell.)

*Adam and Eve Out of the Garden and Down to Earth:
John Updike on Entropy and Family Law*

In literature if not in law, marriage itself is Edenic, traditionally an early
step in adulthood yet bathed in innocence. At consummation, innocence peers over the wall of experience, and with pubescent sexual experience in modern times, as well as our increasing resort to divorce as a
sort of blameless bail-out or corporate reorganization, the literary treatment of family law has become ironic. John Updike provides a particularly fine example of this in "Here Come the Maples," his heartbreaking
short story about the coming of "no-fault" divorce to Massachusetts.
   Although he was a gimlet-eyed observer of just about everything

earthly, Updike wrote little about law. His great subject was ordinary, middle-class life in mid-twentieth-century America. But his writing always concerned the tensions at the heart of law and literature – the interplay of Law and law, law and morality, duty and selfish, material fulfillment.

"Here Come the Maples" first appeared in *The New Yorker*, on October 11, 1976. "Now come Richard F. and Joan R. Maple" its opening paragraph quotes, from the spouses' joint affidavit, "and swear under the penalties of perjury that an irretrievable breakdown of the marriage exists." And sure enough, at the time, such documents seemed as curious to lawyers as they did to the bewildered affiants. "We're all sailing uncharted waters here," Richard's counsel tells him, while advising that his client should have an example of irretrievability handy, just in case.

But as the Maples "had always been a lucky couple," the story's first sentence says, "it was just their luck" that no-fault had come to their home state "as they at last decided to part." All Richard can come up with for irretrievable breakdown is, "She used to make me go on peace marches." The divorcing couple sails those uncharted waters of irony mostly alone – alone together and alone apart, poised at the railings of the sinking vessel that was their joint venture, queasy with panic as they contemplate the rubber dinghies below that might take them independently to a less sickened place, or might not. And that is the story's scarifying point.

The legal language tells nothing like the whole truth, or even, really, anything of the manifold ironies. It must remain clinical and precise, as scapular as Updike's more personalized narrative. For the petitioner and respondent, everything becomes retrospect, such that Richard now sees his fairy-tale marriage gone Grimm, but grimmer: alone together, he recalls of the wedding at city hall, "Hand in hand, smaller than Hänsel and Gretel in his mind's eye, they ran up the long flight of stairs into a gingerbread-brown archway and disappeared." Flash forward to today, the day of divorce, when he has moved from blaming Joan for everything to letting go of her hand: "He had set her free, free from fault. She was to him as Gretel to Hänsel, a kindred creature moving beside him down a path while birds behind them ate the bread crumbs."

Alone together, there is no going back. The black crows of the law eradicate the saving trail of stale food. Everyday middle-class experience, 1976–2013. Paradise, where perfection precludes law, is a fairy tale, a matter of nostalgia made ironic/bitter by experience – Hänsel and Gretel without the happy ending. The marriage made in Heaven has devolved, fallen, with the spouses de-sexualized as young siblings in a world of entropy and evil: Adam and Eve have become Hänsel and Gretel; death has entered the world, a wedge between the living as well as between life and what comes after.

Indeed, the story is exemplary in terms of myth criticism, with its reflections from urbanity (particularly the immutable courthouse where Richard obtains the affidavit and copy of the marriage certificate – the "anti-license," he comes to call it) backwards to the couple's youthful innocence and the beginnings of maturity in the pastoral setting of their honeymoon. There, in the country, they glimpse signs of the decay that will come to dominate Richard's thoughts as he prepares to divorce – the rusting ski-lifts, the derelict industrial buildings, the junk food. The newlyweds shamelessly play naked croquet, but as the divorce hearing looms years later, Richard cannot recall whether they really saw a deer in the mist. Entropy now is everywhere, and often ironically so. The word *luck* appears at least six times in this story about marital breakdown, and when Richard arrives to drive Joan to the courthouse for the *decree nisi* hearing (having constantly ruminated on the passage of time and the increasing imminence of death in his life), she is, again, barefoot – all Paradise lost. Here, even the couple's name, their exemplary modern saga, "The Maples Stories," recalls pastoral innocence, and that, come autumn and the winter of their marriage, innocence falls. What seems to be luck is more precisely fate.

At the honeymoon stage they strain at the illusion that they live in the more rarified world of no responsibility (in the woods, with the magical deer, the fairy-tale world of Hänsel and Gretel where sex is no shame, it's as innocent as walking hand-in-hand with your sibling, playing naked croquet), but the world of experience constantly impinges, the world where we need positive law to avoid Darwinism. In divorcing Joan, Richard comes now to understand that he has always been the weaker "particle" (imagery he picks up from an article on physics, stuffed in his pocket with a copy of the marriage licence), obeying the higher law of nature – Adam, one has to imagine, to the more powerful Eve. He finds the affidavit "shocking." As he and Joan have made the phone arrangements to go together to the

divorce hearing – Richard drives them to court as they chat compan-
ionably about "their cars and their children" – Joan has said the document strikes her as funny: "Here we come, there we go."

But when the judge at last asks each spouse, "And do you believe
that your marriage has suffered an irretrievable breakdown?" Joan, artless as Eve, pauses. When at last she answers, her voice (in Richard's
"peripheral vision") is a rainbow, a covenant of redemption in a disaster, where at the wedding ceremony, in his peripheral vision she herself had been like a rainbow in a fog. Richard answers directly if ironically, despite his lack of concrete evidence, "I do," and once the judge
signs the divorce order, the atmosphere turns almost celebratory, missing only the champagne and confetti. The lawyers merrily discuss no
fault and the Maples become "obsolete at their own ceremony," like
newlyweds. And "Richard at last remembered what to do": he kisses
his ex-wife.

It is a shattering climax[51] and, all at once, denouement. The point
of marriage is largely its legality, a merging of proprietary and parental
interests; but of course no one considers the legal aspects until the
union breaks down in fact, not in law. As the story exquisitely shows,
the laws most keenly at work are those of nature, of entropy – love,
habit, time, and boredom, as Richard puts it, his mind flitting from
his and Joan's honeymoon, when he was a twenty-one-year-old student, to the present, *decree nisi* day, when he has arthritis, his friends
are dying, and the world has moved from myth and fairy tale to science. All else is human vanity, a delusion of stewardship and control
of nature. The only thing that remains unchanged is city hall and the
courthouse, where the couple married and Richard gets the divorce
affidavit notarized. Castle-like, it resembles something out of the
brothers Grimm, symbolizing the persistent need for positive law in
the fallen world of experience. And it was here, once the judge had
pronounced the couple husband and wife, that Richard had forgotten
to kiss his bride.

The divorce ceremony is a heartbreaking parody of the marriage
solemnization (after Richard has had to go *down* to get a copy of the
marriage licence, where he had gone up for the original). That
restored kiss, even when you know it is coming, is a reliable (brilliant
and breathtaking) tear jerker. Updike's writing is that good here, that
acute on the entropy at the heart of family law, never mind our modern attempts – no-fault, collaborative divorce, shared custody – to normalize the tragic.

The Reasonable Person and Other Legal Fictions:
Archetypal Truths Versus Fictional Lies

The Maples are, of course, "everycouple," moving through life from irresponsible childhood into the world of experience, the world where positive law is our bulwark against survival of the wiliest and most brutal. In retrospect, "the honeymoon period" has lived up to its cliché meaning: it is really more a matter of hope or nostalgia than anything persistent. That epiphanic or paradisal world, where everyone behaves well enough that we don't really need law but just the basic rule of love thy neighbour, is the locus of utopian fictions, including legal fictions. Using the latter, the law can make us momentary semi-gods or super-beings, heroes like Moses or the reasonable person. But in the end, this state is only fictive, almost but not quite mythic. The childhood cliché shifts in adulthood from the "do unto others as you would have them do unto you" (of sacred teaching) to the cynical (secular) "do unto others before they do unto you." Nature will out.

In law, a fiction is something that is accepted as altogether imaginary. It is fictive, not mythical, because nobody believes it really exists. In literature, however, fiction is generally understood to present transcendent truths. As we have observed, the reasonable person as a legal fiction harkens back to a state of perfect observance and faith, in Eden; the reasonable person is not god, but then he is no identifiable mortal. He is heroic. In 1935 William Empson published a lovely poem explicating this otherworldly but not quite heavenly quality of fictions in law. The legal fiction he chose, however, was, in the words of his footnote to "Legal Fiction," "the assumption that ownership of land extends into the earth beneath and into the air above." On this basis, he notes that "Law makes long spokes of the short stakes of men," giving us ownership not just in the land we acquire but into that part of heaven above it and the hell below – "Of all cosmos' volume, and all stars as well." In this sense, we are as powerful as a god, but the power is a vain lie:

You are nomad yet; the lighthouse beam you own
Flashes like Lucifer, through the firmament,
Earth's axis varies; your dark central cone
Wavers a candle's shadow, at the end.

The "end" is deliberately ambiguous, of course, signifying both the darkness at the end of life on earth (each of us our own little earth whose brief light spreads out from the self, at one's axis on the earth's surface, into the firmament) and the darkness of hell. As Lucifer is both the morning star and a demon, our lighthouse beam flickers, as much illusion as real. Despite the metaphysics of our law, despite the super powers it gives us regarding real property, despite our strutting about and laying grand claims in a fallen world, we are only mortal, and we don't "own" anything permanently. In the end our self-declared heroism is only a fiction; though glorified with the qualifier "legal," it is still a human construct, almost but not quite mythic.

The Romantic Semiotics of the Courthouse and Litigation

In being run out of Paradise, Adam and Eve become the first outlaws or transportees, revolutionary prototypes of later fallen heroes, moral outlaws such as Robin Hood or the poachers of the traditional ballad.[52] Robin Hood springs up (imaginatively) where the new rule of law – secular law in the fallen world – becomes corrupted or fails to deliver justice, oppressing the masses and leaving them hungry and cold. The machinery that breaks down or is seen as an engine of corruption is largely that of the administration of justice, often litigation, which has its own iconography.

Primarily it is a romantic iconography, a universe of good versus evil, of contests, champions, and dragon-slaying, with plaintiffs and prosecutors as protagonists. The battleground or jousting list is the courtroom. This is what makes it such a splendid setting for novels as well as drama in theatres and on television – this and the fact that a trial superlatively respects the Aristotelian dramatic unities of time, place, and action.[53] Courthouses, in other words, are the original settings of reality television and cinema vérité. Besides Justitia and the seals and sloganeering we already have noted, on older courthouses (and legislative buildings) we find gargoyles meant to ward off evil, in stone as well as human, judicial form. From the counsel table or prisoners' box or well of the court, we mere mortals must look up toward the priestly judge on his dais/altar, with his subalterns sitting just below. Admission beyond the bar, and "permission to approach the bench," are sorts of vouchsafing, allowance onto semi-sacred ground. Judges' chambers are a sort of holy of holies, from which they appear via "secret" (hidden) passageways.

Trial by jurymen (and for most of the institution's history, jurors were men, of course) has evolved, from trials by fire, water, and combat, all of which assumed the intervention of God to show who was guilty or not. Classically, there are twelve jurymen, as there are twelve apostles, signs of the Zodiac, tribes of Israel – culturally seminal, regulatory entities that represent and follow specific, fundamental laws. Graphically, this gives us another version of our quartal hierarchy, whether we are talking about law as or law in literature:

LITIGATION PARADIGM, DRAWN FROM ROMANCE

I   Judge, as trier and highest authority but also priestly symbol of received wisdom/law, either statutory or judge-made.

II Jury of peers, applying fictive ("paradisal") standards of reasonableness. Where there is no jury, it is substituted by legal principle according to which the judge says, "I must instruct myself."

III Plaintiff, prosecutor as quester-protagonist, dragon-slayer in the trenches. The plaintiff's cause of action can also be symbolic, as with "distressed" land or property, assaults on an innocent or "pure" victim, etc.

IV Defendant, accused (antagonist), representing evil.

Darkness and Light

As metaphor, these appear in both law in and law as literature, to symbolize the absence or presence of justice. The metaphors are multifarious and often cliché: bad times and places are wintry, devoid of sun, an unjust or lawless place is dark or gray (as in Conrad's *Heart of Darkness*, Orwell's *1984*), the devil is the Dark Prince (as in *Paradise Lost*), and humans who are evil have often been dark-skinned or have dark hair. In the British traditional ballad "The Twa Sisters," for example, the jealous "dark girl" drowns her sister, who has attracted a lordly lover with her skin "white as is the milk." White is purity, and in this case, as in many others, its power is transcendent, metaphysical, overwhelming the dark:[54] the drowned girl's sea-bleached bones are made into a harp, which bears witness to the crime, singing it out publicly in the hands of a musician.

One finds a modern ironic take on such magic in Cynthia Ozick's Puttermesser stories: Puttermesser creates a golem to restore law and order to New York City, only to be raped and murdered as she mulls over a passage in Thomas Mann's *Joseph and His Brothers* – fatefully, about how earth and heaven are interlocked, as human, and thus imperfect, constructs. (As well, Puttermesser's golem, while embodying Platonic ideals of justice and reason, specifically remarks that she fears the dark.)[55] Such magic is a throwback in the sense that it appeals to higher, or metaphysical, powers and shows evil to be uncontrollable by means available in the physical world. In a fallen, unjust world, supernatural magic intervenes to work justice. But as Ozick and the golem legends themselves suggest, as a creature of the planet, it too is mortal.

Formerly, the "underworld" would have been represented by public executions, heads on pikestaffs, hanged men left on the gallows, perhaps, the gallows themselves, etc., as well as milder forms of public punishment, such as the pillory and ducking stool.

The Symbology of Colour

Finally, colour symbolism in literature parallels such symbolism in law:

- White (as just noted) signifies light, heaven, purity, source of law, justice, and mercy.
- Green connotes the paradisal, pre-law, pastoral ideas of equality; it is, for example, the iconographic colour of Robin Hood as moral outlaw. Its pastoral quality is highlighted in *A Gest of Robyn Hode* when, for sport, the king and his men dress in green so as to seem part of Robin Hood's now massive private army. When the mock coalition reaches an urban setting, Nottingham proper, the townsfolk (unlike the country folk) flee.[56] Soon thereafter, Robin himself goes AWOL from the king's service for twenty-two years, plumping – albeit not with any evident moral purpose – for outlawry, the life and politics he knows and claims.
- Red connotes Eros/Thanatos, love, war, death, strife.
- Black (as above, in the sense of darkness) often signifies evil, hopelessness, anarchy, criminality, etc.

Law is Prose, Justice is Poetry (Reprise)

Every idea behind all of what we have said above, behind law and the culture encompassing it, is a matter (naturally) of human conception and creation. It is all part of how we explain our universe to ourselves, and how we seek to impose some sort of order on it. And that is where law and literature – the prosaic and the poetical – meet. The only pure justice, the most dependable justice, is poetic justice.

IV. THE MOCK EXECUTION OF ISAAC: THE UNJUST TEST AS DIDACTIC ANTI-ARCHETYPE?

Finally, we note one motif that recurs enough that it seems to be an archetype, but is disturbing enough to be anti-archetypal. What I mean by that is that this motif contains two types which seem to work at cancelling each other. It seems to confound the demonic into what Frye calls the apocalyptic pattern, or what we have adapted as the law-as-literature or secular justice paradigm.

From the standpoint of justice, Genesis XXII recounts one of the most troubling narratives of the Hebrew and Christian Bibles, a story that has vexed commentators for centuries. To "prove" or "test" Abraham's faith, God commands the prototypical patriarch to sacrifice Isaac, his first-born son, as a burnt offering. Some say justice prevails: Abraham binds Isaac, hefts him onto the woodpile, and prepares to slaughter him. Having proved Abraham's faith and loyalty, God tells him to stay his hand and provides the ram in the thicket as a substitute sacrifice. Then, too, we can read the text to say that Abraham trusts all along that he won't have to go through with the sacrifice of his first born: accompanying his father to perform what he believes to be the usual animal sacrifice, Isaac asks, "But where is the lamb?" Abraham reassures him, "God will provide a lamb." But if this means Abraham really believes God will provide a substitute for his son (and is not hinting that Isaac is in fact the "lamb"), it is counter-intuitive in the story's context: such a reading mitigates the test of faith, or even nullifies it. It presumes that Abraham goes along with the test believing that God isn't serious. He follows God's command, all right, but on the understanding that he won't have to respect it.

If, however (as is more likely), Abraham is meant to follow God's command in the expectation that he will have to execute it to the letter, there are two core problems of justice, both of them founded in apparent totalitarianism:

(1) At the age of one hundred, Abraham is ordered to kill his young son for no apparent reason other than it demonstrates that he accepts God's absolute supremacy and authority. The justice – if it exists – remains invisible or intuitive. What makes this so uncomfortable, and

pushes us to look for rationalizations – such as that God uses the occasion to show how he turns his back on human sacrifice as a repugnant, pagan practice – is that it feels like dictatorial bullying. On such a reading, the lesson and meaning are obscure, particularly insofar as the God of the Hebrew Bible generally just forbids something rather than stages a melodrama to imply he doesn't like it. As with the test elements in the stories of Adam and Eve, Moses, and Job, to mortal understanding the test seems patently unjust. It is almost as though the unjust test is another archetype – perhaps an instance of what Frye calls "demonic modulation"[57] – that seeks resolution in the story of Jesus Christ, who is bound to succeed at his test as a matter of redemption for all of humankind (just as Adam, Eve, and Moses are bound to fail theirs). This seems to be what Melville conveys in another warhorse of the law-and-literature canon, *Billy Budd*. Budd strikes a fellow sailor who maliciously accuses him of counselling mutiny, and the man dies. Vere witnesses this, and in his role as ship's captain both prosecutes and defends Budd, whom he considers morally innocent. Acutely aware of the injustice of imposing a capital penalty, he anyway argues that Budd must be hanged from the yardarm. He specifically distinguishes between natural justice and law, remarking that it is not the military court who will impose sentence of death but "martial law operating through us. For that law and the rigor of it, we are not responsible. Our avowed responsibility is in this: That however pitilessly that law may operate, we nevertheless adhere to it and administer it."[58] Melville then tells us that Vere privately advises Budd of the verdict, such that "what took place at the interview was never known." The author imagines, however: "The austere devotee of military duty letting himself melt back into what remains primeval in our formalized humanity may in the end have caught Billy to his heart even as Abraham may have caught young Isaac on the brink of resolutely offering him up in obedience to the exacting behest." At other junctures throughout the story, Melville baldly compares Budd to Adam and Christ.

Unlike Adam and Moses, and more or less akin to Job and Christ, Isaac is a complete innocent. Abraham's test regarding this sort of lamb could seem to create a scarifying template for modern suicide bombers, often young men sacrificed by their fathers and elders on the promise that this is a religious duty which will earn them eternal life brightened by sexual connection with celestial virgins. These men are assured they act as martyrs in God's name. The Christ narrative is saved from this difficulty by virtue of the fact that the father is the sovereign: father and sacrificer are the same, who knows from the outset that he is making no sacrifice at all.

(2) Following from that, for all Abraham knows the commandment demands that a blameless young man must sacrifice his life well before he has lived it, as part of a test of someone else's faith and loyalty. Commentary routinely ignores young Isaac's trauma, or very occasionally assumes he bravely passes the test along with his father.

On this reading the test is totalitarian and ruthless – sadistic, even. The fact that Abraham is not obliged to go through with the commandment is obviously mitigating, but in the way of a mock execution (presuming, again, that he does not assume God ultimately will not make him carry through). We are compelled to look for something more comforting and substantial, such as that the legal code now substitutes lower animals for human sacrifice. Yet it remains that to feel any sense of justice we are forced to cast about like this so as to take the sting out of Abraham's "proving" and Isaac's trauma. Then, too, the narrative, if not the legal code (the two, of course, are confounded in the Hebrew Bible, such that it is difficult to know what is law and what might be legal fiction or metaphor) seems to call for further, later instances of human sacrifice, and of sons and daughters – some still sexually immature, at that. These include where:

- Joshua tells the Israelites that Jericho will be rebuilt (after the wall is destroyed and the city obliterated) on the blood of its eldest and youngest sons: "And Joshua adjured them at that time, saying, 'Cursed be the man before the Lord, that riseth up and buildeth this city Jericho. He shall lay the foundation thereof in his firstborn, and in his youngest son shall he set up the gates of it'" (Joshua 6:26).[59]
- The jurist-mercenary Jephthah promises Yahweh that "if thou shalt without fail deliver the children of Ammon into mine hands, then it shall be that whatsoever cometh forth of the doors of my house to meet me, when I return in peace from the children of Ammon, shall surely be the Lord's, and I will offer it up for a burnt offering." Having defeated the Ammonites, Jephthah returns home, where the first to greet him is his virgin daughter "with timbrels and dances." She agrees with her father that he must fulfill his vow by sacrificing her as a burnt offering (Judges 11).

- Yahweh advises David that the cause of a famine is "Saul, and ... his bloody house, because he slew the Gideonites." By way of "atonement," David sends the Gideonites seven of Saul's sons for sacrifice. The Gideonites hang the men at harvest time, and the nurturing rains begin (II Samuel 21).

Then again, an archetypal pattern can have its own logic – here, the Abraham-Isaac narrative establishing a motif that takes us to Moses and Christ, all in the name of fidelity to the Law. Isaac is the sacrificial offering resurrected, but in a trial on the individual level and *not* of the sacrificial figure but of the sacrificer, the messianic father. As we've noted, it is in this last respect that the story fails to fully set the precedent and thereby helps to make us anxious about questions of justice. Abraham and Isaac are patriarchs, but they are not legally iconic in the way of messiahs as ultimate authority figures. In the case of Moses, "God the father" sacrifices the quasi-messiah, an unwilling "lamb" like Isaac but otherwise a messianic "son," his "father's" end being to restore a nation to earthly Paradise – redeeming a people, but without the son of man who has led them to this point. With Jesus, God the father sacrifices the willing – co-conspiring – lamb so as to reunite humankind and Heaven, or humankind and the son reconstituted as the father. Here the son is only a manifestation of the father, with whom he reconstitutes after his mortal mission. He can never really be sacrificed in the way that Isaac or Moses can, which in the end makes us less queasy about the justice questions.[60]

V. LAW AS NARRATIVE

Legal versus Individual Narrative

The legal paradigms – some version of the four steps working from legislative supremacy to sociopathy, or topsy-turvy from sociopathy down – remain static in both law as literature and law in literature. But in the case law, law *as* literature, the judge is the primary author, the priestly interpreter of the law. In *The House Gun*, Nadine Gordimer puts the point exactly, from the point of view of a professional couple whose son is on trial for murder: "A judge knows everything. He's the vicar of the god of justice, as the priest is the vicar of God, he's privy to the confessional of the court, where witnesses and experts and the accused tell what Harald and Claudia would never have learnt. This knowledge, it's the basis of justice, isn't it?"[61]

Legal protocol – displaced ritual – limits a judge's narrative scope with such devices as precedent (*stare decisis*) and other procedural matters. The advocate has a role as co-author – a sort of altar boy, permitted as he is inside the bar, but this is little evident, unless the judge expressly refers to it in such phrases as "Ms. Counsel states the case strongly in her factum ...," "As Mr. Barrister put it in his able argument ..." In any event, like Moses or Luke, the judge has the final, if sometimes plagiaristic, word.

In this sphere, as opposed to law *in* literature, how the static paradigm is expressed, its narrative form, will depend upon the judge's role, or his perception of that role, in the system of government.

Strictly speaking, doctrines of legislative supremacy and precedent dictate that the judge is as much at the mercy of the law as he is its interpreter. In terms of the paradigm and iconography, he is a Moses on Pisgah, slow of speech, forbidden to take onto himself the trappings of the Logos, and ultimately not altogether equipped for his task. But then of course there are the activists – or, where the jury is trier, the nullifiers – who do what they think is just, never mind the law. Thus we have Lord Denning, possibly the most notorious activist judge in Anglo-American history, distinguishing himself from his colleagues: "They go by the letter and I go by the spirit of the law."[62]

This is rightly regarded as dangerous, because, first of all, the law depends on precedent (predictability, stability), which itself depends on a community of interest and decision-making, not on idiosyncracy. The activist judge is – again in the historic sense – a Prometheus, who would steal the gods' fire, ostensibly for man's sake. And only true messiahs can get away with that. Sometimes they do, even if it takes them years of railing in dissent (as was the case with Denning, Chief Justice Oliver W. Holmes in the US, and with Bora Laskin in Canada). They are allowed Creative trappings, as creator-interpreter, with the legislator. Sometimes their evangelism withstands appeal and makes new law, and a new branch of the narrative, a sort of new church founded on historic principles.

Albert Camus's *The Outsider* is exemplary in showing how the law's narrative – which is communal – can differ from our own, individual version. In such instances, law in literature approaches law as literature. Writing (however idiosyncratically) about a sort of outsider in the Alabama of 1935, the liberal lawyer of Harper Lee's *To Kill a*

Mockingbird, Stephen Lubet notes that a law trial is essentially a presentation of competing narratives.[63] And Northrop Frye has written that "the action of comedy in moving from one social center to another is not unlike the action of a lawsuit, in which plaintiff and defendant construct different versions of the same situation, one finally being judged as real and the other as illusory ..."[64] Rhetorically, this movement is from opinion to proof, but I would suggest *The Outsider* and other works such as Kafka's *The Trial* demonstrate that other literary modes can show the same relationship to legal actions. *The Trial* has many comic elements, of course; it is a tragicomedy. But *The Outsider* has none. And neither moves toward the desired society that comedy strives for in the end (the new Earthly Paradise); the prevailing "proof" leads to tragic death in each case.

Camus's protagonist Meursault sees himself as an ordinary man acting in an extraordinary circumstance: his mother and he were not particularly close, as often happens in life; when he killed the Arab man, he was overcome by sunstroke and possibly some fear for his life; he was not himself. The law's narrative is that he is a psychopath, with no fellow feeling or even love of his own mother. He is completely self-involved. The difference at the surface is largely rhetorical: evidence becomes semantics, a matter of subjective description of events. (The prosecutor even makes speeches about Meursault's bad character, without leading evidence to support all of it or otherwise justifying any argument – unlawful in some settings – for "propensity" to commit murder.) Only as Meursault watches his own trial, and hears the prosecutor's version of his life since the death of his mother, does he see that law's narrative is distinct. It is as though he is a spectator at a performance that has nothing particular to do with him.

The more objective listener will hear the discord among the chords – the uses and misuses of legal language, which can render more or less innocent acts as evidence of criminal character. ("Innocent" in this context means blameless legally if not morally.) In many respects, Meursault's behaviour has been hyper-reasonable. For example, given his character and circumstances, his view that his mother would fare better in a nursing home than in his care, and that after her death it was hypocritical to show grief he did not feel, are rational. In other ways, he is dispassionate to the point of recklessness, making love with his new girlfriend before his mother is cold in her grave, and indifferently befriending the cruel and immoral, helping his neighbour Raymond exact revenge on that man's estranged Algerian girlfriend.

(And of course, in Meursault's time and place, generally society expected children to be more solicitous of their aged parents.) Still, all of this could be put down to his rejection of bourgeois convention if only he had not subsequently committed the brutal murder, emptying a gun into a man he knew he had killed with the first shot.

The law views everything in that light, retrospectively, as part of a pattern leading to what lawyers call "the culminating event." But for the senselessness of the murder, even Meursault's agreeing to help defend a brutish friend could be "accepted" as part of a macho moral code of his era and geography. The murder breaks through the barrier of idiosyncracy into psychopathy. The law's narrative, as presented by the prosecutor, confounds the two, which is the law's error. It leaves out the evidence that contradicts psychopathy – Meursault's pleasure when others feel happy, for example, his kindness to Salamano (the repulsive, lonely man who abuses his dog but loves it all the same) and even to the less *sympathique* if equally lonely Raymond. While Meursault exists mostly at the animal level of immediate self-centredness, he is not unaccommodating and often, in fact, goes along to get along: he does his work dutifully but without ambition; he "doesn't mind" being Raymond's friend, marrying Marie. Compared to Salamano and Raymond, he actually looks supremely reasonable. On this view, many readers see Meursault being sentenced to death simply for his coldness to his mother.

Claude Lévi-Strauss gives an interesting version of this bifurcation of narrative, used in this instance by the accused person himself, during an actual trial at the beginning of the last century. A young boy, of the Zuni of New Mexico, had grabbed a twelve-year-old girl by the hands. She then suffered "a nervous seizure" and the Zuni accused the boy of sorcery, a crime punishable by death. Believing on apparently reasonable grounds that pleading innocent would be fruitless, the boy gave several versions of how he was led to or practised sorcery, improvising more elaborately every time the triers rejected his explanations. At last he explained that he came from a family of witches who could transform themselves at will into murderous cats. The family changed shape, he added, by using certain kinds of plumes. When the court demanded that the boy produce the plumes, he claimed they were hidden in a wall in the family home. The triers forced the boy to pull down a significant amount of plaster in the residence until at last, by great fortune, he found a feather in a wall. Returning to the public forum, the boy proffered the feather as evidence, made further elaborate improvisations on the magical cat narrative, and apologized. Upon finding him guilty on this narrative, the judges set him free.

The accused boy, Lévi-Strauss explains, "gives the group the satisfaction of truth, which is infinitely greater and richer than the satisfaction of justice that would have been achieved by his execution." By "truth" Lévi-Strauss of course does not mean what actually caused the girl's seizure. He means that the boy provided the triers with a narrative that accorded with their beliefs and related justice system. Fiction, as the cliché has it, tells a higher truth. "Through the defendant, witchcraft and the ideas associated with it cease to exist as a diffuse complex of poorly formulated sentiments and representations, and become embodied in real experience." At the same time, the boy's impromptu short story – "his ingenious defence," Lévi-Strauss calls it – serves as "a corroboration of their system (especially since the choice is not between this system and another, but between the magical system and no system at all – that is, chaos)," and so does the group transform a terrible criminal in its midst to "the guardian of its spiritual coherence."[65] Then, too, by creating a necessary fiction, the boy shows his desire to participate in and build the culture; he makes clear, in other words, that he is no outlaw. Cultural truth over justice; structure over chaos: legal narrative has its own, culturally satisfying truth, even if the result is not objectively just.

This shift from actuality to fictive truth throws into relief another principle: the rule of law is not the highest achievement envisioned for our legal culture, even from just a secular point of view. Civilization constantly strives to regain the utopian state of being law-free, where duty is implicit and automatically respected, and personal freedom balances perfectly with personal responsibility – the ultimate liberalism. (Like everything else on Earth, society seeks equilibrium – a pre-law state. Consider again George Steiner's comment on the fall of communism.) Reconfiguring our schema for the secular "fallen" world, the Nietzschean, "godless" society of a Meursault, we find (contrary to what some of Camus's more learned readers say) that his behaviour still merits condemnation:

1 Rational civilization, or a state of paradisal lawlessness, an earthly, utopian environment – a restored Eden, free of predation, where one needs no law because cooperation is reflexive as central to

enlightened self-interest – the ultimate achievement of man as against nature

2 Urbanity – a state of developed, "artful" society that requires the rule of law to control human impulse and selfish behaviour; a more developed tribalism, with political and economic motivations which the law supports

3 Innocence/natural law, where man remains artless, in a state of nature, childish and therefore not morally corrupted or malicious, but without having developed the equipment to govern his behaviour. Social behaviour is limited to basic pack needs for individual survival; that is, tribalism. (Thus do some attribute Meursault's behaviour to the "new paganism.")

4 Anarchy/Social Darwinism/law of nature – man in a state of animal lawlessness

Meursault is comfortable at level three, but because conventional society and its legal system conduct themselves at level two, his behaviour obliges him to interact at that level. While he admits dispassionately that he committed a homicide (the admission itself being a legally mitigating circumstance), he does advance (if incoherently) a perfectly legal defence in at least mitigation of what he has done: non-insane automatism. He blames his crime on "*le soleil*" (which is also his focus as he languishes on death row), but which remark – or the absurdity of its terseness as an explanation – provokes hilarity in the courtroom. The popular mind labels the condition he means to describe "temporary insanity" – as, for instance, the result of a greater "personality disorder" (more jargon that can signal the twisting of unconventional behaviour into some more socially acceptable dysfunction), and as such it can be at least mitigating. To the extent that it is mindless, it can constitute a complete defence to a crime of violence. But even were the defence advanced more effectively, the character evidence is particularly damning against it, because there is nothing that shows Meursault to have been under any particular psychological compunction or stress that led to the behaviour. He would in fact assert this strenuously, against his own interest – which one could interpret as another sign of mental disorder, on the one hand, or a highly reasoning, if non-conformist mind on the other. (Ironically, he himself suggests a link to his mother's death: "It was the same sun as on the day of Mother's funeral." Depending on the narrative context and rhetorical thrust given, this could be evidence for either the prosecution or the defence.)

In viewing the proceedings against him as a sort of theatre, and in his final words to us as readers, Meursault demonstrates a deliberation or *mens rea* that before was unclear. He is not an outlaw, but having chosen to be an outsider he fits the French way of describing outlawry – *hors la loi*, literally: outside the law. In the book's last paragraph, as a prisoner he at last comes to identify with his mother's situation in the retirement home: "With death so near, Mother must have felt like someone on the brink of freedom, ready to start life all over again." At the same moment, he feels reborn, "for the first time, the first, I laid my heart open to the benign indifference of the universe" – the indifference that, ironically, makes positive law necessary. He feels the indifference to be "so like myself, indeed so brotherly," that he realizes how happy he has been. Finally, he concludes: *Pour que tout soit consommé, pour que je me sente moins seul, il me rester à souhaiter qu'il y ait beaucoup de spectateur le jour de mon exécution et qu'ils m'acceuiellent avec des cris de haine*: "So as to resolve everything, so that I can feel less alone, my final hope is that there will be many spectators on the day of my execution, and that they will welcome me with howls of hatred."

Only here does it become clear that Meursault seems to reject not only "bourgeois convention" but the rule of law, the bulwark against the universe's indifference. Then again, one could argue that this is a coping mechanism, rationalizing what he has done and the fearful punishment he faces (to the extent that such a sentiment can be described as rational). It is anti-redemptive, affirming in the sense that his way of living becomes a point of principle, even in the face of death.

It has become common to characterise Meursault's outlook on life as "absurdist": among humans, all is vanity; any attempt at interpretive order is a fantastical imposition on nothingness; life has no necessary meaning, no matter our attempts to impose rhyme and reason. The trouble with this view is that it still assumes a level of civilized behaviour, a sort of innate goodness in people, at least to the extent that we understand that our mutual self-interest rests in cooperating with our fellows. If everyone acted more or less on selfish impulse, only the most brutal and canny would survive. Although Meursault only half-heartedly comes to accept some responsibility for his predicament, his own experience in the short period covered by the book walks a continuum towards social Darwinism, a descent from not crying at his mother's funeral to homicide. In other words, he himself has not known where to draw the line on his egocentrism. Here is where the law's narrative of his life gains some credence. Viewing life as "absurd" might account for resisting bourgeois sentimentality, but where along the following continuum is it no longer an excuse for what the conventionally reasonable person would consider bad behaviour?

- not crying at your mother's funeral;
- kicking a scabby dog (as Salamano does);
- luring a woman into sexual humiliation;
- standing by while your "friend" (Raymond) beats the woman;
- fighting with someone for whom you feel no personal enmity, in support of your friend;
- homicide, on the vague ground that the victim might have been threatening you;
- shooting someone you've just killed an additional four times (after all, you feel sun-stricken and he's already dead)?

The latter part of the book concerns the absurdity of contingency. (This has to be the point, at least in part, of the blackly comic news clipping Meursault finds under his prison mattress – about the man who, separated from his mother and sister for twenty-five years, decides to surprise them with his newfound success, only to have them murder and rob him when they mistake him for a rich stranger. Contingency – the conflicting narratives at work – turns his "comic" ending to tragedy.) On this view, it is the individual in bourgeois society who suffers from non-insane automatism as he follows meaningless cultural rituals and is buffeted by events that might not have happened if the events leading to them would have been skewed however slightly by some other event. It's all a matter of narrative. To the extent that Meursault's behaviour "means" anything, it suggests that he views ritual and convention as empty, as futile attempts to impose order and meaning on essentially pointless existence. In his refusal to "accept God," Meursault's attack on the prison chaplain concerns living honestly, not on false hope and convention. (As Camus has said in an afterward, Meursault "agrees to die for the truth," a man "in love with a sun that leaves no shadows." Here we recall Empson: "You are nomad yet; the lighthouse beam you own / Flashes like Lucifer, through the firmament, / Earth's axis varies; your dark central cone / Wavers a candle's shadow, at the end.") His mother dies and "nothing had changed" – a matter of "benign indifference" to the universe, which indifference is precisely why mortal law exists. Meursault's brand of "reasonableness" or hyper-rationality – the refusal of individuals to obey laws they view as pointless – is at base a way of intellectualizing social Darwinism. Peace, order, and good government[66] often require that we buy into the fiction that the world is not absurd. This is what the prosecutor means when he tells the jury that the "negative ethic" of tolerating aberrant behaviour must give way to the "loftier ethic of justice." He means "justice" in the figurative way that lawyers use it on a daily basis, in the sense of protecting the social order, even if the disaffected minority must suffer disproportionately.

In fact, Meursault moves beyond indifference to disdain for human society, and a need to justify the way he has lived. His concern at the end is to reaffirm his disgrace. This is why it is more sensible to translate the title not as *The Stranger* but as *The Outsider*. Under the shadow of the noose, he persists in his desire to live outside conventional society and closer to the visceral, Darwinian or less "civilized" (more "honest") world. While the protagonist of J.M. Coetzee's *Disgrace* similarly embraces anti-conventionalism, a sort of libertinism bordering on benign anarchy, finally he is interested in redemption – re-attaining grace.

Against the backdrop of South Africa's emergence from apartheid, the protagonist, David Lurie, ultimately rejects the possibility of earthly justice, accepting, instead, a sort of poetic justice, the ironic concept that justice is perfect only metaphorically. Like Meursault, Lurie lives a hedonistic, selfish life that lands him in disgrace: he loses his job after seducing a listless student. He scorns "earthly," quasi-legal procedures (the university discipline committee) as compelling repentance he does not feel; here, in his view, resides the actual "political correctness" of the situation, not community outrage about sex. He then submits to the procedure while passively resisting it, in a sort of harrowing of Hell. This leads to his exile to his daughter's farm, like a scapegoat in the wilderness, where his real trials begin – horrors that include a house invasion and the gang rape of his daughter Lucy, leading to the burglary of his apartment in town – until he at last has nothing material left, and no material interests. Paradigmatically, he moves from urbanity – the "world of experience" – into the limbo of the pastoral, awaiting redemption, which comes only after "Paradise" is well and truly lost. (It has, of course, been only a false paradise, in any event, standing on the quicksand of apartheid.) The attack on the farm is an instance of *Et in Arcadia ego*, death and sin entering Paradise, reminding us that we are still in the material world and realm of laws, and lawlessness. Until the end, a skeptic's Job, he accepts the idea of grace – redemption, not necessarily earned – but, Meursault-like, rejects rehabilitation.

As Lucy has given up redemption in the material world, so does David, at last, give it up for spiritual pardon (as he helps euthanize a dog and imagines its soul twisting out of its body but unable to ascend to Heaven, not subject, by convention, to grace). He is the sinner redeemed, not the criminal rehabilitated. Along the way, inadvertently suffering sentence, he learns humility in various ways, first with the terrible attack at the farm, then with Lucy's black hired hand Petrus, who symbolizes the new world order that in many ways is just as malevolent as the old – apartheid – and who, he and Lucy see, is the future of the country. Ultimately Lurie develops a compassionate relationship with Bev (the lay veterinarian whom he otherwise finds ugly and pitiable – he allows her to use him, it seems, as if in expiation for his sexual exploitation of his student), pays an abortive visit to the student's family (the father being a sort of self-appointed Christ figure/redeemer whom Lurie rejects in that role), and, upon the ransacking of his Capetown apartment, lets go of everything substantial, including secular law, notions of earthly justice, and his worldly ambitions as symbolized in an operetta he is writing about Lord Byron. Ironically, it is his turning away from the material world that has unleashed his creativity with the latter. To the extent that this conceit works, it seems to make graphic Lurie's need to redeem, romanticize, and satirize all at once, his licentious urbanity.[67]

Dogs appear regularly throughout the novel, seemingly to reflect humankind's relationship with grace: as the universe – or fate or the godhead – may grant grace to man, so may man grant grace to the animals we husband and exploit. Mostly we don't (at least for Coetzee, who, mildly here but more pointedly elsewhere,[68] is an animal-rights exponent): a dog is beaten for expressing its natural sexuality; dogs are abandoned, sadistically shot in their kennels, euthanized because they are inconvenient to the people ("gods") around them. In the last pages, Lurie adopts one of the mutts at the shelter, only to "give him up," with everything else, to early euthanizing. And then there is his conversation with Lucy, after he offers to send her away from post-apartheid danger to Holland, where she was born, or "to give you whatever you need to set yourself up again somewhere safer than here." She decides, instead, to marry Petrus, polygamously, despite the fact that she is a lesbian, and to cede him her land. She agrees with her father that this will be humiliating, but thinks perhaps she "must learn to accept" that she must start over. "With nothing," she tells him. "Like a dog," Lurie replies. "Yes," Lucy says, "like a dog."[69] Coetzee is too careful a writer and reader not to be aware he is echoing what Joseph K. says at the end of *The Trial*, as his final words before execution: "'Like a dog!' he said; it was as if the shame of it must outlive him." Like K, Lucy, and perhaps Lurie (and the rest of us), are victims of history, a fate that seems arbitrary or at least oblivious to the dictates of justice. Grace, redemption, is a matter of chance or luck, and, finally, spent hope.

It's a Dutiful Day in the Neighbourhood: Duty as the Fulcrum on the Scales of Justice and the Centre of Community

I. WHO IN LAW IS MY NEIGHBOUR?

Like sacred law, secular law assumes that there is a single truth, and that the narrative conforms to that truth. It accepts that there are various narratives toward that truth, and perhaps an infinite variety of narrative voices and interpretations, but in the end it is exclusive. Judgment is determinative. So we need something outside of narrative to determine what justice really is: otherwise, the narrative of the Nazis or of the megalomaniacal officer in Kafka's "In the Penal Colony" would be just. That outside measure, which we often call morality, will vary over time: it might be an interpretation of received wisdom, such as the Bible or Koran, or it might be a more secularized standard of duty or rightness. Under sacred law, duty is always presumptively statutory, as it begins in the sacred texts but can be interpreted (or distorted) by sages and priests. Under secular law, it can have a statutory basis, but secular priests – judges and other official arbiters – can themselves create it, based on community standards of reasonableness. Occasionally, a Promethean jury can steal their fire, practising nullification or perverse verdict.

We said earlier that, as a juridical benchmark for lawful behaviour, the reasonable person evolved from the exemplary person of faith, such as Moses or Job. In secular law he evolves into a person of duty – one who respects his duty of care. He owes that duty, in Lord Atkin's famous dictum, to his neighbour, the formulation of whom Lord Atkin borrows from a sort of sub-commandment in Leviticus (19:18) and the parable of the good Samaritan:

The rule that you are to love your neighbour becomes in law you must not injure your neighbour; and the lawyer's question, Who is my neighbour? receives a restricted reply. You must take reasonable care to avoid acts or omissions which you can reasonably foresee would be likely to injure your neighbour. Who, then, in law, is my neighbour? The answer seems to be – persons who are so closely and directly affected by my act that I ought reasonably to have them in contemplation as being so affected when I am directing my mind to the acts or omissions which are called in question.[1]

Lord Atkin is aware that he is writing metaphorically, calling upon something profound in the legal and wisdom literature of our culture. Parables – fictive, often didactic narratives – are of course common in sacred law, including aboriginal or "primitive" law as well as in classical, Islamic, Hebrew, and Christian law.[2] In the latter two, the Ten Commandments, that prototypical constitution for western societies under the rule of law, also forbids us from coveting or appropriating our neighbours' property, employees, and spouses. Secular law adopted this but restricted the broader formulation – thou shalt not harm – at least insofar as Jesus had counselled, in the Samaritan parable, that your neighbour includes (and your duty extends to) a stranger suffering harm from third parties. Lawyers employed the early formulation of the common law neighbour principle as shield more than sword: defendants' counsel would often successfully plead, particularly before *Donoghue v. Stevenson*, that their clients owed no duty of care to the plaintiff suing. Time and industrialization expanded the duty of care, such that the bottler of the ginger beer owed a duty to provide May Donoghue an uncontaminated beverage, never mind that he had no dealings with her. Even unseen, and having no contract with her, she – a stranger – was the bottler's neighbour. (The duty was no longer limited to what could be laid at the door of Minchella, the restaurateur who served Donoghue the drink, which would have been no duty at all, given that the bottle was opaque and Minchella presumably was as surprised about the decomposing snail in the bottle as Donoghue was.) Today, the law has evolved further such that many jurisdictions have "good Samaritan" legislation requiring not just that we avoid harming others, but that we *intervene* if we observe someone in need of assistance. Canada and England still view this as a radical departure: "duty" in law does not impose a positive obligation to do good; it imposes liability, in the breach, for causing harm. This of course can be characterized as the distinction between law and morality: we lawfully can take advantage of loopholes in tax law, but we cannot steal; in many jurisdictions, we can lawfully engage in fornication and even adultery, but we cannot have more than one spouse.

In terms of legal iconography, or law as (literary) culture, we've said that the reasonable person is symbolic of epiphany, the way people would behave in a world that was altogether cooperative and sensible, if not quite heavenly. They wouldn't need to be "civilized," because they would live in a state of natural innocence (prototypical natural law) under a tacit social contract. The defining trait of that evolving symbol (the reasonable person) is a reflexive obeisance – a faithfulness – to received wisdom, a wisdom that orders society and keeps it peaceful. In the everyday material world, where we often need to work at being civil, against the laws of nature, this faith devolves into duty, and it requires at least a minimum of intentional "proper" behaviour, an enlightened self-interest.

Of course, law more generally is about community, with duty as the fulcrum balancing individual against community interest: "Love thy neighbour as thyself." Iconographically, duty is also the fulcrum on the scales of justice, mediating law and morality, putting in the balance whether we've met our community obligation. This is implicit in Martin Luther King's famous "I Have Been to the Mountaintop" speech (which is literary in its use of rhetoric – particularly the hortatory use of repetition – and imagery), delivered on April 3, 1968, at a rally to support striking garbage collectors in Memphis, Tennessee. "And so," King said, in his explication of the parable of the good Samaritan,

the first question that the Levite asked was, "If I stop to help this man, what will happen to me?" But then the Good Samaritan came by. And he reversed the question: "If I do not stop to help this man, what will happen to him?" That's the question before you tonight. Not, "If I stop to help the sanitation workers, what will happen to all of the hours that I usually spend in my office every day and every week as a pastor?" The question is not, "If I stop to help this man in need, what will happen to me?" "If I do not stop to help the sanitation workers, what will happen to them?" That's the question.

For students of law and literature, the speech makes the larger point that their subject cannot be divorced from history, never mind that some literary critics insist that the work speaks for itself, no matter its historical or biographical context. On this day before he was assassinated, King eerily alludes to the personal dangers, serious threats on his life, he has faced in leading the civil rights movement:

> It really doesn't matter what happens now. I left Atlanta this morning, and as we got started on the plane, there were six of us, the pilot said over the public address system, "We are sorry for the delay, but we have Dr. Martin Luther King on the plane. And to be sure that all of the bags were checked, and to be sure that nothing would be wrong with the plane, we had to check out everything carefully. And we've had the plane protected and guarded all night."
>
> And then I got to Memphis. And some began to say the threats, or talk about the threats that were out. What would happen to me from some of our sick white brothers?

There follow the famous words that end the speech, in which the great leader and rhetorician proves that he is, indeed, a new Lawgiver, bringing into modern times more individualized legal protection under the umbrella of community interest, coalescing the Christian teachings on "Who is my neighbour?" with modern secular law, while rationalizing it with the Mosaic tradition from which it derives. King has had his glimpse of the Promised Land from Pisgah. Even if he doesn't enter, he knows his people will. His mission is accomplished. Which is to say, he has done his duty:

> Well, I don't know what will happen now. We've got some difficult days ahead. But it doesn't matter with me now. Because I've been to the mountaintop. And I don't mind. Like anybody, I would like to live a long life. Longevity has its place. But I'm not concerned about that now. I just want to do God's will. And He's allowed me to go up to the mountain. And I've looked over. And I've seen the promised land. I may not get there with you. But I want you to know tonight, that we, as a people, will get to the promised land. And I'm happy, tonight. I'm not worried about anything. I'm not fearing any man. Mine eyes have seen the glory of the coming of the Lord.

We of course know today that thirty-nine-year-old King was not happy and worry-free that night. He was ill with flu, and seems to have felt strong foreboding that his time was not long. He was engaging in fiction to tell the greater truth.

Before reaching a conclusion about neighbourly duty, W.H. Auden's "Law Like Love" (1940), another law-and-literature staple, is largely about narrative perspective: gardeners say law is nature; old codgers say it "is the wisdom of the old," while their grandchildren mock them and say it "is the senses of the young." The priests say law is what emanates from their books and pulpits, while their secular counterpart, the judge, "looks down his nose" and impatiently reminds us "Law is The Law." Legal scholars insist that law is "neither wrong nor right," but simply anything the powerful make it to be. Almost unobtrusively, before the poem veers off to tell us law's narrative is as subjective and slippery as love's, Auden remarks on how dangerous such relativism can be:

> And always the loud angry crowd
> Very angry and very loud
> Law is We,
> And always the soft idiot softly Me.

When it's a lynch mob, the neighbourhood does not have the community interest at heart, any more than does the selfish idiot next door. As with love, while we might not be able to define law in a definitive way, we find it to be a force of life. Somehow it is necessary, objectively and subjectively, to human society.

It is important to note that this iconographic duty is a legal one in western cultures, though it pre-exists positive law. When Lord Atkin says that "Who is my neighbour?" is a "lawyer's question," he is talking about the law of duty in the case before him, but also something that transcends it, as its foundation. Luke 10:25 tells us that it was "a certain lawyer" who cross-examined Jesus on this issue – a lawyer seen to be baiting Jesus, "tempting" him by asking "What shall I do to inherit eternal life?" (Even in Luke, and even on this occasion of neighbourliness, lawyers suffer unsympathetic prejudgment.) Jesus turns the question back on the lawyer, asking, as one would do with a law student who has forgotten to consult the rules of procedure, "Well, what does the law say, as you read it?" The lawyer replies that the law commands complete love of God, and love of thy neighbour as thy-self. Jesus tells him he has his answer, then, but the lawyer persists: "And who is my neighbour?" Which leads to the literary event, or parable, which itself is a prototype of law in literature: to make his point about duty and the law, Jesus tells a story, using metaphor.

He recounts how a man travelling between Jerusalem and Jericho is mugged. As he lies half dead in the road, two passersby – a priest and a Levite – walk by without stopping. At last a man from Samaria rescues the traveller, and pays the bills for his rehabilitation. What is important for our purposes is that, having presented the parable, Jesus asks the lawyer, "Which now of these three, thinkest thou, was neigh-bour unto him that fell among the thieves?" And the lawyer correctly answers, "He that shewed mercy on him."

Note that the phrase, at least in Jacobean English, is "shewed mercy on him," not some version of "showed concern for him" or "helped him." The word-choice helps point up the importance of the Levite and priest, whom Jesus (or Luke) "writes into" the parable by way of contrast against the Samaritan, a non-Jew whom Jesus would have identified with, given his people's history of persecution (sometimes at the hands of Jews). Levites were Jewish but not of the priestly class, so what Jesus/Luke seem to be saying is that, until the Samaritan showed up, neither aristocrat – the so-called holy man – nor com-moner stopped to help the traveller. The priest and Levite seem to embody an "Old Testament" austerity: there was no positive legal duty to get involved in this unpleasant mugging business, so it was better to keep to oneself. By contrast, the non-Jewish Samaritan is accorded an innate Christian nature. The "New Testament" view is *merciful* (or at least its proponents say so, never mind that some of them have per-petrated genocide and global religious persecution), tempered, as equity tempers the common law. And in the industrial age, the House of Lords extended that mercy so as to make a manufacturer the neigh-bour of a consumer completely unknown to the manufacturer, out-side any pre-existing legal contract between it and the consumer. The equitable, social contract forged a new link in the legal contractual chain.

Literature often concerns the fact that duty is outward looking and requires an object, the community, at the sacrifice of the self, at least to the extent that self-interest conflicts with the common good. The so-called "duty of care" can sometimes be subjective – "a reasonable person in the defendant's circumstances," for instance – but the duty is always to some third party or parties, or to the world at large. The presumption is that the self finds its most secure development in a society of the like-minded.

Underlying this is the aforementioned central precept of law and literature: *Law begins and ends with Eden.* In Eden, there was only one rule (or, as we've said, restrictive covenant): do not eat of the Tree of Knowledge of Good and Evil. When the first humans broke that condition (as the sacred narrative goes), they opened the door to evil and death, making mortal law, founded in outward-looking duty, necessary to human survival. This is the point Milton makes when he has Eve tell the serpent:

> But of this Tree we may not taste nor touch;
> God so commanded, and left that Command
> Sole Daughter of his voice; the rest, we live
> Law to our selves, our Reason is our Law. (IX, 651–4)

Until the Fall, Adam and Eve have only themselves to consider: acting reasonably they will remain in a paradisal, pre-law state, like perpetual children. So does Wordsworth pick up Milton's language here in the first line of his "Ode to Duty": "Stern Daughter of the Voice of God!" Duty is a "dread Power" but also "victory and law/ When empty terrors overawe." Wordsworth explains his own mortal backsliding as part of the poem's motivation: "Many and many a time have I been twitted by my wife and sister for having forgotten this dedication of myself to the stern lawgiver."[3] Making poetry of this forgetting, he writes,

> Yet being to myself a guide,
> Too blindly have reposed my trust;
> And oft when in my heart was heard
> Thy timely mandate, I deferred
> The task, in smoother walks to stray;
> But thee I now would serve more strictly, if I may.

He has listened too much to ego and not enough to Duty. And so Wordsworth looks to Law, earthly duty's source, as solace. A strong sense of duty informs and governs the freedom of choice that led to the biblical fall and personal lapses, and it is also responsible for what is most beautiful in the fallen world:

Me this unchartered freedom tires;
I feel the weight of chance desires
My hopes no more must change their name,
I long for a repose that ever is the same.

Stern Lawgiver! yet thou dost wear
The Godhead's most benignant grace;
Nor know we anything so fair
As is the smile upon thy face:
Flowers laugh before thee on their beds
And fragrance in thy footing treads;
Thou dost preserve the stars from wrong;
And the most ancient heavens, through thee, are fresh and strong.

And the poet concludes by asking:

Give unto me, made lowly wise,
The spirit of self-sacrifice;
The confidence of reason give...

In less Romantic times, both language and sentiment here are
ripe for parody, and in his "Kind of an Ode to Duty" Ogden Nash
relies entirely on the sentiment that duty is self-abnegation, which
is to say, not very fun. Writing with self-criticism equal to Wordsworth's, but also in more honest confession, the poet shows he is
more than ambivalent about the task of celebrating the dread
Power. Even his title qualifies the honorific, and he uses the high-
falutin' language of "litrichoor" (Ezra Pound's mocking term for
arts and letters) as a shredded veil over his true feelings, the naked
imperatives of Self:

O Duty,
Why hast thou not the visage of a sweetie or a cutie?
...
Why art thou so different from Venus
And why do thou and I have so few interests mutually in common
    between us?
Why art thou fifty per cent martyr
And fifty-one per cent Tartar?

Why is it thy unfortunate wont
To try to attract people by calling on them either to leave undone
   the deeds they like,
or to do the deeds they don't?

Again, where ego says "Me first," law and conscience say "love thy
neighbour." In a parody within the parody, Nash gives a new answer
to Emerson's "When Duty whispers low, Thou must." Emerson's
Youth, a potential Union recruit in the American Civil War, replies, "I
can"; but Nash, ever Falstaffian about discretion and honour (particularly where the youth is now "erstwhile"), responds, "I just can't." Then
again, we can all take comfort in George Peele's homiletic, "Beauty,
strength, youth are flowers but fading seen; / Duty, faith, love are
roots, and evergreen." The mature self finds fulfillment in duty, based
on "the confidence of reason."

The larger point in all this for law and literature is that with the Fall
not only does death enter the world, but so does duty. As Milton puts
it, referring us back to Adam's prototypical duty in Eden, prefiguring
Nash but in a different mood:

Many there be that complain of divine Providence for suffering
Adam to transgress. Foolish tongues! When God gave him reason,
he gave him freedom to choose, for reason is but choosing; he had
been else a mere artificial Adam, such an Adam as he is in the
motions. We ourselves esteem not of that obedience, or love, or
gift, which is of force: God therefore left him free, set before him
a provoking object ever almost in his eyes; herein consisted his
merit, herein the right of his reward, the praise of his abstinence.
Wherefore did he create passions within us, pleasures round about
us, but that these rightly tempered are the very ingredients of
virtue? They are not skilful considerers of human things, who
imagine to remove sin by removing the matter of sin; for, besides
that it is a huge heap increasing under the very act of diminish-
ing, though some part of it may for a time be withdrawn from
some persons, it cannot from all, in such a universal thing as
books are; and when this is done, yet the sin remain entire.
Though ye take from a covetous man all his treasure, he has yet
one jewel left: ye cannot bereave him of his covetousness. Banish
all objects of lust, shut up all youth into the severest discipline

that can be exercised in any hermitage, ye cannot make them chaste that came not thither so: such great care and wisdom is required to the right managing of this point.[4]

We act dutifully only so far as we resist selfish temptation. Otherwise duty is meaningless, including (especially) man's easier, singular duty *before* the Fall. Elaborating some years later on this tension or co-dependency, this legal necessity of free will, Milton's God feverishly asks, of his fallen angels but, by extension, of Adam and Eve:

> ... what praise could they receive?
> What pleasure I from such obedience paid,
> When Will and Reason (Reason also is a choice)
> Useless and vain, of freedom both despoild,
> Made passive both, had serv'd necessitie,
> Not mee...
> ... nor can [they] justly accuse
> This maker, or thir making, or thir Fate;
> As if Predestination over-rul'd
> Thir will, dispos'd by absolute Decree
> Or high foreknowledge; they themselves decreed
> Thir own revolt, not I ...[5]

And so does law begin and end with this notion of innocence breached. As we shall investigate more fully when we talk about the revolutionary mentality, or reasonableness without civil duty, at the Fall humankind moves from *Homo ludens* – a childish, playful existence free of rules – to a state that requires watchful responsibility enforced by rules: the daily world as we know it is circumscribed by duty and death. How we answer duty determines not only how we survive this life, but how we outlive ourselves, in name and spirit.

II. DEFEND THE CHILDREN OF THE POOR; PUNISH THE WRONGDOER: BREACH OF DUTY AND THE SEARCH FOR JUSTICE

On its publication in 1966, Mordecai Richler's *St. Urbain's Horseman* was regarded as satire – exotically ethnic, funny, "edgy," a Canadian expression of what Philip Roth, Bruce Jay Friedman, and Saul Bellow were doing in the US. Today, it has more the feel of a meditation, if a neurotic one, on justice in the twentieth century. It is, in fact, as chivalric as *Don Quixote*, with which it bears more than a passing resemblance.

As a wealthy filmmaker resident with his beautiful wife and accessory children in posh Hampstead Heath, protagonist Jake Hersh lives the 1960s liberal dream in the shadow of bristling nightmare. Cocooned by wealth, secular humanism, "free love," he constantly anticipates personal holocaust even as the capital H version remains palpable, in danger of flaring back up. He frets over his own conventional liberalism, escaping into quixotic fantasies about his gangster cousin Joey – St. Urbain's Horseman – hunting down Josef Mengele in Paraguay. But whenever Jake tries actually to break out of his middle-class complacency, miserable disaster ensues. He confronts an uncle about his supposed gruff treatment of Joey and his family, only to have the reality of Joey's ruffian, self-centred life thrown back at him, along with a reminder that the uncle pulled Joey's family out of desperate straits. And, fatefully, when Jake slums around with Harry Stein, the *farbissener* (misery-guts) who works for Jake's accountant, he ends up convicted of an indecent assault he didn't commit – on a German girl, yet. (So much for free love.) He is not Joey, never mind his dream at the book's end when, momentarily, he seems to take his cousin's place after reading of his death. "It's just a nightmare," he reassures his wife Nancy. *Just* a nightmare. And at last he abdicates, climbing back into complacency, if a battered one, telling himself that Joey is only "presumed" dead. After all, Joey, messiah, has resurrected himself before, after a car wreck (possibly staged). And after 1939, every Jew is a survivor.

Although it occurs at the end of the novel, the trial, and the events surrounding the death of Jake's father which just precedes it, is its centrepiece. Stein, whom Jake has allowed to use his home while Jake attends his father's funeral and wife Nancy is away with the children in Cornwall, stands charged with sodomy, rape, indecent assault, and possession of cannabis. Jake – involved in the incidents at bar only because he arrives home a day early, fleeing Montreal after the confrontation with his uncle – faces charges of aiding and abetting sodomy, indecent assault, and possession of cannabis. The truth seems to be that the marijuana belonged to Ingrid Loebner, a German student who consented to the salient sexual acts (albeit at first, before Jake arrives to find Stein and the girl in his home, under the impression that Stein was Jake Hersh, the trendy film director), and in fact performed fellatio on Jake without his explicit invitation. But in his own self-disgust, Jake thereafter has treated the girl contemptuously, throwing her out of the house in the wee hours of the morning.

In his first appearance at the Old Bailey – the Central Criminal Court – Jake Hersh notices the famous inscription over the door, leaving the reader to ruminate how it could be Hersh's own idealistic motto, if only he could live up to it: "Defend the Children of the Poor" – Joey and his siblings, those who died at Hitler's hands – "Punish the Wrongdoer." But he is painfully aware that he has not lived up to it as a matter of justice.

The letter of the law, of course, is another matter. Though Hersh and Stein have used Loebner, no doubt, "objectified" her, she has been at least a party to that offence. And it has been a contentious point in British law whether one actually consents to sex with somebody who represents himself to be someone else. *R. v. Collins*, for example, decided seven years after *St. Urbain's* was published, concerns the case of an eighteen-year-old woman who had drowsy intercourse with an odd jobber under the mistaken belief that the man, who had worked occasionally at the woman's home, was her boyfriend. On the theory that the young woman had consented to the "nature and quality" of the act, and therefore was not raped, the Crown prosecuted Collins for burglary – illegal entry with intent to rape – insofar as he had climbed a ladder and entered the woman's bedroom as she slept. He was convicted but acquitted on appeal on the argument that, confusing him with her boyfriend, the woman might have invited Collins to enter the bedroom while he was still outside on the ladder.[6] As one commentator archly put it, on this view "burglary may well ... vary with the length of a part much more private than the prisoner's foot."[7]

In literature, this sort of sexual duping – where A engages in sexual relations with C upon mistaking C for B – has an archetype, lately called "the bedtrick."[8] *Measure for Measure* supplies another notable legal-literary instance of it. In *The Sirens Sang of Murder*, Sarah Caudwell borrows the ruse from *All's Well That Ends Well*, but in a manner that has only a coincidental relationship to the legal aspects of the novel. In *St. Urbain's Horseman*, once the student learns Stein has duped her, she engages in further sexual acts with him and attempts to seduce Hersh. A brave barrister might argue retroactive consent but would still have to address the fact that, by the time of Jake Hersh's unexpected arrival, she has been smoking cannabis and drinking, such that her judgment was likely impaired.

In any event, the jury convicts Stein on both sexual-assault counts and the judge sentences him to seven years in prison. The popular modern view would no doubt construe this as his just deserts. But it is clear that, as Stein suggests, the student more than consented to the nature and quality of the acts and, in a sense, condoned his fraudulent seduction of her. The convictions will of course inflame his already overwrought, self-involved apprehensions of injustice, which are predominantly material, betrayed in his seething, often hilariously repulsive, jealousy of the access the Jake Hershes of the world enjoy to worldly pleasures and fortune. Just before the trial, Richler conveys Stein's perverse concept of justice with poetic concision, as Stein shares a half-bottle of scotch with Hersh and narrates the details of his prior conviction for extortion during the Korean War era. Just starting out as a bookkeeper, Stein had read in a tabloid newspaper that a merchant banker's wife had gone missing and might have been kidnapped. He sent a ransom note to the husband, then went to collect the money, oblivious that the police had found the woman at the seaside in Sussex, "none the worse for a post-menopausal fit of amnesia." A court sentenced Stein to three years in prison, never mind that "he had not, after all, kidnapped the lady, which was undeniably true, and he had intended to turn over the money to the defense fund for Julius and Ethel Rosenberg." At least that was his story.

Hersh's conviction is, however, genuinely unjustified as a matter of law. When a police officer informs him he could spend seven years to life in prison for aiding and abetting, "he said as British law seemed to value property above everything else, and he quoted the thirty-year sentences of the Great Train Robbery as an example, then it would seem to follow that there was no property on this island quite so precious as Miss Loebner's bottom."

In the end, as it were, Hersh gets off with a fine of £500 plus costs, the jury convicting him of indecent assault alone. Worse, he falls into a depression which seems to have nothing to do with the conviction, wrongful or not. Never mind the law, justice is another matter. Hersh's liberal guilt reasserts itself, all the more vigorously because it is the "downtrodden" Harry – both the poor and the child of the piece – paying the real price.

Slumming with Stein, in a bid to shake up his complacency, has been like slumming with his own Id. All the while, Hersh seems tacitly to have fallen in with Stein's view of him: Stein is the person

Hersh would have been without the good fortune and materialist comforts that prop up his liberal superego. (In having Hersh affectionately call Stein "Herschel," the Yiddish version of Harry, Richler plays with this doppelganger theme.) And where is the justice in that?

The paradigm here – the literary mode – is perverse Romance. The quest for the ideal, for perfect justice, remains fantasy. In the end, Jake Hersh's chivalry is ironic, the chivalry of cynicism. He would be a Jewish Don Quixote if only he were not weighed down by the material world, by his freighted, ambiguous, complacent liberalism. His ironic Dulcinea has always been his slutty, foul-mouthed cousin, Joey's sister, who like Hersh has betrayed his people by marrying a Christian. Harry Stein, his Sancho Panza, his ironic Virgil as the men tour Hell where – in his Horseman dreams – Hersh longs to harrow it, would bear the weight gladly for him, if only fortune would declare it.

III. NARRATIVE DUTY:
WHAT WE REQUIRE OF THE STORYTELLER

The Narrative Roles of the Players

In law as literature in particular, but also sometimes in fiction or poetry about law cases, the principal players have a narrative role that conforms with their status in our basic paradigm – the cultural hierarchy underlying the narrative:

Supreme authority/legislator	Law creator: language of fiat (imposed or received wisdom)
Realm of judges/legal fictions	Juristic/interpretive/mediative: language of justice
World of experience/lawyers	Advocacy: language of legalism
Underworld	Anti-legislative/Reversal of the legislative "mean": antonymic language

In a democracy, the legislature is meant to stand above bias and create law for the common weal. With statutory law, it creates the regulatory mean or starting point. In their role as secular priests, judges interpret this imposed language – now a "received wisdom" – for everyday use, either on referral ("by reference") from the government or – coming from the other way – through advocacy by lawyers. From above, the principles of precedent and legislative supremacy – received wisdom – impel them not to get too creative: in everyday life we need consistency and predictability, and previous law reflects the will of the community – which elects the politicians who (often) appoint the judges ... Creative is for the legislator.

From below, the judges have advocates getting clever in the individual interests of their clients, making arguments that don't necessarily serve the communal good. As the priest mediates between the language of God and the vulgate, so does the judge mediate between legalese and the vernacular. The judges' duty is to respect legislative supremacy, and by inference from that, the good of the larger society. They are meant to work justice in the broad sense.

As advocates for paying special interests, the lawyers often use language that stresses legalistic, one-sided argument over judiciousness. Comparable to what we will see with "moral outlaws," they do not attack the political system as such, but assume a duty to a much smaller community than do the judges working for the larger social good. When lawyers seek to change the law, they act on revolutionary impulses. The demonic language of Big Brother turns democratic, legislated language on its head. (Even there, we might assume that judges who have fully bought into the system believe they work for the general good.)

We will soon see that law-breakers occupy a continuum of evil, from moral outlaws like Robin Hood to totalitarian dictators such as Orwell's Big Brother. This is also a continuum of selfishness, which finds expression in how the law-breaker defines what he does: a poacher or low-level scofflaw such as Robin Hood will claim he breaks the law to restore justice: the rule of law is broken and he is fixing it in the interests of at least his family or neighbourhood, and sometimes for the people at large. An anti-democratic dictator completely recreates the language to justify his oligarchy by way of perversion and parody: war is peace, love is hate, Big Brother knows best.

We will consider all this in greater depth in Chapter Five, when we discuss legal philology in case law – how these paradigmatic roles cause lawyers and judges to create a dialect of "legalese." At this point, our focus is narrative duty in law IN literature, which often presents the lawyer as quester or champion, romantically, if ironically (as in *St. Urbain's Horseman*).

Lawyer as Quester/Champion

Generally speaking, if not always, the hero as reasonable person in literature corresponds to his model in law cases: he does not go looking for just causes but, when confronted with them, he must respond, in the name of duty. Most fiction with lawyer-protagonists has this romantic, quest theme, in which the hero, armed with a bar ticket, engages in a straight-ahead or ironic mission for justice. Lawyers have their own sub-genres in crime and suspense novels on this account, albeit sometimes as clone of the angst-ridden gumshoe, but with a law degree. Yet it is perhaps the more ironic treatment of the quixotic lawyer that comes closest to serious literature, even if it is often comic.

The most colourful and vibrant example is probably Sir John Mortimer's Horace Rumpole, the "Old Bailey hack" who trolls the grey environs of the Inner Temple for clients to flag him down like a cab for hire. Because Rumpole's first duty is to the presumption of innocence, argued before a jury of his clients' peers, he never pleads guilty, except when he does. The Magna Carta never boasted a more ramshackle knight (even his hat and wig are notoriously tarnished "armour"), a fact that Mortimer exploited in the years just before his death, as he worried about the erosion of civil liberties in Britain. Reacting in fear of political terrorism, successive governments had rolled back basic due process, imposing detention without charge and "anti-social behaviour orders" against rough-housing children, sometimes on unchallenged hearsay evidence. Taking arms against these attacks on the finest traditions of Anglo-American law, an aged Rumpole came as close as ever to Quixote.

But larded with irony as much as with Yorkshire pudding, he generally is not as deluded or blinkered as his literary forebear. Many of Rumpole's peers take him for a fool, but the wiser see him as a gadfly, puffing himself up – ignobly, in their view – in impossibly noble causes. He is a classic liberal, the really reasonable man who values community over personal gain: some of the nicest people he ever met were murderers – most of whom, he says (echoing Mortimer's personal experience as a barrister), do not act out of evil but in a moment of mindless passion – and career petty criminals who got that way because society blocked them from more conventional approaches to sharing the wealth. They can't afford high-priced Queen's Counsel like the bankers and industrialists and Jake Hershes of the world, with their Ponzi schemes and tax scams that do far more social harm.

Though a perpetual junior even in old age, Rumpole is like the fool in Lear: he sees better than his putative betters. In the jargon of myth criticism, he is an *eiron* (albeit an evolved one, moving towards *alazon*). Though he is sometimes compared to Shakespeare's Falstaff, there is a crucial difference: Rumpole is not a buffoon or roustabout. He wears his social conscience on his sleeve, a conscience comprising a firm, if ironical, belief in the rule of law.

We find the same thing in Sarah Caudwell's series of four comic mysteries, the "lead investigator" being Hilary Tamar, a professor of medieval legal history at Oxford. Tamar (whose sex Caudwell never reveals) is drawn into the fray, the world of experience outside the ivory tower, by trendy young friends at a barristers' chambers in Lincoln's Inn. With affectionate condescension, the London barristers view Tamar as an out-of-touch don, a pastoral bumpkin in their urban midst. The double irony, of course, is that they are mostly foolish and superficial where the mature Tamar, like Rumpole, sees what they do not. (In each case, the younger barrister-colleagues are concerned with Romance literally, the pleasures of the flesh – an irony Caudwell emphasizes in *The Sirens Sang of Murder* in describing how Julia Larwood and Michael Cantrip write a romance novel, during working hours, based on their life in chambers set against their fantasies and entanglements.)

This itself is almost iconographic, Quixotic with a capital Q insofar as it repeats the mythic theme (from Adonis to Christ to the Little Prince) that only the innocent really understand the Truth. (Thus are *Sirens'* young barristers nauseously at sea in the tax-haven netherworld of the Channel Islands, pacific and luxurious in daylight, mortally dangerous at night.) Rumpole, however, is a pathetic figure, a loser in material life, and therefore a truly comic figure where Tamar is not. (At least Tamar doesn't appear to be; although we might suspect that the professor is lonely, we see little of the law professor's private life.) We are meant to laugh a little with Rumpole, even as we admire his pluck, partly because he has benefitted from a leg up, before he kicked the ladder out from under himself. He has had a public (i.e., private) school education and is married to the daughter of the former head of his chambers. He would be on the inside track, in other words, even head of chambers, were he not a "stirrer," a rebellious friend of the little guy, like the idealistic law student (he is, again, a perpetual junior) who never got around to selling out for the big bucks in Chancery. (Like Mortimer, Rumpole did poorly in his legal studies, and frequently opines that the law – meaning justice – has nothing to do with law books.) A devotee of physical pleasure, he must nonetheless remain content with spiritual reward, like the Christ of Handel (who turns the wisdom literature of the Hebrew Bible to his Christian purpose), "despised and rejected of men; a man of sorrows and acquainted with grief" – an *eiron* who would be king.

The archetype here is David the giant-killer, although in Tamar's case its expression is subtler. Mostly more passive than Rumpole, Tamar is the prototypical officious bystander (now common in commercial law), an outsider who can view matters dispassionately. Like Rumpole and his socially-conscious ilk, the professor isn't a conventional fit in the very material world of law practice. At best, Tamar's young friends class the professor with the greyer members of the Chancery bar who believe (as Caudwell puts it in *The Sirens Sang of Murder*) "that any serious study of the law requires an atmosphere of dust and antiquity." That Rumpole would share their disdain for this view of law shows how profoundly he and Tamar are the ultimate outsider-insiders, so much alike as to be the archetypal *eiron* of their respective adventures but different enough that they would not find much common ground should Tamar stumble into Pommeroy's Wine Bar – Rumpole's second home – looking for a change from The Corkscrew, the Inner Temple "local" favoured by the professor's friends.

The quest aspect in Caudwell is partly the vindication of scholarship and maturity; though Rumpole is also anti-material, in spite of himself, his quest is, in its ironic way, nobler: justice in spite of the law – the greater social justice associated with the Christian Bible, as against the black-letter law that literature has associated, not entirely fairly, with Shylock, an equally pathetic figure of Hebrew biblical lineage.

Even while in the fray, Rumpole, like Tamar, is above it. The two are perfect reasonable persons, quixotically (transcendentally) superior to their peers in the ways that count, never mind that their colleagues regard them as clownish. They are the champions that no one really asked to serve in that role. Neither quite belongs in the evanescent, material world.

As neither does Ruth Puttermesser, Cynthia Ozick's lawyer-scholar. To her, Paradise is sitting under a tree and eating fudge while she reads omnivorously – "anthropology, zoology, physical chemistry, philosophy" – all about earthly things. "To postulate an afterlife," Ozick tells us, "was her single irony." She is, from the start, more self-involved than

Rumpole or Tamar, her concept of public duty arising only after personal insult in both her professional and love lives.

Only then does the disorderliness and sociopathy around her motivate her, in a sort of trance, to create a golem, a Jewish Frankenstein's monster or Robo-Cop. Following the legendary method of Judah Loew, the Chief Rabbi of Prague who is said to have created a golem in 1580 to protect the city's Jews from pogroms, Puttermesser constructs a teenaged female superhero – a very modern golem – to restore law and order to New York City. Even before Giuliani, the city becomes an earthly paradise where "lost wallets are daily being returned to their owners ... Gangs of youths have invaded the subway yards at night and have washed the cars clean ... The streets are altered into garden rows ... There is unemployment among correction officers ... slums undo themselves." Civility abounds. Poets and intellectuals become high city officials. Venereal disease takes a holiday and crime disappears, including the corruption that caused Puttermesser to lose her job as a city solicitor. She becomes the ironic quester. Her motto is "Justice, justice shalt thou pursue." Rappaport, her ex-lover, praises her: "It's one terrific town, I mean it. Utopia. Garden of Eden."

And of course it is no accident that she calls the engine of all this, the teenaged golem, Xanthippe, after Socrates' wife. The restored rule of law is based on rationality, thoughtfulness, civilized taste, intellectual refinement – Truth, the English translation of the word inscribed on Xanthippe's forehead, *emet*, that gives her life (and death, when the first e is erased, leaving the Hebrew *met*).[9] Ozick mentions several times that Puttermesser is a rationalist, and just before creating Xanthippe in a delirium, she has been reading Plato's *Theaetatus*, a dialogue about the nature of knowledge and how the philosopher has been the "midwife" of wisdom among his students. (The dialogue completed, he goes to court as accused in the trial that ends in his being sentenced to death for his teachings and belief.) As Puttermesser somnambulistically breaks potting soil out of its containers, the book lies on the floor beside her bed, sublime next to the day's *New York Times*, with its "record of multiple chaos and urban misfortune," abandoned there by her lover. He has stomped out and back to his home in Canada because Puttermesser prefers reading Plato to immediate sexual pleasure with him. Her political party, as named by Xanthippe, is Independents for Socratic and Prophetic Idealism, betraying that at heart she is more poet than philosopher queen, the rationalist – ironically – as utopian dreamer, and the centre cannot hold. Soon she is returned to anonymous citizenhood, and a sadistic burglar murders and rapes her (in that order, we are advised several times, so that the violation is all the more sordid) in her book-filled East Side apartment – as she mulls over a passage in Thomas Mann's *Joseph and His Brothers*, a passage about how earth and heaven are interlocked, apparently as human constructs.

Naturally, there has been all manner of foreboding. In creating Xanthippe in her own image, Puttermesser has mimicked the method of God in creating Adam, using mud (from her potted plants) and breathing into its nostrils. The archetypal lineage here is graphic: God making Adam, Moses striking the rock, Rabbi Loew creating the golem, Frankenstein creating his homemade manchild, Puttermesser constructing the mute child Xanthippe. In each case, the creature becomes wilful and spurns the control of its creator, such that, one way or another, it fashions the conditions of its own destruction. (The muteness of the human creations, not their wilfulness, is what distinguishes them from Adam, divinely made. Humans, however moral or right-minded, can only approach the godhead so far; otherwise they become Promethean, violating capital Law and subject to punishment.)

The scheme for restoring earthly paradise, the PLAN, as drawn by the golem, is full of the bureaucratese of the old regime, the managers who demoted then fired Puttermesser at the Department of Receipts and Disbursements: "Was it not possible to dream a dream of City without falling into the mouth of the Destroyer?" Puttermesser wonders. The answer turns out to be resoundingly No. *Et in Arcadia ego.* The dream is still a dream, in a fallen world. The pleasure principle reasserts itself, social Darwinism defeats the rule of law. The golem herself falls victim to overweening lust, Adam and Eve's shame – their motive for disobeying the one covenant God has decreed for them. Similarly, grieving Puttermesser must destroy Xanthippe to control her, for the world's sake. The day of judgment has not quite arrived.

Then, too, in making Rappaport her co-conspirator, the bait to bring Xanthippe back for destruction in her own seed-stained bed, Puttermesser indulges in the patronage she excoriated: as payment, she offers her former lover a job heading up ... Receipts and Disbursements. *Et in Arcadia ego.* Death enters the world, on human seed, mortal shame. We cannot save ourselves. The lynch mob that killed Plato, all nerves and feelings, drags the criminal code back from the moribund, recalling the old joke that ending crime is simple if we just repeal all laws. And though Rabbi Loew kept his dead golem in the attic at the Old-New Synagogue, Puttermesser cannot do the same at the very secular, very unsacred Gracie Mansion. Human law has moved so far away from the sacred that God has turned his back on us. The golem that began in homely pottery is returned to the garden, an unEden, this time across the street from the mayor's residence, in an unmarked grave.

In other words, in the fallen world even magic provides at best a temporary solution to evil. Like Moses, earthlings who indulge in magic off their own bat will bring judgment down upon themselves. Knowledge is power and supernatural knowledge is über-power. Magic is a form of revolution, a final resort when order or justice cannot be restored by appeals to conscience or positive law. The magician faces judgment for stealing the gods' fire, for approaching omniscience and omnipotence.

The PLAN, that is, is foredoomed. The inevitability of Puttermesser's failure is archetypal insofar as she enacts a parody of messianism or what anthropologists call "the dying god motif." To redeem entropy, the fatalism of earthly existence, Christian law gives us an omnipotent god who creates the "son of man" and immortal life on high. Fatalistically, Puttermesser creates the unredemptive "daughter of woman."[10]

Inside and outside the minds of its gods, earthly paradise is fated to fall back on itself. And so, while after the burglary Puttermesser achieves "genuine" Paradise on high, her suffering does not abate: she is permitted to live out her fantasies there, but then, because Paradise is eternal yet still linked with our earthly conception of it, a *human* dream, happiness is whisked away: "Paradise is a dream bearing the inscription of Solomon's seal: *this too will pass* ... The secret meaning of Paradise is that it too is hell." Like Puttermesser makes the golem, we create our own Paradise, as we make the bars of our own private prisons.[11]

(In this light, we recall what Vladimir Nabokov says inspired *Lolita*, his narrative about the ambiguity of biological imperatives and the soulless legalism meant to govern them: "As far as I can recall, the initial shiver of inspiration was somehow prompted by a newspaper story about an ape in the Jardin des Plantes who, after months of coaxing by a scientist, produced the first drawing ever charcoaled by an animal: this sketch showed the bars of the poor creature's cage.")

Of course, this is a very "Mosaic" or legalistic view, as opposed to the more Christian or "equity-based" postulate of mercy and redemption.

Speaking more broadly, the fact that Puttermesser must rely on magic – because the rule of law has failed – suggests that Frye is right: in our imaginative life, after irony we cycle back toward myth. We are not quite there, given that the mythic fails in works such as Ozick's. But for some time now "magical realism" has been a growing feature in fiction. In the broader culture, there is a resurgence of religious fundamentalism, even as science and atheism push back. With Winston Smith in *1984* – who puts his faith in the Proles, at a devolved level of sophistication insofar as it is more visceral – we become Rousseauist Romantics, yearning for a simpler state in which positive law is less oppressive or unnecessary.[12]

(Occasionally literature uses magical realism to work justice in specific instances: the rule of law isn't necessarily broken, but neither is it working to resolve a particular injustice. In the traditional ballad "Bruton Town," for instance, two brothers murder their sister's lover, their servant, during a hunting trip. The dead lover visits the girl in a dream, tells her what happened, and indicates where she can find his body. She sits with the body, grieving for three days, but her sorrow becomes a little suspect in one version, once she abandons the corpse because she missed dinner.[13] We see something similar at work in Toni Morrison's *Beloved*, with the ghost of a murdered child haunting a house, and in the ballad "The Twa Sisters," where a harp made of the body parts of a young woman sings out to the royal court that the dead girl's "darker" sister is the murderer.)

As we suggested above, the archetypal relationship of lawyer protagonists with questing knights associates them more broadly with champions. The champion lawyer goes that extra mile, risking his own life and limb, or at least bread and butter, putting his reputation and sometimes his bar ticket on the line. It is no accident that in such a role these literary lawyers are at least partly comic or ironic, for often their setting parodies the David and Goliath story, even insofar as the lawyers being champions that no one expected or solicited. This, after all, is the most thrilling aspect of David's little-guy story. (It is no coincidence, of course, that like Moses and like Christ in the metaphorical sense, David is a shepherd, becoming a shepherd of men only by dint of trial by battle.) In the case of Rumpole, and other unconventional lawyers such as Harper Lee's Atticus Finch and John Grisham's Rudy Baylor, these David-lawyers mirror (and parody) the champion in the old legal sense, "at common law," as *Black's Law Dictionary* describes it, "the person who, in the trial by battel, fought either for the tenant or demandant." As with other forms of trial – including the forms depicted in Mortimer, Grisham, Earl Stanley Gardner and so on – this form was highly ritualized, stipulating what weapons could be used, which oaths were to be sworn, and how long the fight was to last (until, indeed, "the stars appear in the evening.")[14] In this case, however, Goliath is usually the system or some iteration of "the Establishment," heartless and corrupted, or viewed as such.

Grisham has made his literary fortune on legal thrillers whose thrill is mostly visceral, and therefore not normally the province of "litrichoor." But *The Rainmaker* (1995) is more substantial, partly because the author so skillfully handles this David-and-Goliath motif.

When the book opens, Rudy Baylor is in his last weeks of law school at Memphis State University. In an extremely tight market, he has found the last law-job available to him, with a small, respectable firm. Suffering the law student's characteristic cynicism and burnout, he emerges from campus with some clinical experience gained in "Codger Law," officially known as Legal Problems of the Elderly. Even if he passes the imminent bar exam, seven years of university could leave him without much of a living. His contact network consists principally of a fellow student – whose legal interests run to low-profit civil rights cases – and, secondarily, the owner of the bar where he works after classes. Prince, as the owner is known around town, is a big player in the Memphis underworld, specializing in the skin trade and tax evasion. We know he's nasty because he is fat and has a lot of hair. Then again, he's very good to Rudy.

Never mind the student-as-bartender schtick, this is not *The Paper Chase*. Rudy's firm merges with a multi-national law partnership, a regular Grisham demon. Caught in the middle, his job is squeezed out. By graduation day Ruby is broke and in trouble with various creditors. What ensues, to a certain extent "Rudy's Revenge," is a rare, possibly unique, phenomenon: a thriller about insurance litigation. And how do you write thrillingly about insurance litigation? You write a morality play. Corporations in black hats, ordinary folks in white. Sitting at the bedside of a client, a man dying of leukemia, Rudy observes:

So this is how the uninsured die. In a society filled with wealthy doctors and gleaming hospitals and state-of-the-art medical gadgetry and the bulk of the world's Nobel winners, it seems outrageous to allow Donny Ray Black to wither away and die without proper medical care. He could've been saved. By law, he was solidly under the umbrella, leaky as it was, of Great Benefit [Insurance Co.] when his body was afflicted with this terrible disease.

This is not literature. But by this point Grisham has convinced us that Rudy Baylor is the greatest lawyer in America. What gives *The Rainmaker* substance is its view of the profession in general: here he transcends the black-hat, white-hat dichotomy, in which lawyers typically side with wealth and power in some perversion of the rule of law. He gives us a legal thriller with nuance: lawyers as a group are depicted in grey hats. The rare specimen is a David, a real champion. This would be as cliché as the black hat-white hat business if it were designed simply as the usual "lawyers are boring crooks" routine. But Grisham tempers his anger about some of the nasty things lawyers do with the goodness, the *reasonableness,* he knows that is in many of them, at least in their early idealism. Inching towards literature, Grisham seems to be hinting that it wasn't just best-sellerdom that led him to abandon legal practice for full-time writing. It seems he got tired of grey.

IV. RECONFIGURING THE PARADIGM, FROM TRADITIONAL BALLADS TO NOT EXACTLY PORTIA MEN

The "Good Outlaw" Archetype

Sometimes when literature is concerned about social justice, it tells us that the powerful have perverted the law to their own ends. They view the duty owed as, primarily, a duty to the self, not the community. By way of answer, it becomes necessary to adjust the paradigm. This is different from turning the whole thing on its head, as in Orwell's *1984,* for instance, where utopia and dystopia are confounded and evil is given primacy. Here, what is rejected is not the rule of law, but how it has been corrupted by those exploiting it for their selfish advantage. As the magistrate Angelo puts it in *Measure for Measure,* just before he gives in to the temptation of extorting sexual favours from a novitiate nun in return for saving the life of her brother, condemned for fornication, "Thieves for their robbery have authority/ When judges steal themselves." (II, ii, 176).

Although this is predominantly a comic motif, we see at least hints of it in tragedy such as *King Lear* (of which Frye says, "the sense of life under the law is present everywhere,"[15] law again being distinct from justice), and revenge drama (whether tragic or structurally comic) such as *Hamlet* and *The Eumenides* of Aeschylus. Thus does a villain like Robin Hood become a romantic hero, where normally he would inhabit the bottom of the basic paradigm (in the world of sociopathy): an Ur-socialist, he (heroically) takes from the rich to give to the poor, or at least the temporarily embarrassed. The earliest ballad we have recounting his adventures – "A Gest of Robyn Hode," which dates from the fourteenth century if not earlier at least in some of its parts[16] – ends:

Christ have mercy on his soul,
That died on the rood.
For he was a good outlaw
And did poor men much good.

(I have modernized the spelling.) In a sense, Robin is a Christ figure or knight-champion, best friend of the ordinary fellow, in a world that has corrupted the law of the "Old Testament God." For Pharaoh, after all, Moses was no freedom-fighter. To redeem the situation in folklore, the quest motif itself is made perverse.

Some, such as the poet Shelley and the critic William Empson, would say that this is John Milton's technique, more or less, in *Paradise Lost*, given that God has been so bloody-minded with Adam and Eve, setting them up for failure and, worse, mortality. "Justifying the ways of God to man" ends up making Milton put much of the justice advocacy into the mouth of the devil.

If we view Adam and Eve as the first convicts sentenced to transportation – God sends them "forth from the Garden of Eden, to till the ground from whence he [Adam] was taken" – we see their descendants made heroic in traditional ballads such as "Van Diemen's Land." Britain used this island in the south Pacific, today called Tasmania, as one of the centres to where its judges transported convicted criminals. The ballad concerns such a sentence passed on a poacher who is sometimes Irish, sometimes Scottish, sometimes English. (Folk tradition includes many such poacher-as-anti-hero ballads, and Robin Hood himself is constantly found to be "taking of the king's deer.") A version collected in Newfoundland in 1951 tells the story this way:

Come all ye boys of Liverpool, I'd have you to beware,
When ye go a-hunting with your dog and gun and snare,
Watch for the land keeper; keep your dog at your command,
And think on all the sorrow going to Van Diemen's Land.

We had two Irish lads on board, Jimmy Murphy and Pat Malone,
And they were both the best friends that any man could own.
The land keeper he caught them and from old England land
They were fourteen years transported to plough Van Diemen's
    Land.

We had an Irish girl on board, Mary Brophy was her name,
And she was sent from Liverpool, for a playing of the game.
She took the captain's fancy and he married her out of hand,
And the best usage she gave us, going to Van Diemen's Land.

The first day that they landed us all on that fateful shore,
The planters gathered round us, full twenty score or more;
They led us round like horses and sold us out of hand,
And yoked us to the plow, me boys, to plow Van Diemen's Land.

As I lay in the bed one night a-dreaming all alone,
I dreamed I was in Liverpool down by a purling a stream,
With my true love beside me, and her at my command,
I awoke all broken-hearted, lying in Van Diemen's Land.

Like Jean Valjean and his famous loaf in *Les Misérables*, the poachers presumably are only trying to feed their families. For them, Britain
is a sort of Promised Land, but with its promises denied the poor, who
are then banished to savage lands. With some irony, the banished
poacher dreams of England and his family there. Van Diemen's Land
becomes a Hell on earth, like exile did for Adam and Eve (there being
no subterranean Hell at the time). Hell, itself, is exile and mortality,
returning to dust instead of eternal life in Paradise. But in other versions of the ballad, the poacher is rehabilitated *in situ* by being made
a farm worker or even a bookkeeper, and adopts his new land as
home, a far territory of milk and honey:

As we marched into Sydney town without no more delay,
A gentleman he bought me, his bookkeeper to be.

I took the occupation, my master loved me well.
My joys were out of measure, I'm sure no tongue could tell.

It is particularly interesting in these versions that a city – though a foreign one to the convict – remains the earthly paradise: after suffering in jail and aboard ship, the convict is marched into town, Jerusalem restored, to be redeemed. A version quoted by Robert Hughes lays on the irony of this with a trowel: the convicts are marched into "Hobart Town" where the narrator is bought by a "gentleman farmer" who makes him ... gamekeeper. "My master loves me well," the transport again assures us, and his joys are (again) ineffably immeasurable.

What we have called the moral outlaw is an instance of what Northrop Frye labels displacement (after Freud) and "'demonic modulation,' or the deliberate reversal of the customary moral associations of archetypes." He elaborates:

Any symbol takes its meaning primarily from its context: a dragon may be sinister in a medieval romance or friendly in a Chinese one; an island may be Prospero's island or Circe's. But because of the large amount of learned and traditional symbolism in literature, certain secondary associations become habitual. The serpent, because of its role in the garden of Eden story, usually belongs on the sinister side of our catalogue in Western literature; the revolutionary sympathies of Shelley impel him to use an innocent serpent in *The Revolt of Islam. Or a free and equal society may be symbolized by a band of robbers, pirates, or gypsies ...* Diabolism is not however invariably a sophisticated development: Huckleberry Finn, for example, wins our sympathy and admiration by preferring hell with his hunted friend [the slave Jim] to the heaven of the white slave-owners' god. [Emphasis added.][17]

While plagued with doubt over whether he is an apostate, an unconfessed abolitionist, Huck makes a moral choice to team up with an escaped slave to become an outlaw. He even accepts that, in helping Jim, "I'll go to Hell." (The fact that Jim is a man of principle and morality heightens the irony of this, reassuring the reader about Huck's faith.) At the symbolic level here and in the ballads, the outlaw or convict harrows Hell only to renovate it, really, where usually the hero harrows Hell to emerge into a regained paradise. Of course, the new home is not a real paradise, but a new beginning in the same old fallen world, as one is "awaitin'" that "better home... in the sky, Lord, by and by." More generally, because the law has itself become corrupt and no longer serves justice, the reconfigured paradigm offers a real world solution: given that everywhere on earth is "fallen" (subject to corruption), even Robin Hood ultimately must inhabit the same world as the Sheriff of Nottingham, no matter how judiciously Robin tries to redistribute its wealth. Wealth and power have become a parasitic disease on the old paradigm, with its politicians and judges at the top, making all the rules, such that it has lost its legitimacy. The home society's rule of law no longer promotes justice, so a new start must be made. And so does Hughes adopt the title of his history of Australia, *The Fatal Shore*, from a line in some versions of "Van Diemen's Land":

> The very day we landed upon the fatal shore,
> The planters stood around us, full twenty score or more;
> They ranked us up like horses and sold us out of hand,
> They chained us up to pull the plough, upon Van Diemen's Land.

If Adam and Eve were our first transportees, their son Cain was the first outlaw, when far short of signifying someone romantic like a Clint Eastwood gun-for-hire, the word described a person literally outside the law's protection: under old British law, you lawfully could kill such a criminal on sight. (As Charles Rembar pointedly observes, "The merry men of Robin Hood could not have frequently been merry.")[18] Having killed his brother (and thereby having become the first criminal in the fallen world we still inhabit), Cain is at similar risk, prompting him to plead with God that such punishment is more than he can bear. "Thou hast driven me out this day from the face of the earth ... and I shall be a fugitive and a vagabond in the earth; and it shall come to pass that every one that findeth me shall slay me." His parents have brought death into the world, and now he risks it everywhere he turns. So the Supreme Lawgiver shows mercy, marking Cain's flesh as a way of signalling that he is not to be harmed, a sort of prototype in reverse for what English law would later call benefit of clergy: the convict was branded so that he carried his own record, showing that he was in mercy.[19]

You would think that living at mercy makes Cain distinct from "good outlaws," and particularly different from the prototypical good outlaw, Robin Hood. However, "A Gest of Robyn Hode" shows the latter and his crew enjoying the king's mercy. It also makes him a devotee of the Virgin Mary, putting him firmly on the side of the forces of good combating evil in the fallen world, represented here by greedy monks, an archbishop, a bishop, and a chief justice. Robin might not be law abiding, but he is just. And he supports the king insofar as the sovereign is an agent of Perfect Justice.

In this ballad, he specifically instructs his followers not to attack commoners, nor even selected knights and squires:

"Thereof no force," than said Robin;
"We shall do well enough;
"But look ye do no husband harm,
"That tilleth with his plough

"No more ye shall no good yeoman
"That walketh by greenwood show;
"Neither no knight nor squire
"That will be a good fellow.

"These bishops and these archbishops,
"Ye shall them beat and bind;
"The high sheriff of Nottingham,
Him hold ye in your mind."
                    (Verses 13–15; I have modernized the spelling.)

A knight – Sir Richard at the Lee – arrives on the scene and Robin tests him to make sure he is "a good fellow." It turns out that not only is Sir Richard a fellow servant of "Our Lady," but he is down on his luck: the abbot of St. Mary's at York has loaned him £400 against his land, and with the year-term on the mortgage up, the knight cannot pay the debt. Having feted Sir Richard, Robin outfits him with horses, lends him Little John as squire, and gives him the mortgage payment, so as to save his livelihood and family.

But the abbot wants the land, and has paid off the chief justice and sheriff to secure it:

The high justice of England
The abbot there did hold.

The high justice and many more
Had take in to their hand (honde)
Wholly all the knight's debt
To put that knight to wrong.

At first, before thumping Robin Hood's money down on the table, Sir Richard plays with his creditors, seeking to extend the term of the loan. But the chief justice rules, "Thy day is broke" and the land is forfeit. "I am hold with the abbot," he adds, "Both with cloth and fee." Sir Richard then turns to the sheriff, fruitlessly begging relief from forfeiture.

The scholarship on these stanzas clarifies the corrupt ethos that makes Robin more saint than sinner, or at least more revolutionary than terrorist. In his comprehensive notes on the ballad, Francis James Child writes: "The abbot had retained the chief justice 'by robe and fee,' to counsel and aid him in the spoliation of the knight ... All the English judges, including the chief justice, were convicted of bribery and were removed under Edward I, 1289."[20]

The statute 33 Edward I, 1305, stipulates, "They who receive persons of peace to their robes or their fees for maintaining their evil undertakings and suppressing truth, are conspirators, the recipients as well as the givers."[21] Yet the next fifty-four years saw such abuse metastasize – the normalizing of what lawyers call "maintenance," "an officious intermeddling in a suit which in no way belongs to one, by maintaining or assisting either party" (*Black's Law Dictionary*, fifth edition). As J. Lewelyn Curtis points out in *Notes and Queries* for November 20, 1852, new law under Edward III specifically required that, "you will take no fee so long as you shall be justices, nor robes, of any man great or small, except of the King himself." The statute explained that this was because otherwise "taking robes and fees" had seen "many persons disherited, and some delayed and disturbed of their right, and some innocent persons convicted and condemned, or otherwise oppressed in undoing of their estate, and in notorious destruction and oppression of our people." In other words, giving robes and fees could mask judicial bribery.

And so does Robin ride as Justitia's knight, virtually a reasonable person. (A truly reasonable person would perhaps run for Parliament.) He manages to extract double the loan amount from a travelling monk and thereby forgives the knight's debt, explaining that the Virgin has repaid it twice (never mind that this sounds suspiciously

like a highly unChristian, usurious interest rate). Robin's men then
lure the sheriff of Nottingham into a trap, so Robin takes him prisoner. Robin forces the sheriff to strip to his underclothing as the
start of a year-long object lesson on the depredations of the outlaw's
daily life. Accustomed to greater comfort, the quavering sheriff plea
bargains:

> "All this twelve months," said Robin
> "Thou shalt dwell with me;
> "I shall thee teach, proud sheriff,
> "An outlaw for to be."
>
> "Or I be here another night," said the sheriff,
> "Robin now pray I thee,
> "Smite of mine head rather tomorrow,
> "And I forgive it thee."

The sheriff agrees to give Robin free reign thenceforth, and even to
be at the service of his gang, but later breaches the agreement and
Robin kills him. But a note of ambivalence (moral and legal) hangs
over the sheriff's entrapment by (and *entente cordiale* with) the outlaws, reverberating from a more generalized feeling in the good-out-
law ballads that they protest too much: this third "fit" begins with Little John on a spy mission, infiltrating the sheriff's headquarters – and
apparently his domicile – by offering himself up as a servant. The
reader is told that, from the beginning, he plans to make a poor job
of it, gumming up the law-enforcement works in accordance with
his job as secret agent. Yet near the end John says he has delivered
the sheriff into Robin's hands because he was ill treated during the
employment, and by the sheriff's cook, not by the sheriff. This is jus-
tification after the fact for disloyalty to his erstwhile employer. The
overall sense is that part of the thrill for the outlaws is that they know
they are scofflaws: it is not the rule of law that is wrong, but those
who pervert it to their egocentric gain. Robin serves a higher power
than the sheriff, although ultimately he knows he is not above the law.

In the seventh fit Robin hosts an abbot to a feast of game poached
from the king's inventory, but not before extorting from the cleric the
£40 on his person. (And it is here that we see the "merriment" of
Robin's men is no later gloss: "Robyn took the forty pound / And
departed it in two parties; / Half he gave his merry men / And bade

them merry be.") Characteristically, Robin then glibly returns the other half to the abbot, as though it were a gift from his treasury – perhaps making a socio-political point about wealth distribution, but then again, perhaps not. The abbot turns out to be the king in disguise (the reader/audience has known this all along), who enjoys slumming with Robin to the extent that he and his entourage exchange their "grey" religious disguise for the outlaw ("Lincoln") green of an *hors la loi*. As the now re-inforced merry gang rides through Nottingham, the townsfolk flee, signalling to the cagey reader that trouble is on the horizon for Robin. He is no folk hero in the urban, courtly world, the world of experience and the Establishment.

But still infected with the pastoral spirit, the king pardons Robin on terms of parole that require the outlaw to work in royal service, as part of his court. Robin accepts the terms but can't stomach being co-opted, particularly as he has lost his treasury and most of his colleagues have deserted him. So he absconds for twenty-two years, plumping – albeit not with any evident moral purpose – for outlawry, the life and politics he knows and claims.

Child calls the ending mere epilogue, and perhaps it was tacked on, to lend narrative as well as archetypal coherence. Taking us full circle back to Eve in the garden, a "wicked woman, the prioress of Kirklee," betrays Robin to Sir Roger Donkesly, who kills him at last. There is a sort of rush to judgment here, that makes the skulduggery an obscure afterthought. A duenna who is both religious (at least overtly) and seductive beguiles our hero, or purportedly does so, never mind that she is Sir Roger's lover, and never mind that Robin says he is going to Kirklee "craftily to be letting blood," not necessarily for some romantic assignation. All this suggests a reverberative power in the prioress's duenna character, to the extent that she is also a double agent, for Robin Hood on the one hand but ultimately for the Establishment on the other.

At once too good and too bad for this world, Robin Hood has strong mythical qualities, such that his iterations reverberate even in the popular culture of today – in the character, for example, of the renegade cowboy or biker bad-boy who is on the side of moral good against a justice system corrupted by the powerful and greedy. The setting always has a pastoral aspect – even if the setting is the city – and the outlaw can be comic, as in "the Fonz" good-bad boy on the television series, *Happy Days*. Of course, Robin's home base, the Sherwood Forest, has Edenic echoes, as a place where human (corrupted) law is suspended. Green is his emblematic colour, instead of pure white: as we have said, he is firmly an earthbound hero. His "trystell," or meeting tree which sometimes he calls "the greenwood tree" and marks where he transacts all important business, recalls Eden's Trees of Life and Knowledge, and the cross on which Christ died. In "The Sacrifice," George Herbert has Jesus say:

> O all ye who pass by, behold and see;
> Man stole the fruit, but I must climb the tree;
> The tree of life to all, but only me:
> Was ever grief like mine?

You've committed the crime, I must pay.

Politically speaking, the moral outlaw character is grassroots, a way for the conventionally powerless to express their frustrations and aspirations for real justice. Robin returns the law to those it was meant to serve, the community. He co-opts the basically feudal view that the law is for other people, the view of the suzerain that law is his tool to control the underclasses. And while he might symbolize the waning of feudalism, the wealthy and powerful continue to use the law as a form of class control, having learned to work around guarantees of basic human rights and even support legislation that placates the masses. To a certain extent, John Mortimer's Rumpole is a modern Robin Hood, dodging inside and outside the law – working the system, in the modern way – as it suits his purpose and personality. (It seems a law degree gives you licence to do this, something Robin, with all his native intelligence, should have considered.) Then, too, the golem, from his appearance in the days of Robin Hood to modern novels, is as much Robin Hood as Frankenstein's monster – an outlaw, but also a *creation* of the secular world using means borrowed from the divine. Through such creations, which are palpably connected with divine law (again, the golem is a neo-Adam created with God's holy name placed in his mouth, and Robin Hood constantly pays obeisance to the Virgin Mother), the disenfranchised assert moral authority. Truth is equated with justice in him, insofar as the Hebrew word for truth, "*emet*," is imprinted on his forehead or the paper that enlivens him, and insofar as he gives the lie to the antisemitic blood libel. (See *infra*, at 101–5, 190–2.) Then, too, he is deprived of speech, arguably because, unlike God, mortals cannot create a complete human.

The literary Jew has needed such a champion because often he has been made an outlaw himself, first literarily, then, with awful tragedy, in history. We have already seen this not just with Ozick's magic realism, but in the idealized Joey Hersh of *St. Urbain's Horseman*. The conventional terminology for such outlaws or outcasts is "pariah," but if we approach the problem anthropologically, mythopoetically, we have this more refined answer to the perpetually vexing question: why are Jews so consistently despised in the popular imagination of the west?

Part of the answer we have already suggested: the Mosaic worldview can seem unforgiving; its god is routinely described as vengeful, stern, unrelenting. Jesus proposes what Christians see as more evolved Law, and it is not uncommon to hear that he was, after all, an enlightened Jew. Jews have viewed this as apostasy, a fundamental breach of received law and settled precedent; a false messiah is one who remakes new rules to suit his own claims and convenience as a putative moral outlaw. Because the Jew refuses to conform to the "evolved" law – the law that western culture equates with the development of equitable remedies in our secular law – he is an unmitigated outlaw.

The view literally and metaphorically has been that Jews are not entitled to "Christian justice." Consider the Grimm brothers' tale number 110, "The Jew among Thorns." A dwarf grants a poor man three wishes and the man asks for a rifle that always hits what he aims at, a fiddle that compels all listeners to dance, and the ability to get what he wants from anyone just by asking. The man comes upon a Jew on the road who admires a bird and would like to have it for himself. The dwarf shoots the bird and tells the Jew that if he wants it, go get it from the bracken. The dwarf then plays the fiddle to make the Jew dance among the thorns until the Jew's skin is torn and his clothes are shredded to rags. "You have fleeced people often enough, and now the thorn hedge shall do the same to you," the dwarf advises, until the Jew pays him a purse full of gold to stop his fiddling. Catching his breath, the Jew calls in the law, saying the fiddler stole the purse. The judge sentences the fiddler to death. On the gallows, the fiddler asks the judge to grant him one last tune, and though the Jew protests, the judge cannot resist. The fiddler sets the whole town to dancing, including the local dogs, until the judge says he will spare the fiddler's life if only he stops fiddling. The fiddler threatens to start playing again if the Jew doesn't confess that he gave the purse willingly. The Jew agrees and the judge has him hanged on the spot.

Apparently the judge has never heard of the defence of duress. Indeed, to the modern eye the story – in some ways a perversion of the Orpheus myth – betrays itself, and betrays its compounding of the injustice, inasmuch as justice is denied the Jew because of his race. But what has made the "fairy tale" acceptable (as such) is that, historically, the dominant culture viewed Jews as undeserving of Christian justice.

Then too (and much more recently), in an insurance case can Lord Denning, an assertively Christian judge on England's Court of Appeal, declare himself a "Portia man" against settled law, which he equates with Shylockian, "Old Testament" legality. The very fact that Shylock would seek a pound of flesh, even assuming one can make a contract that involves serious bodily harm, attests to his being "outside the law" in temperament as well as in public perception.

The poor *Merchant* has been done to death in law-and-literature treatises, but from the perspective of *Sydall v. Castings Ltd.*, [1976] 1 Q.B. 302, we perhaps get a fresher view. Sydall had left five children, an estranged wife, and a lover who was the mother of his youngest child, a baby girl named Yvette. His trustees wanted to include Yvette as a beneficiary of Sydall's life insurance policy. But following the old common law on illegitimacy and "descendants," Lord Russell and a majority of the Court of Appeal held that "'descendant' is to be construed as descendant in the legitimate line."

Lord Denning dissented. "Because Yvette is illegitimate," he wrote, "she is to be excluded from any benefit. She is on this view no 'relation' of her father: nor is she 'descended' from him. In the eye of the law, she is the daughter of nobody. She is related to nobody. She is an outcast and she is to be shut out from any part of her father's insurance benefit." She was, in some ways, an outlaw. So the master of the rolls excoriated the common-law view of descendants as Victorian, old-fashioned, and vengeful.

Lord Russell rose directly to the challenge. He compared Lord Denning to Bassanio in *The Merchant of Venice*, Bassanio being the friend of debtor Antonio, and intended of Portia. In the famous trial scene, Bassanio pleads with Judge Balthasar not to make Antonio pay with a pound of his flesh in default of his bond, even though Antonio has agreed to such a term. Balthasar is of course Portia in drag. "Wrest once the law to your authority," Bassanio begs Balthasar/Portia. "To do a great right, do a little wrong."

Lord Russell quotes these words, and continues: "But Portia retorted:

It must not be; there is no power in Venice
Can alter a decree established:
Twill be recorded for a precedent,
And many an error, by the same example,
Will rush into the State: it cannot be."

In other words, she refuses (at first) to let Antonio off the hook for his pound of flesh because she does not dare establish a precedent that would allow defaulting debtors to escape their obligations. And that was when Lord Russell got in first with the declaration: "I am a Portia man."

He meant that it was his legal duty – according to the doctrine of *stare decisis* – to follow settled law, holding that "descendant" included only children born in wedlock. More pointedly, he meant, "I am not a Lord Denning man." Lord Denning objected, sustainably, that *he* was the Portia man: "I cannot believe that Russell L.J. would be a 'Portia man' if it meant aligning himself with Shylock – in support of a strict law of penalties which could not be relieved by equity."

In fact a deeper reading of the play suggests that no fair judge would be a Portia man or woman. Siding with Portia is to declare kinship with one of our culture's worst sexual teases, most determined sadists, and a woman who epitomizes everything the ordinary person despises about law and lawyers.

Most of Portia's time in *The Merchant of Venice* is spent fighting boredom by flaunting her wealth and power – spurning suitors, cracking witticisms, and playing practical jokes, not only on the despised Jewish moneylender, but on her innocent intended, Bassanio, making him give up his engagement ring in payment to Balthasar just so she can berate him for it later as Portia unmasked. True, she makes a very famous and beautiful speech about the quality of mercy, but it is the speech of a jaded academic, a Machiavella. At law, she is a savage parodist, twisting and hair-splitting to the last micron. And, in stringing everyone along (including the "doomed" Antonio) by pretending at first to be on Shylock's side, she is, as well, a skilled amateur of torture. With the aplomb of a practised show-off (and coquette), she gives judgment: she tells Shylock, yes, he may have his pound of flesh, but the bond says nothing about blood.

Tarry a little, there is something else.
This bond doth give thee here no jot of blood

The words expressly are a pound of flesh.
Take then thy bond, take thou thy pound of flesh;
But in the cutting it, if thou dost shed
One drop of Christian blood, thy lands and goods
Are, by the laws of Venice, confiscate. . .

This is the worst sort of lawyering: Portia does not say that a contract to do mortal harm to a person is illegal and therefore unenforceable. That would not be clever and flashy enough. (Of course, dramatically, it would also be boring.) So, surely Lord Russell does not really want to be a Portia man. Portia makes an ass of the law with the proclaimed end of saving a life, when really it is for her own amusement and self-gratification, Jew-baiting as in "Jew among the Thorns," and putting one over on her fiancé.

Then again, Lord Russell ends up denying 600 dollars to a fatherless baby. And Lord Denning, if he had thought more equitably about it, would rather have been a Robin Hood man.

The depiction of the Jew as outlaw is among human history's most extravagantly blood-soaked injustices. Blood, in fact, seems to be its central attribute, in history and in literature, emerging from the ideas of sacrifice and scapegoating.

Arguably, the blood libel that has served as the excuse for countless murders and pogroms – the canard that Jews sacrifice a Christian child and mix his blood into their unleavened bread at Passover – begins in the iconography of sacred law. The archetypal evolution from Hebrew to Christian law could well account for the persistence of what in fact is a slander, usually – orally made, often by the illiterate – even into pockets of ignorance and malice in our own day. The evolutionary link – the legal anthropology – is that connecting Passover and Easter. The Israelite Exodus of the Passover story begins with God's killing the Egyptian first born and the doors of the Israelites being marked with lamb's blood to protect their children from the same fate (Exodus XII, 3–13). The lurid symbolism only makes the apparent injustice of this more graphic. I say "apparent injustice" because biblical law has its own logic, through which the deaths are seen as justified and legally as well as theologically necessary: why the innocent? The seder, culminating in "the Last Supper" just before Christ's self-sacrifice as the Lamb of God, includes the Paschal lamb. Wine is deliberately spilled at the seder table to commemorate the ten deadly plagues on the Egyptians and blood spilled by Israelites in their struggle for freedom. Blood, innocence, and sacrifice are linked with ultimate justice and the return to a paradisal home. And as we have seen in the evolution of the messiah theme, the Christian version of the story emphasizes blood sacrifice leading to eternal paradise on high, not just a return to Eden, the "next year in Jerusalem" with which Jews greet each other at the seder. Ironically, Christian law mixes blood with unleavened bread in a central rite, the Eucharist, hearkening back toward human sacrifice. As Francis Child notes, regarding the notorious example of the blood libel in the ballad "Sir Hugh, or, the Jew's Daughter," Jews have been "equally taxed" with "the absurd sacrilege of stabbing, baking, or boiling the Host."[22] And the pound-of-flesh bond in *The Merchant of Venice* could easily be founded in such slander (as well as "on the provisions of Roman law which allowed creditors power over the lives and limbs of their debtors").[23]

The blood slander is often related to the golem story, and in the case of the Prague golem we have the chief rabbi attempting to explain to the authorities (as Jewish leaders repeatedly tried to do across Europe, throughout history) that murder, human sacrifice, and the consumption of blood are fundamentally repugnant to Jewish law. But the urge to scapegoat has its own illogic. In his notes on "Sir Hugh," Child writes, "And these pretended child-murders, with their horrible consequences, are only a part of a persecution which, with all moderation may be rubricated as the most disgraceful chapter in the history of the human race." That is, only now and then were Jews accorded the rule of law in these cases, with the occasional acquittals at trial and, even more rarely, sanction against the lynch mobs attacking, torturing, and murdering them. "It would be tedious and useless," Child adds, "to attempt to make a collection of the great number of similar instances which have been mentioned by chroniclers and ecclesiastical writers." He then cites perhaps fifty examples that "come readily to hand without much research" – 600 killed in one case (during 1883 in Smyrna), houses and synagogues burned down, ridiculous confessions extracted by torture in others. Writing long before the Holocaust, Child notes that Germany and Russia were particularly fertile ground for blood slanders, even into the nineteenth century. Although an imperial ukase of 1817 formally prohibited criminal prosecutions, forty-three Jews were indicted in 1823, Child's research reveals. Proceedings spread over the next twelve years, only to conclude in acquittal for all "on account of the entire failure of proof."[24] But that was not the end of such prosecutions in Russia, as the case of Mendel Bellis shows, which prosecution Bernard Malamud used as the basis for his Pulitzer Prize-winning novel, *The Fixer*.

Malamud depicts the slander there as deliberately vengeful and exploitive of popular ignorance, elaborating it in its truly defamatory light, concocted as it is by an angry lover and jealous workers whom the victim supervised as foreman. But the slander's literary lineage, among non-Jewish authors, treats it mythically, allying Jews with Satan. As Chaucer's "Prioress's Tale," the principal literary analogue for the slander (although apparently it is easily more than 850 years old), has it:

Our firste foe, the serpent Satanas,
That hath in Jewses' heart his waspe's nest,
Upswell'd and said, "O Hebrew people, alas!
Is this to you a thing that is honest,
That such a boy shall walken as him lest
In your despite, and sing of such sentence,
Which is against your lawe's reverence?"

On his way to and from school through the Jewish quarter, the boy in question has taken to singing, apparently in the way of tuneless whistling, the "Alma Redemptoris Mater," paying vocal homage to the Virgin:

As I have said, through the Jewery,
This little child, as he came to and fro,
Full merrily then would he sing and cry,
O Alma redemptoris, evermo.

And of course he sings it after death, though a Jew has cut his throat. The ballads usually have the boy playing with his friends, until their ball goes over the wall of "the Jew's" garden or through his window. Once tempted inside the house, the boy is often tortured in the way of Christ, then rolled in a "cake of lead" and cast into a well fifty fathoms deep. The versions collected by Child and MacEdward Leach[25] do not have the boy singing, nor do they pick up Chaucer's especially vile detail that the body's dumping ground is a public privy. Child, however, says folk associations with "Our Lady's well" emanate from the prioress.[26]

Generally speaking, and perhaps unexpectedly, the ballads are more sophisticated than the tale of the prioress, which seems merely puerile, motivated by thoughtless bile. In the ballads, the killer is a woman, "the Jew's daughter," who tempts the victim with an apple, and in one case, a fig, before "sticking" the child "like a swine" or sheep, then laying him out with Bible and prayer book. That is, in a demonic parody of Eden the killer is associated with Eve, the original scofflaw who caused the Fall and "all our woe." The parody of sacrifice (of the innocent, including Isaac and Christ) is deliberate, it seems, even insofar as it offends not just secular or canon law, but Jewish law. And where Chaucer sees justice done in the summary execution of the Jewish murderer, the ballads leave to the imagination the fate of the Jew's daughter.

Of course the death of children most sharply engages our attempts to reconcile law, sacred and secular, with notions of justice. To make that point, Peter De Vries titled one of his most powerful novels *The Blood of the Lamb*, its basis being the death of his young daughter from cancer. The protagonist, Don Wanderhope, rejects "those consolations called religious" as belonging "to the childhood of the race." His hope has wandered such that he must find redemption in the natural world, the world of experience with its own physical laws. But this is when he thinks his daughter, Carol, will recover. As she nears death, he begins a debate with God as to whether he exists and asks God if he and Herod are not one and the same. "Who creates a perfect blossom to crush it?" he asks. The God in his brain forgives him, to which Wanderhope replies, "I cannot say the same."

   A neighbour has baked a cake for the daughter and her friends on her ward. As Wanderhope carries it to the hospital, he sees Carol's night nurse turn into the church of St. Catherine. He follows her in to talk with her, forgets the cake on a pew, and proceeds to the hospital. A scalding series of tableaux begins. As Carol dies, Wanderhope touches the "stigmata" on her needle-pricked, scalpel-pierced body, praying over her. Immediately after she dies, he drinks heavily at a nearby tavern until the bartender cuts him off. Walking home, he passes the church, recalls the cake is inside, and retrieves it. Once again outside, he pauses before the statue of the crucified Christ at the church's entryway.

   I took the cake out of the box and balanced it a moment on the palm of my hand. Disturbed by something in the motion, the birds started from their covert and flapped away across the street. Then my arm drew back and let fly with all the strength within

me. Before the mind snaps, or the heart breaks, it gathers itself like
a clock about to strike. It might even be said one pulls himself
together to disintegrate. The scattered particles of self – love, wood
thrush calling, homework sums, broken nerves, rag dolls, one Phi
Beta Kappa key, gold stars, lamplight smiles, night cries, and the
shambles of contemplation – are collected for a split moment like
scraps of shrapnel before they explode.

He throws the cake into the icon's face, and then hallucinates
that it patiently wipes the icing from its eyes and tells him, "Suffer
the little children to come to me ... for such is the kingdom of
heaven."

The moment, evisceratingly comic, serves little as catharsis, and no
consolation at all. And so does Wanderhope experience the ambivalence of the seeker of justice in a fallen world:

Progress doubles our tenure in a vale of tears. Man is a mistake, to
be corrected only by his abolition, which he gives promise of seeing to himself. Oh, let him pass, and leave the earth to the flowers
that carpet the earth wherever he explodes his triumphs. Man is
inconsolable, thanks to the eternal "Why?" when there is no Why,
that question mark twisted like a fishhook in the human heart.
"Let there be light," we cry, and only the dawn breaks.

V. UP THE REVOLUTION:
REASONABLENESS WITHOUT DUTY

Duty always presumes reasonable behaviour, but reasonableness does
not always presume duty. Reasonableness can exist without an expansive sense of obligation, as where a group of people – a family, a sect,
a tribe – hive themselves off from the greater society. The neighbour
principle is weak or absent insofar as the group operates on the principle that the prime or only duty owed is to the group, or sub-group,
itself. This is the universe of Idaho survivalists but also our commercial law in its earlier, involuted days; before *Donoghue v. Stevenson* in
1932, privity of contract often dictated that a manufacturer had no liability to an end user damaged by the product. Where there is reasonableness without duty, the smaller society exists within, but rejects, the
larger. It privileges what it perceives to be *moral* reasonableness over
legal reasonableness. Thomas More's *Utopia* illustrates this, where the

survivalist tribes of *Lord of the Flies* do not: the children do not reject an alternative (ostensibly better) society, they adapt to their predicament (and unsuccessfully attempt to establish a legal system). So, too, do Winston, Julia, and Offred in the dystopias of *1984* and Margaret Atwood's *The Handmaid's Tale*. Note that these latter inhabit large totalitarian societies. In tribal or self-styled utopian regimes that purport to favour moral reasoning over a wider social and legal duty (though usually these societies often prove to be more idiosyncratic or monomaniacal than reasonable), the neighbourhood principle gives way to "chosenness," excluding people who do not fit within the social structure: they have not "seen the light." Everybody outside the group is damned, even if "the light" has nothing to do with religious or supernatural beliefs.

The archetype here has evolved from the narrative of the Tower of Babel, in Chapter 11 of Exodus, which is part of a cycle connecting the narrative of Eden to that of Moses and eventually to that of Christ. In other words, Babel is, figuratively, the last of three falls, or more precisely, cyclical risings and fallings: the tragic fall from Eden; the fall of Adam's and Eve's descendants at the time of the great flood, which is comic insofar as it has a "happy ending," the recreation of humankind in its post-lapsarian context, a rehabilitation signified by the covenant of the rainbow; and the fall from Babel, which is ironic or tragicomic, providing the basis for God to start again with a Chosen family group and leaving them to their free will under the Sinaiatic system of Law. Christianity, of course, provides the alternative, "equitable" resolution of Christ, but it builds on the Hebrew resolution, as the Christ or chosen-man narrative builds on that of Moses.

EDEN – FALL	NOAH – FLOOD	BABEL – CONTENDING CULTURES/TRIBES
One couple	One family	One people reduced to contending tribes, and finally a chosen tribe.
Fall from Paradise	Fall into water	Fall from manmade height
Creation	Reconstruction	Resolution (tribalism -> Chosen People -> chosen man in Christianity)
Thesis (pre-law)	Antithesis (positive law)	Synthesis (movement toward choosing one people from many under law, awaiting final judgment)[27]
Tragedy	Comedy (new beginning in fallen world)	Irony (tragicomedy)

With Babel, God seems to have been concerned that he had another Eden on his hands, where mere mortals sought to be god-like, seeking knowledge of all good and evil, but this time on a mass scale. When the First Couple had eaten of the protected tree, he evicted them from Paradise Manor, and the world filled with their scofflaw descendants. By way of further sanction there came the global flood, which, the narrative goes, killed every animate being on earth except selected specimens of each species. Beginning under the mortal lawgiver Hammurabi in Babylon, Noah's descendants constructed a tower with a temple at its top. God came down for a look and the first thing he noticed (so says Genesis 11) was "the people is one, and they have all one language." He worried that this powerful monoculture had constructed the seven-storey building "whose top may reach unto Heaven." The tenants seemed literally to be getting above themselves again.

The Law's solution this time was preventive, and, for a change, not altogether violent (at least not immediately). "Let us go down," God said to himself, "and there confound their language, that they may not understand one another's speech ... Therefore is the name of it called Babel; because the Lord did there confound the language of all the earth: and from thence did the Lord scatter them abroad ..." So Babel becomes the tragicomic resolution of the original Fall, as our cultural narrative (moving from general deterrence against an individual couple to the communal) accepts that, this side of Paradise, justice will remain imperfect and peace elusive. People, or tribes, will contend, for their selfish ends. The mortally tragic is mitigated by the Supreme Ruler's choice of a certain people and their journey toward earthly paradise, whence God becomes hands-off. The covenant inherent in the Law completely redeems the Fall, in both the Jewish and Christian traditions, by grace and final judgment, which redemption restores us to Heavenly Paradise, as one big, happy family.

When we look back at what we've said about narrative duty in litigation, we see how the Babel archetype operates in positive law as literature: charged with interpreting law's meaning in a specific circumstance, law courts juggle the interpretations proffered by litigants and advocates "from below" with "received" meanings as promulgated or suggested by legislators from on high. As priestly mediators, judges attempt to re-establish a single "tongue" or set meaning. That is, they establish a "chosen" meaning.

In law IN literature, both the moral outlaw and the Chosen One see conventional authority as corrupt. But unlike the moral outlaw, the moral chosen do not accept that conventional authority and its concept of the rule of law could ever be legitimate. Robin Hood feels a broad responsibility to his "neighbour," who happens to be any decent person (any conventional Christian of his day, anyway) who needs help. Ruth Puttermesser and Horace Rumpole feel similar commitment, although they are more in the "Mosaic" tradition of community: while their motivation is rooted personally, they understand that their self-interest lies in the common weal. As Rumpole occasionally notes of his troubled clients, "There but for fortune go I." Personal salvation is tied to the social good.

The poacher of the traditional ballads is closer to the Chosen One insofar as he feels a duty principally to himself, his family, and possibly his cohorts. They are chosen to suffer, as it were, under an unfair distribution of wealth enforced by supposedly lawful authority. Resorting to self-help, the poacher-protagonist is pre-revolutionary; and revolutionary behaviour, thinking bigger in a larger group, can render him more "moral." At the other extreme, we have tribalism without transcendent reasonableness, as with Nazism. Thus does a warped sense of duty slide into evil.

The Chosen One is driven by messianism that hasn't become mythic: the "messiah" here has only a small following. A fine literary example of this is Paul Theroux's novel, *The Mosquito Coast*. The protagonist Allie Fox believes that America, his homeland, has lost its bearings and is on the brink of self-destruction. It has gone soft, cocooned, suicidally industrialized – fatally alienated from humankind's natural environment and the common sense of natural law. The central metaphor for this is, in Fox's sardonic, *reductio ad absurdum* mind, cheese paste in a tube. Making all sorts of chiliasmic pronouncements about paradise lost – the end of days, or at least of an empire – he removes his family back to nature, to primitive tribal life in the jungles of Honduras.

There he purports to recreate civilization, which to his mind is all work, no school (it corrupts), with only family singalongs and boardless games as luxury. It never questions that the prelapsarian world needs improvement. As cult leader, Fox practises a well-intentioned totalitarianism, but of course George Orwell has shown us where this too often leads. When things go south, as they easily and quickly do, they slide into evil. Inevitably, chosenness is a sort of oligarchy. Fox declares that there is no God – or, with Nietzsche, that God has abandoned Creation (he can't really make up his mind) – so that it is up to man to make the natural world a better place. To

effect this, he invents a giant ice machine – refrigeration and air con-
ditioning for the jungle – and literally runs organized religion off
his jungle patch to "start over again," in a new, refrigerated Eden.
With unconscious foreboding, he compares the ice machine, "Fat
Boy," to hellfire:

> And the funny thing about hellfire is, it's imaginary. But not Fat
> Boy! He's got more poison in him than a century of hells. Oh,
> gaw, I could teach those missionaries a thing or two about chemi-
> cal combustion. If they saw hydrogen and ammonia get loose
> they'd believe in me, instead of the dead top-spinner [God, acting
> like a distracted boy].

"I am the last man" he repeats as a messianic mantra, at once the new
Noah and the sacrificial lamb of God, a new iteration of the Christ,
who embodies the Word: he talks ceaselessly, in self-justification that is
equal, and complementary, parts self-reassurance, self-justification,
mollification of his family and followers, and excoriation of modern
America. "This is why I came here," he messianically chants of his
machine in the new Eden (after his son has dreamt Fox has been crucified by Honduran primitives), until his fanaticism really takes hold
as denial and he declares his family "the first family" (as with Noah)
even as his successive jungle Edens – the darkness enlightened – dete-
riorate and he abandons them as miscues, each one starting and ending at a lower point than the one before. He moves from Eden to the
Great Flood, from arrival in the Garden to sailing away from it on an
ark (formerly the family's new, spartan home after he destroys their
purported paradise) – from one fall to another, ending ironically as
a failed, oblivious Noah, leaving his teenaged son (the real man of
the family, at fourteen) to salvage the clan by returning it to fallen
America, the purported Hell on Earth. He is a missionary who is his
own god, Kurtz without the savagery, which in many ways makes him
more dangerous – and causes him to devolve into the savagery he
mocks.

Nature never quite brings Fox down to its Id level (as Conrad seems
to suggest happens with Kurtz), but it enlarges him, enables his sense
of supremacy. He is a user, bringing people into his family (his tribe)
only to the extent that they agree with him or provide manpower to
his "plan." He is Jim Jones without the Kool-Aid,[28] likeable and obsessive in the same way, an apocalyptic liar in his higher cause (once in

the jungle, as his mythography becomes expansive, he persuades his family that America has been destroyed in a nuclear holocaust), lawless but frighteningly sensible – reasonable even in prehistoric environments, bravely if dogmatically working toward his own version of earthly paradise. Everyone admires him, and that anti-charisma makes him a devil in angel's clothing. Like Milton's Anti-Christ, he has all the best lines, and best lies.

Fox's ambivalence about a higher power creeps through, however, revealing a denial that is pathological, but which, like every other hitch, he exploits (with often admirable pluck). Speaking of the danger in the ice machine, he says (as reported by Charlie, the book's narrator and Fox's teenaged son),[29]

"You feel a little like God..." His clothes were soaked from the ice bricks and sweat. His fingers were red from handling the ice. His hair was long and his face like a hatchet. He turned his bloodshot eyes on me and went on in the same tired wondering whisper, "God had fun making things like icebergs and volcanoes. Too bad He didn't finish the job. Ha!"

Fox's utopian idea is of a *Homo faber* paradise. Man-the-maker exploits nature and in this sense the ideal is self- or human-centred. At the mythic level, this is why Fox never succeeds: man cannot steal the gods' fire without consequence. Such an act violates not one but two central or constitutional (and natural) Laws: man is not god and man should not steal (especially not from the gods). Then, too, Fox's is very much an idiosyncratic utopia, improperly founded on misanthropy and disdain for natural law expressed in the human. (All of this is symbolized by the fact that he has long since mutilated himself in an inventing accident: one of his index fingers is a stump that horrifies everyone who meets him.) Only very late in the book does Fox finally admit his hatred of humankind, indirectly, explaining that he obsessively detests and enjoys killing scavenger birds (ignoring that they play a crucial part in nature's plan, in the fallen world) "because they remind me of human beings." Ironically, he has himself been a scavenger from the start, "shopping" in American dumps and throughout the Honduran jungles and swamps, taking from them the material for his tools and inventions. After the ice machine apocalypse, he complains, "'I thought I was building something ... But I was asking for it to be destroyed. That's a consequence of perfection in this world – the opposing wrath of imperfection. Those scavengers wanted to feed on us!'"

A foundational law or principle in many other utopias would say that killing any sentient being, even for food, is wrong. Pain and death are dystopic. Yet Fox has no compunction about killing, particularly if the prey can be used for any human purpose or whim, such as soap, lubrication, etc. (not just clothing or food). When (in a fallen world) his most precious tool, his ice-maker, blows up everything he has created and triggers his final descent into madness, he is obliged to "retool" without tools, becoming pure *Homo "sapiens"* – the irony being, of course, that he has monomaniacally reduced himself and his family to a parody of Adam and the first family, guileless, toolless, and, ultimately, mindless. Mirroring his perverse obsessiveness, the jungle ice machine ("Ice is civilization," he has insisted before this, because man improves nature by making the substance artificially, on demand) has set fire to Eden, razing it to the ground. He is forced to retreat to the real Eden, "Acre," not coincidentally created by the children, a place where all is play based on the modern developed world, a sanctuary from their otherwise sweaty, Spartan existence, jealously kept secret from Fox. The wisdom even of this discretion (for here, the child is indeed the father of the man) is borne out when, true to form, Fox ridicules Acre even in desperate refuge there. It inevitably relies on all the conventional human improvements Fox despises: a school, a church, a store which trades goods for "cash" pebbles. In this real paradise, there is no real work: Eden is home of *Homo ludens*, man the player.

In Acre, husbandry and ice are beside the point; as drought sucks all water from the main camp, fresh spring water in the children's camp "brimmed to the grassy edge." Food in Acre is ready for the plucking and harvesting. Here is perfection, where *Homo faber*, as Fox admits, is a product of an imperfect mortal world. But *as* imperfect man, Fox can't help himself: against his most sincere efforts to eradicate the worst depredations of the military-industrial complex on natural life, his attempts to civilize the jungle have destroyed it. *Homo faber*, he that would steal the gods' fire, is man the ravager. Congenitally (as by Original Sin) he violates nature's law.

In the end, Fox is a theist who doesn't believe in the Law. He views *Deus faber* as "a hasty inventor of the sort you find in any patent office," a fellow who doesn't finish the job. At his convenience, he is a proponent, now, of *Deus otiosus* – there is a god, but he's left man to his own devices – and then, *Deus absconditus*: God has turned away from man out of indifference, disgust, or something unknowable. Such views make positive law a necessity, as they otherwise leave impulse and the "laws of nature" without a governor. They also make positive law open to immoral abuse. When justice seems to turn its back on us, we might feel that God has done the same – that, in fact, the two are congruent. Thus is faith sometimes killed by tragedy, as where a Holocaust victim loses her religious belief.

I enclose "laws of nature" in quotation marks in deference to a remark by Northrop Frye that Nietzsche's infamous "God is dead" version of *Deus absconditus* is

> incidental to his more important aim of de-deifying of "law" from ordinary consciousness to describe the operation of nature. There are no laws of nature, Nietzsche says, only necessities; but the metaphor "law of nature" carries with it a vestigial sense of a personality who commands and other personalities (ourselves) who have the option of obeying or disobeying; and this vestigial metaphor, for Nietzsche, is a superstition in the most exact sense of an inorganic survival of tradition.[30]

Accepting these views (or not), for our purposes here "laws of nature" remains a valid metaphor. Just as we purport to refine Law with Mercy, legalism with equity, Allie Fox seeks to improve on nature, blaming an absent deity for its fallen state. It is an Oedipal theme echoed by his relationship with Charlie, as narrator, who slowly comes to see that his father is crazy like a fox, but no messiah. As self-appointed Lawgiver, Fox is often wrong, and worse, regularly unjust, subjecting others to his megalomania and whim. Egocentric in the way of all false messiahs, he lacks compassion or even the capacity for empathy. He is a soft psychopath – soft at least until he murders three armed intruders (with no apparent regret), triggering the really apocalyptic explosion and Fox's increasingly manic downward spin. Death enters the world.

Frye suggests that literary depictions of this sort of obsessiveness are themselves archetypal in comedy (here, of the blackest sort), usually featuring

> someone with a good deal of social prestige and power, who is able to force much of the [work's] society into line with his obses-

sion. Thus the humor is intimately connected with the theme of
the absurd or irrational law that the action of comedy moves
toward breaking ... Shylock, too, unites a craving for the law with
the humor of revenge. Often the absurd law appears as a whim of
a bemused tyrant whose will is law, like Leontes or the humorous
Duke Frederick in Shakespeare ... Or it may take the form of a
sham Utopia, a society of ritual bondage constructed by act of
humorous or pedantic will ... This theme is also as old as Aristo-
phanes, whose parodies of Platonic social schemes in *The Birds*
and *Ecclesiazusae* deal with it.[31]

For all his genius, and despite his core reasonableness and crafty
spunk (a revolution against Cheez-Whiz bespeaks transcendent sanity,
after all), Fox scorns the community, and even, at last the tribe. In the
language of duty, he is a bad neighbour. "He invented for his own
sake!" Charlie realizes at last. "He was an inventor because he hated
hard beds and bad food and slow boats and flimsy huts and dirt" – for
himself. "And waste – he complained about the cost of things, but it
wasn't the money. It was the fact that they got weak and broke after
you bought them. He thought of himself first!"

This in itself is not bad or unlawful; it is adaptive. Motivation usually begins with self-interest, but self-interest flourishes with the community interest. Fox's hubris is that he never has this insight, the banal
concept that no man is an island, even on an island. Fox is pure
Prometheus, the oligarch's dictator, arbitrarily declaring, enforcing,
and amending his own tribal law. His messianism is all self-regard.

And so, envisioning himself as a messiah, he devolves from Adam
to Moses to Noah, homeless and sick and adrift with his terrified
young family on a raft, navigating savage waters as civilization passes
in the opposite direction. Even in the deepest jungle, he finds that
the natives associate the Christian church, via its missionaries, with
civilization – health and comfort (including refrigeration) ... with salvation. It is not industry – human tools – that have gone wrong, but
how colonizing humans have used them. "A Zambu passed by one
day ... He was going to church. It was Sunday he said. Father said, 'I
wish you hadn't told me that ... If God hadn't rested on the seventh
day, He might have finished the job.'" Particularly infuriating is that
they have ignorantly substituted indigenous superstition for the
colonial, plasticized version, brought down from the sky by white
men in an Iron Bird. The natives can recite the Lord's Prayer, all

right, although they think "hallowed be thy name" is "hello bead name."

And so in the end is this version of Prometheus, this self-styled god who would be a law unto himself by appropriating to himself not just fire and ice but the Word – Law and Creation rolled into one – punished by the scavenger he reviles: having been shot by a Christian missionary (the same man who has offered Fox's sons Kool-Aid), he lies helpless in the sand of "paradise" as vultures tear out not his liver, à la Prometheus, but his tongue. It is not enough that he is anyway dead and thereby silenced. In the Moses narrative, we find a lawgiver who stutters to show us he is no god. Theroux gives us a blathering false messiah dealt the ultimate poetic justice. Speech, some say, is what makes man Earth's supreme ward. Then again, maybe not.

4

The Evil That Persons Do:
Unreasonableness and the Rejection or
Abnegation of Duty

Where the rule of law is corrupted, we have seen how the collective imagination makes the outlaw "good," moving him up the reconfigured paradigm. It does not do the same thing, of course, with someone who is a scofflaw for his or its own sake. Everyday bad-acting is not heroic, but neither is it sociopathic evil: in John Mortimer's Rumpole books, it is often humorous, with its "officer of the court" protagonist viewing the administration of justice as a game, but still well worth playing. As a barrister, Horace Rumpole's banner, as it were, is the proud legacy of British justice, with (specifically) its presumption of innocence and the "beyond a reasonable doubt" standard for criminal convictions. Rumpole has his feet firmly planted in the everyday human world; his gentle cynicism is not directed at the rule of law, but at its corruption, at "unneighbourly" behaviour. Generally, the "villains" he defends are less blameworthy – morally, anyway – than bankers and equity traders whose licensed greed compromises world economies, not to mention the pension funds of millions of ordinary working people. More harrowingly, for all his rationalism and heroic charisma, Milton's Satan is still in Hell, and James Kelman's *How Late It Was, How Late* gives us a sort of Meursault in the funhouse mirror, a man who has no rational basis for his rejection of the rule of law. A man who feels no investment in civil society but is not sociopathic, he acts viscerally and therefore unreasonably, but is not evil.

Though *How Late It Was* has enjoyed critical praise, some serious readers do not consider it serious literature. We expect our "litrichoor" to be redemptive in the same way that law, as another reflection of our culture, is meant to be normative. We want our fiction to make sense of things, and crime – particularly crime among the underclasses – is often base or apparently senseless, and therefore terrifying. In this light, detective fiction seems artificial, too baroque in its motives and contrivances, and too neat in the way it ties up the loose ends. We want meaning, we accept that art is artifice, but we also understand that life is full of ambiguity. *Crime and Punishment* and *The Trial* are literature; *Rumpole of the Bailey* and *The Sirens Sang of Murder* are (supposedly) facetiae.

It seems likely that when Rabbi Julia Neuberger declared this winner of the 1994 Booker Prize "a disgrace," she meant the novel was not redemptive: in her cultural context, it had no saving grace. It was not litrichoor. There was insufficient artifice according to western literary convention. Her outrage reverberated because she was one of the judges on the panel that made the award. Apparently she called *How Late It Was, How Late* "crap," but it won anyway.[1]

For Kelman, fiction is a sort of Molotov cocktail. He uses his novels and short stories to engage in class warfare and often perverse Scottish nationalism, which no doubt is why the *Times* columnist Simon Jenkins called him an "illiterate savage," and compared the experience of reading *How Late It Was* to being stuck next to a "drunk Glaswegian" (translation: low-life) on a train journey.

How Late It Was is written stream of consciousness from the point of view of Sammy Samuels, a Glaswegian petty villain whose world is rendered even more claustrophobic when he becomes blind, in the first few pages, after a "doing" by the police. Bizarrely, given the novel's contemporary context when just about anything goes in public, some readers have thought it unworthy of prizes because every other sentence contains "fuck" and "cunt" – although in the case of the latter, no sanctimony has been possible in the arena of gender politics: Sammy uses the word exclusively for males, and the only sex in the book comprises passing, even limp, allusions to "a wank" (without any depiction of same) or, perhaps twice or three times in 374 pages, the sexual attraction of a particular woman. One would have thought a young man in Sammy's condition might have sought more refuge in sexual reverie. Yet the objections to his verbal "obscenity" are no different from those that have featured prominently in our legal history, in biblical prescriptions about language and swearing to criminal code obscenity provisions today. The offended readers seem to be reacting from the artistic, legal, and political climate of the 1950s, making Kelman's shocking book more artificially shocking than it is. Neuberger's broader shock and disgust have played into Kelman's hands. What better way to crown Kelman's achievement as a literary form of class warfare than to officially – establishmentally – judge it disgraceful crap.

But beyond sociology, one can appreciate the rabbi's visceral reaction. The first time I tried to read the novel, I could hardly breathe. On the edge of private hysteria, living totally inside the head of a blind hooligan in a holding cell, I had to put it down after just a few pages. Kelman does not play the game, never mind the obscenity charges. He gives us no quotable quotes to note down in our commonplace books or to use as epigrams in our own writing. But this is really the point. And as a judge in a literary competition, Neuberger had a duty to rise above the visceral. Her job was to see past it to what artifice there was, which, in its execution, is the book's brilliance, no matter that she found it wanting.

It is true that in the end a compelling tale lets us down. Part of the novel's pleasure, if you can call it that, or at least part of its motive force, is the reader's idea that he has guessed some of the conclusion: the compensation "rep" is a cop and Sammy's girlfriend is dead. Kelman cheats the reader by giving no hint of anything definite there. Presumably a "lesser" work, something that wasn't litrichoor, would have tied those strands, which can hardly be called loose ends. Leaving us hanging is too clever by half. It accomplishes "art" only in the sense that hanging a side of beef in a gallery to rot is artistic. It is happenstance, realism, "slice of life," but not, finally, narrative. It is all right to play with the formalistic trappings of art – as Godard does with cinema, Picasso with painting, Schoenberg with music. But once you engage in narrative, you cannot altogether abandon it simply because your energy runs out. Rabbi Neuberger is right, for the wrong reasons: there is insufficient artifice in *How Late It Was, How Late*.

Then again, conventional narrative these days is often anti-heroic: the traditional expression, in which right or good prevail, is turned on its head. Antagonist becomes, at least perversely, protagonist. And to the extent that legal narrative mimics imaginative narrative, the perverse gains the day – as where, say, Nazi, South African apartheid, and Jim Crow statutes established a perverse "rule of law." What is troubling about *How Late It Was*, and what probably most troubled Neuberger, is that it presents a non-productive, less than "good," person as the narrative voice and complete (claustrophobic) focus – the reader's guide to human experience. And Sammy is not an anti-heroic guide in the sense of Blake's *Songs of Experience* or Milton's Satan, with his beautifully plausible arguments about truth and justice. There is nothing redemptive in Sammy, even perversely. At the end of the novel, his fifteen-year-old son, whom he has de facto abandoned, comes to help him and to ask his father if he might accompany him on the run – a perverse father-and-son outing. Abandoning the child yet again, Sammy immediately accepts the boy's offer of his savings, £80 he sneaks out of his mother's home.

Still, the reader who accepts this fiction for the anti-conventional narrative it is never abhors Sammy. We are aghast, but we get the sense that he simply isn't equipped to do better. As his narrative gains momentum, we yearn for him to cope with his blindness, get some help, turn his life around. Bereft of Satanic glibness, he is no psychopath, just, as one says in Yinglish, a no-goodnik. He actually seems to love his son, and (in his fleeting moments of empathy) to feel he is not worthy of him.

In other words, if Sammy is evil, his badness is equivocal, ironic. He brings a taste of Hell into the world of experience, but in the end it is a personal hell, not Hitlerian. It wins no battles, let alone the war, accomplishing nothing, not even anything criminal or perverse. It is unclear that he has done anything worse than cold-cock a police officer, for which his sentence is blindness. If this makes him a Tieresian or Samsonian prophet, his message is obscure, banal, so intensely personal as to be socially almost useless. And to the extent that legal narrative parallels his experience, we never know whether, as he takes to the road blindly, it is the path to rehabilitation or his final comeuppance. In the cross-over language of law and literature, his fate is Kafkaesque, yet recounted in language that disposes some judges to dismiss his story as anti-litrichoor, and to throw away the key.

Kafka has resonance here on a second point: his work, the familiar instances being *The Trial* and "In the Penal Colony," does not depend on a change to the paradigm. The system is perverse because of the perversity of its designers and users. Joseph K is not superior to any of his persecutors: he has bought into the system and sees it as his duty (to himself, but also to his society) to somehow make sense of its senselessness. The paradigm is turned on its head in dystopic or sociopathic narratives, not normative ones, as in Kafka, that take a surrealist turn.[2]

George Steiner writes that "the key fact about Kafka is that he was possessed of a fearful premonition" of Nazism.[3] With its machine that kills convicts by slowly carving the indictment into their bodies, absent a trial or even permitting the prisoner to answer the charges, an instrument controlled by the Eichmannite petty bureaucrat whose passion is that machinery, "'In the Penal Colony' foreshadows not only the technology of the death factories, but that special paradox of the modern totalitarian regime – the subtle, obscene collaboration between victim and torturer." The obscene collaboration becomes possible at the next, lower stage (which is why the colony's machine only foreshadows it), when the law is twisted to make genocide "legal." And decent people, the victims, believe in justice under the rule of law as an article of faith. When law fails, we have Hell.

Experience tells us that as the rule of law and civil society break down, humaneness fails and we return to a state of nature. But it is at least at first a state of nature in a fallen world, survival of the most ruthless and cruel. Societies, like their myths, tend to follow such cycles. This is particularly worrisome as we seem to inhabit a new or more deeply fallen world, in the wake of the horrors of two world wars and the surge of religious fundamentalism amid the proliferation of weapons of mass destruction. Kafka's machine of "In the Penal Colony" has been systemized and perfected on a mythic scale. No wonder there are deniers among those too lazy or credulous to consider the evidence. Of course, this is often the subject of modern literature, the problem of justice where law is at best a tool of the complacent, self-justifying bully.

Abuse of Authority: The Charming Rogue v. the Moral Outlaw

We have seen how the traditional ballad can, by displacement, make outlaws moral, at least where the rule of law has been corrupted and it becomes reasonable to disobey it. But sometimes the heroes of this medium are truly equivocal: they have no really redeeming qualities beyond a certain tribalism, a loyalty to their fellow criminals and sometimes remorse over their alienation, once imprisoned, from a lover, family, and country.

This lamentation is a convention in many ballads about transportation. In "Botany Bay," for example (the title locale being a centre for convicts transported from England to Australia during the eighteenth century), the prisoner admits to being light-fingered and violent, but he provides neither excuse nor explanation:

T'aint leaving old England we cares about,
T'aint 'cause we mis-spells what we knows;
But because all we light-finger'd gentry
Hops around with a log on our toes.

These seven long years I've been serving now,
And seven long more have to stay,
All for bashing a bloke down our alley
And taking his ticker away.

Oh had I the wings of a turtle dove,
I'd soar on my pinions so high
Slap bang to the arms of my Polly love,
And in her sweet presence I'd die.

Now all my young Dukies and Duchesses,
Take warning from what I've to say.
Mind all is your own as you toucheses,
Or you'll find us in Botany Bay.

This is from a version attributed to Henry Stephens and William
Yardley in their 1885 burlesque, *Little Jack Shepherd*, but it borrows
from an earlier street ballad, "Farewell to Judges and Juries" – itself
attributed to John Ashton – and bears other similarities to "purely
folk" versions. (Which came first, this author cannot say, but the his-
toricity is irrelevant here, as our interest is in the conventional
imagery, wherever it arose.) In one of those folk versions, the convict
is a Londoner and describes the setting of his trial at the Old Bailey:

To see my aged father dear,
As he stood near the bar,
Likewise my tender mother,
Her old grey locks to tear.
In tearing of her old grey locks,
These words to me did say:
"O Son! O Son! What have you done,
That you're going to Botany Bay?"

This version shares with other outlaw ballads the fact that the convict has been

Brought up by honest parents
For the truth to you I'll tell.
Brought up by honest parents,
And rear'd most tenderly,
Till I became a roving blade,
Which proved my destiny.

So, though the convict might not be a sociopath, or at least he experiences emotional pain for which we feel sympathy, he offers no evidence in mitigation of his crime, only aggravating circumstances. The rogue ballads evoke pathos, even some admiration, but leave us to provide remorse (and mercy); the outlaw – or more properly for this sub-archetype, the rogue – makes no plea for himself.

The Irish ballad "Roger O'Hehir" is a fine example in this regard, as well as for what it says about the old-versus-new order that we've seen as a motivating factor in not just the outlaw ballads but more generally in law-and-literature archetypology. Young Roger's petty – rather pathetic – criminal career begins when he does nothing more unconventional than jilt a lover. Like the protagonist of the London version of "Botany Bay," he

had honest parents of fame and renown
Oh had I been obedient and kept the command
I never would have broken the laws of the land.[4]

The parents get Roger an apprenticeship with a weaver but his attention wanders to one "beautiful creature, Jane Sharkey by name." "I own I did entice her," he confesses – yes, even here he takes full blame, not saddling Jane with the Eve-temptress role – and the couple runs off. When Roger leaves Jane "forlorn" (and who knows in what other difficulties), her father takes him prisoner.

Here lies one of the features that often makes these ballads equivocal. We note, again, the *senex iratus* of literary convention, the grumpy old man imposing his will, taking the law into his own hands as the aristocracy does in *Measure for Measure*. It is a recurrent motif throughout this particular ballad and occurs in others, even where the suitor remains faithful and loving, as in the more familiar "Matt Hyland." Hyland's wrong is nothing greater (but nothing less common in the popular imagination) than being poor, "the servant" of his lover's father. The girl overhears her parents say that "in spite of me, they will transport you." The Robin Hood ethos creeps in no matter what: there is a class war, implicit even in the "rogue ballad" like "Roger O'Hehir," and the apparent abuse of power by the wealthy. The latter have private recourse to law enforcement, apparently (or so it sometimes seems to the underclasses), so as to arrange severe punishments for the poor, such as transportation to the colonies, even when they've done nothing criminal. So we can't help but be sympathetic, even with Roger.

Indeed, jilted Jane's father has Roger imprisoned in the Newry guardhouse, where he learns he is to be whipped the next morning. So begins his progress from rake to outlaw. In fear of bodily harm, he breaks out of the guardhouse and stows away on a boat to England. Hungry and "loathe to beg," in Wales he steals a horse so as to sell it. He gets away with this, apparently, but upon re-entering Ireland and "up to his tricks again near a fair in Newry town," he steals a hat, whose owner takes him back to the Newry guardhouse.

When Roger learns he is to be hanged, he knocks down the turnkey and swims across Newry Lough. The Newry guards recapture him, this time in the act of robbing a peach tree, and he is finally hanged. Assuming that he has not been charged with horse theft, his recorded crimes are seduction (apparently), stealing a hat, and attempting to steal peaches. But he remains sanguine about his fate, and perhaps even repentant:

> Now Roger was taken but often did get free.
> It's come now his turn for to march to the tree.
> And all his foolish actions he there did declare,
> And that put an end to old Roger O'Hehir.

Again, it is left to the reader or hearer to excuse him, our charming rogue, perhaps by pleading abuse of authority. At least in "Matt Hyland" the harsh father conventionally relents, giving us the true "comic" ending in which the lovers are re-united in a new (Edenic) order, and the father repents his abuse of authority:

> The lord discussed with his daughter dear
> One night alone in her bedchamber
> Saying, "I'll give you leave to bring him back
> Since there are none you style above him."
> She wrote a letter then in haste,

Still for him her heart entwined.
She's brought him back, to the church they went
She's made a lord of young Matt Hyland.

As in Dickens, society is reformed one poor man at a time; or perhaps Shakespeare is the better example, insofar as in John Falstaff he
gives us the sub-archetype in a particularly compelling form, contrasting him with inconstant if ultimately reformed Sir Hal: where
Falstaff remains (very charmingly) roguish, the future Henry V, self-
consciously destined for greater things, merely slums in his company.
In any event, this gravitational pull towards comedy – in the sense of
a truly happy ending instead of an ironically cheerful one – can be so
strong as to be supplemented by the folklore surrounding a ballad.
When Sarah Makem provided collectors her version of "The Derry
Gaol," about a man rescued at the last minute from hanging, as his
lover rides up with a Queen's pardon, she explained:

A young gentleman that fell in love with a rich lady and her parents didn't want him to get her, and she fought hard to get him
and she went away to the Queen and got pardon.
She took her Willie and she married him and defied her parents.
She was right. I didn't blame her one bit. He was the fellow she
wanted and she was right to take him.[5]

The ballad itself makes no reference to the girl's family or their
wealth. She simply gallops in at the last moment, a prototype for the
eleventh-hour phone call from the governor's office.

With "Roger O'Hehir," tragedy is avoided only insofar as we admire
and identify with O'Hehir's pluck, his willingness to thumb his nose
at priggish conservatism, and his roguish acceptance of the legal consequences, no matter that they seem unjust as out of all proportion to
what he has done. Because he never really shows remorse, he draws a
sort of *cordon sanitaire* around himself: we must remain content with
the old order he flouts, perhaps reassured that if we, too, are not roguish, we remain safe from bourgeois legalism. The rule of law, even if
skewed or ruthlessly conservative, is preferable to the survival of the
wiliest in a society of rogues. Or in the vernacular, two wrongs don't
make a right.

The well-known "Black Velvet Band" provides a cynic's antidote to
the *gallant manqué* aspects of Roger O'Hehir and Matt Hyland both.

Like O'Hehir, and at least similar to Hyland, the protagonist is an apprentice. In this case, however, as narrator he casts the love interest as an Eve-like temptress. "Many the happy hour" he's spent in Belfast, until he meets the girl whose "eyes shone like diamonds," and who tied her shoulder-length hair in a black velvet band (which phrase the ballad uses ambiguously, possibly also to indicate "gang colours" for an organized crime ring, the Black Velvet Band?).

> The girl steals a watch and
> slipped it right into my hand.
> Then she gave me in charge to the policeman.
> Bad luck to the Black Velvet Band.

What's worse, the Lord Mayor sentences the narrator "to plough upon Van Diemen's Land" for sixteen years – an unusual punishment given that the standard terms were seven and fourteen years.

The effect of tragedy is mitigated first by a sort of parody of what mitigates the tragedy in "Roger O'Hehir." Where O'Hehir cheerfully admits his bad behaviour and accepts its consequences, the "Band" narrator seems to be trying to shirk any responsibility, even caddishly blaming a lady. If there is any doubt that we are not to feel all that sorry for him, the ballad's conventional, jaunty melody eradicates uncertainty.

In "Old Judge Duffy" the roguishness reaches the judiciary, and the charm (such as it is) has fallen victim to more sensitive[6] times. A particularly interesting wrinkle is that, as a judge and unlike other charming rogues, Duffy has a sense of outward-looking duty. It is perverted, though, by the rogue's flippant self-regard, and in the ballad's most common version, by a failure of empathy. Because Duffy confounds this foolish selfishness with a sense, though jaundiced, of community, the ballad tells us that though he knows "nothing of the rules of the law / For judge he was one of the best." In the ballad's satirical logic, this is exemplified, at a time when overt racism was rampant in North America, by the way he tries a murder case. In two trials, juries (it seems) convict the town's "only good" blacksmith; he was, after all, caught "red-handed." But Judge Duffy discharges the murderer, ruling, "We've two Chinese laundrymen, everyone knows. / Why not save the poor blacksmith and hang one of those?"[7] Once again, law is distinguished from justice, although to the truly judicious ear the latter comes off much the worse in this case. The moral compass – in this case, of the entire community (which of course is the source of the ironic humour) – is not just broken, it is smashed.

A version that MacEdward Leach collected in Newfoundland makes the judge more bumptious and ambiguously empathetic, morally and legally, despite his persistent characterization as "one of the best" jurists: it is, after all, titled, with some sense of truer justice, "Duffy's Blunder." The judge acquits a young black man accused of stealing "a new pair of pants" on the ground that "you can't make a suit out of one pair of pants." While the ballad's narrator uses the "N word" to describe the accused, the judge addresses him politely as "young man" and judiciously tempers the law with mercy. Subsequently, Judge Duffy buys two blind mules for his wagon, only to have them stolen, one after the other. He is, in other words, a sort of wise *schlemiel*. His motive for sacrificing the innocent Chinese laundry-man to save the blacksmith, after three convictions in this instance, is more clearly utilitarian: as the smith is the only such tradesman in town, "they hated to take his dear life."[8] Though crude, it is also a roguish, popu-list illustration of the sophisticated argument made by Rawls in favour of justice as fairness over utilitarian approaches.[9] With cracker-barrel wit, Judge Duffy leans toward Rawls in the first instance, only to strain cleverness later by resorting to populist, Benthamite racism.

In Marcel Aymé's story "The Wife-Tax Collector,"[10] we find a more modern, ironic iteration of the charming rogue. Though proudly scrupulous in his work, title-character Gauthier-Lenoir tempers it with mercy. His wife's lavish spending on clothes and the beauty par-lour have made him sympathetic to those who are short of cash come tax-payment time. He is harsh with only one taxpayer, Rebuffaud, pre-cisely because the latter always pays his taxes long before the deadline, gloating about it as his civic duty. Perplexed, at first, as to why this troubles him as a tax collector, Gauthier-Lenoir has an epiphany, otherwise feeling outcast on the dark, rainy streets outside his local bistro, the dreaded taxman when he'd rather be everyman. (He has, after all, just posted to himself the same demand letter he has sent his neighbours, and later justifies this to his wife, remarking, "'I'm a tax-payer like everybody else.' Gauthier-Lenoir's eyes shone with pride as he repeated, 'Like everybody else.'")

[H]e now understood clearly the meaning of the vehement if mute reproach M. Rebuffaud's attitude sparked in his heart. ... In

making good what he owed straight away, or nearly so, he avoided
the risks most taxpayers took of wilfully forgetting to pay, and of
enduring the consequences. To the taxation officer's mind, the
notion of duty, of taxpayer's duty, was inseparable from temptation, hesitation, come-back, peril. By forbearing from demanding
immediate payment of tax, the Revenue accorded the taxpayer a
sort of free will of the purse, a testing period during which he
could commit imprudence, spend his tax-money on bad works,
but also triumph over all temptation and succeed fully at his fiscal
duty. By the very fact that he paid in cash, M. Rebuffaud robbed
himself of these austere triumphs and succeeded at only one part
of his duty, the tiniest, most negligible.

Archetypal duty is Kantian, or at least Ogden Nashian: you have to
suffer for it, like Adam and Eve, Moses, and Jesus before you. Selfish
temptation is duty's necessary nemesis. At law, the reasonable man,
the Rebuffaud, pays his taxes promptly. In life, the really reasonable
man allows for contingencies, grace, tender mercies. Justice, the spirit
of the law, demands it.

When Mme. Gauthier-Lenoir leaves the collector for a handsome
soldier, Gauthier-Lenoir copes by deciding she has been collected as a
form of tax by the Ministry of Revenue. He goes to his office to complain to himself of the injustice, taking either side of his desk to make
both sides of the argument, always temperate. He doesn't contest the
taxation of his wife, taxpayer G-L argues, but revenue authorities
failed to give him proper notice, and the bailiff never served him with
a writ of execution. Had correct procedure been followed, G-L "could
have enjoyed [his] wife for several more weeks" before she was forfeit.

Sure enough, he is describing what more recently we have come to
call breaches of natural justice. As is his sympathetic wont, tax collector G-L admits that there were procedural irregularities in taxpayer G-
L's case. But he satisfies taxpayer G-L that, while he has "the right to
hope that the authorities would return his wife for five or six weeks,"
it would take years, decades, even, to accomplish this. In the interim
his wife would have become "wrinkled, altogether old, toothless, her
skin gone gray and her head balding." And besides, as a tax collector
by profession, taxpayer G-L was professionally obliged to set a good
example.

The capper, though, is when collector G-L sends other taxpayers
notices requiring them to forfeit their wives to the treasury. When

Rebuffaud complains, G-L advises him that, for once, maybe he shouldn't be in such a hurry to pay his bill.

Clearly the tax collector is no moral outlaw. (Aymé is never more than ambivalent about such figures, as in "La traversée de Paris" – concerning the black market in meat during the Nazi occupation of France – and in his post-war novel, *Uranus*.) He has the utmost respect for the status quo, and his "revolt" against it is entirely personal, a coping mechanism that by chance is adopted by the community as more or less desirable. When Gauthier-Lenoir goes to his local bistro to see how the husbands are reacting to their new wife-tax notices, he watches the "pastry chef Planchon, widowed the previous year, [trying] unsuccessfully to incite the taxpayers into rebellion. 'Surely you're not going to give up your wife?' he said to Petit, who owned the hardware store. 'If necessary,' Petit replied, and others repeated, 'If necessary.'" And when the Minister of Revenue visits the local taxation centre and happens upon a roomful of the forfeited wives, many of them attractive – or at least they seem so, having titivated for the outing, sporting their most expensive jewellery – his thoughts turn to his own appetites, personally and on behalf of the Republic. He promotes Gauthier-Lenoir to Tax Collector First Class and institutionalizes wife taxation.

In spite of his normally dull, bourgeois self, but because of his narrow-minded selfishness, Gauthier-Lenoir becomes a charming rogue: a tool of corrupted law, and law corrupted to phallocratic self-interest. He might rationalize his behaviour as outward-looking duty, but its motivations and goals are purely selfish.

Finally, with John Sayles's story "At the Anarchists' Convention,"[11] we reach rogue literature at its most ironic, beginning with the very idea that anarchists would hold a convention. The group's extreme views have always kept them from being heroic, despite their vociferous support of the working classes, related in some cases to frayed alliances with the Communist Party. Now, in old age, never mind that the story is set more than a decade before the fall of the Berlin Wall, they can barely manage to be a rabble, and then only to bicker with hotel staff who, having double-booked the dining room, insist they take a smaller one so the hotel can accommodate the Rotary Club. The incident is a gift, a chance to relive former (if imagined) anti-Establishment glories, for these days their rabble-rousing is generally limited to squabbling among themselves, picking at the scabs of old grudges and ideological battles. They have become charming to the

degree that they are quaint: they hold on to their ideals as their iden-
tities; they are all about the final gasp of the Self. Having sacrificed
most else to the cause, it is all they have left. To their last breath, they
propose absolute social justice, extravagantly, never mind that a life-
time of experience tells them that it's usually a matter of two steps forward, one step back, and sometimes no steps forward, two or three
steps back. Their bitterness is amusing, even to them.

II. FEAR OF FLYING: FRUSTRATED DUTY

Whether scofflaws are equivocal, lazy, or sociopathic, they increase the
burden of duty for everyone else. They are, in the vernacular, spoil-
sports, and while one bad apple might not spoil the barrel, it requires
more vigilance of the conventional order. Take, to confound metaphors past redemption, the airport example.

When this author was a child, it was common for families to drive
out to the city airport for free entertainment. You could park your car
and picnic at the edge of airstrips as you watched take-offs and land-
ings, which at the time was a thrill comparable to the space missions
that came shortly thereafter. You could sit with Auntie Lena from
New York at the departure gate and wave her off from there, a few
yards from the airplane. Then, political activists from Cuba began
hijacking airplanes. Mostly they were regarded as terrorists, but some,
of course, called them freedom-fighters. Aviation authorities imposed
new restrictions of movement at airports, but they did not install
metal detectors, nor was anyone searched, and it was still possible for
anyone to visit the departure gates. Yet it had become clear that skyjacking was a politically effective form of violence: it had brought
back to consciousness, and aggravated, the danger inherent when
wingless animals take flight. There was a new, or at least revivified,
narrative. Having become hostages of various "revolutions," in which
conventional legal systems were seen as oppressive or evil and in
which skyjacking was now a chosen means of ending the oppression,
the flying public experienced a neo-Fall. Our wilful innocence, our
airstrip picnics and long departure-gate goodbyes, ended. Then came
the airborne terrorist attacks of September 11, 2001, in the US, and
airports have become paramilitary redoubts. Patrolled by scruffy, gun-
toting, obscurely and peripatetically trained sentries, our air terminals
can now look like Latin American cities the day after a junta. Similarly, governments have increased surveillance and security measures

at national borders on the ground, notably the border between Canada and the US, previously boasted of as "the largest undefended border in the world." In other words, whether one sees skyjackers or other political criminals as freedom fighters, selfish fools, or terrorists – which viewpoint is a matter of legal-literary narrative and relativism: who tells the story? – their rejection of conventional duty has exponentially increased duty's burden on the rest of us.

You can read Graham Greene's *Our Man in Havana* as a sort of parody of this, where, more or less thoughtlessly, an apparently reasonable man becomes a sort of freedom-fighter, but for completely selfish ends (affording a better lifestyle for his spoiled daughter). Conrad's "Heart of Darkness" and Forster's *A Passage to India* show how we sometimes even manufacture such a burden – the "white man's," so called – taking it up heroically, in our own view, but arrogantly and ethnocentrically from outside. This is the core, in fact, of George Macdonald Fraser's Flashman series, where this self-regarding heroism is very effectively lampooned in the character of a charming rogue burdened with conventional duties. Like Forster, Macdonald shows that the burden becomes doubled, and doubly frustrating, its imposition being both on invader and invaded. *Disgrace* resonates here as well, insofar as post-apartheid Africans continue to engage in very rough justice while Lucy Lurie, a more or less innocent, white scapegoat for that impulse, insists it is morally wrong to prosecute. The rule of law remains suspended, but ostensibly in the name of a higher duty.

In *A Passage*, Forster is particularly canny in showing these basic problems of justice in colonialism. The only person with a fully developed sense of justice is, ironically, Adela Quested, the Briton visiting in Chandrapore, who wrongly accuses Dr. Aziz of trying to assault her as he fecklessly escorts her, out of an almost idiot sense of duty, through the Marabar Caves. She eventually realizes she has been hysterically mistaken, and against the full weight of her community – which, predictably, decides she is an apostate – insists on her error in open court. She sees her prejudicial hysteria for what it has been, and feels the shame of it, overturning what otherwise promises to be a kangaroo-court verdict affirming the presumption of Indian guilt. The unfortunate accused man, Aziz, likeable but peripatetically ignoble and in many ways as silly as his accuser, thinks the worst of her and her reluctant friend Fielding, never mind that both bravely have defended Aziz to the cost of their standing in the British ruling class, far away from home. Aziz never realizes that this accommodating discomfort among them (which ultimately he rejects in favour of blunt opposition to the Raj) mirrors their good faith efforts to meet India half way, blunting the sharp edges on British imperialism. He fails to comprehend that they feel as compromised as he does, and that they experience keenly his sense of double duty: to one's own community but also the deeper, moral burden to the larger society. They feel the Muslim Aziz's historic humiliation, if only from safer, higher ground. As one of the "invaded" (the unconquered conquered, really), Aziz feels his first duty to be to his own people (while harbouring his own prejudices against Hindus), but also, earlier on, a duty to make life work – at least in the name of enlightened self-interest – "within the system" of the Raj.

III. THE PARADIGM TURNED ON ITS HEAD

We mentioned earlier that in the iconography for the reversed paradigm, light becomes dark, white becomes black. Midway there, where the paradigm is altered but not reversed, white becomes green, the pastoral shade that pervades the Robin Hood ballads and other Romantic literature. More recently, political arguments have been made toward the greying of black-white dichotomy, but our principle focus here is the convention and its evolution – how we got here, not whether the contrast is hurtful or prejudicial to any particular group.

Still, Nigerian novelist Chinua Achebe is persuasive that in many ways Conrad's "Africa as setting and backdrop ... eliminates the African as human factor" in *Heart of Darkness*. Conrad really does not consider the bigger picture. His Congo, Achebe adds, is "a metaphysical battlefield devoid of all recognizable humanity, into which the wandering European enters at his peril." This protests too much, but certainly the novella's standing as a classic lends itself, among less thoughtful readers, to such stereotypes.

These social and political questions, such as whether it is appropriate to portray African native society as savage and uncivilized, whether we can properly call the novella racist, are irrelevant, finally, to what a work tells us about the imaginative culture of the law-and-literature context, in the same way that the verminous nature of a rat would not prevent a scientist from studying the creature. Literature is its own world, with its own truths, that are, however, not "real" and lack morality.[12] They can stimulate discussions of morality, and might be written maliciously, but motive or authorial intention is a matter separate from the cultural ethos it uses to express itself. Conrad's novella is useful for our purposes here partly because of what Achebe finds objectionable: it is virtually allegorical in contrasting the European view of the rule of law with that culture's conception of its colonies, particularly in Africa, as uncivilized or primitive. Then again, claims of racism must account for the fact that Conrad focuses on the hypocrisy and brutality of European imperialism. (This is a version of the double burden, here, the "white man's" and the guilt the imperialist might feel over his incursion.) Kurtz, finally, is the totemic savage, all the worse because he has imposed himself and his values, for the supposedly civilized world, only to transcend primitivism to exploit the local, more "primitive," culture. This is clear even in the story's mechanics: many of the "locals" – including the unlucky helmsman who personifies narrator Marlow's ambiguous feelings on what exactly we mean by "civilized" – have more dignity and honour than the mostly vulgar white imperialists and traders he meets and transports.

Marlow clearly throws his lot in, though, with positive law, which, after all, is his cultural context. In fact he finds and admires a reasonable-man totem in between the light and dark worlds, a character so apparently minor that Conrad deftly – subversively – puts him forward as an aside, in just two paragraphs, never mind that he is the fulcrum of the narrative.

Marlow has been hired to ferry people and goods upriver, toward the headquarters of Kurtz, the ivory trader, and to escort the mysterious man-god, who is dying, back to civilization. The ship's captain is an imperialist only by association, which lends to his objectivity, such as it can be, as a narrator. For Marlow, the voyage becomes a sort of anti-pilgrimage, a voyage backwards into the lawless heart of darkness. At the jungle outskirts, where the other signs of colonialism are tired, brutal, and absurd (the rusted boiler overturned like a dead animal, the ship firing its gun blindly into the dumb, seething jungle), he comes upon the trading company's chief accountant, a white Briton in a starched collar, "snowy trousers, a clean necktie, and varnished boots." Marlow admires the man's demeanour, remarking, "in the great demoralization of the land he kept up his appearance. That's backbone ... achievements of character," partly accomplished by "civilizing" a local woman as a laundress. Even here whiteness and lightness, physically and spiritually, are set against the dark, and what used to be called the Belgian Congo is made to seem a hell. Marlow's admiration of the accountant's demeanour suggests that he (and probably Conrad) would answer yes to that old law school debate, "Is there a prima facie obligation to obey the law?"[13] He insistently observes social correctness, as European society perceived it at the time, where the law of nature otherwise prevails. Of course, in the accountant's "tutelage" of the local woman, we have a first glimpse of imperialism's arrogance, the missionary ethnocentrism we have seen in North America in the treatment of aboriginals and Africans.

He remains pure white, without even a grass stain on his clothing; a deliberate Other, otherwise marginal to the tale. "I wouldn't have mentioned the fellow to you at all," Marlow says, "only it was from his lips that I first heard" Kurtz's name, Kurtz personifying the irredeemable journey from lightness to dark – the black side of imperial, ethnocentric "reasonableness." He stands in stark contrast to the accountant and his deliberate choice to resist that fall downward from "civilized society" and its positive law standards. In a fallen world, civilization requires effort: it is a matter of duty.

Kurtz is the novella's other totem, in other words, standing for the idea that civilization and the rule of law are a veneer, against which our baser natures bang their heads or cruder body parts. He has gone virtually mad with this realization, and his shame at shirking his imperial duty, having made himself a sort of local god by giving himself over to savagery (so graphically portrayed in Francis Coppola's depiction of the story in the film *Apocalypse Now*). He has taken the devil's part and regrets it too late, having descended into the darkness as a sort of missionary, only to allow his vanity to pervert the mission. He loses any sense of the civilizing influence of the law (or the Law) and becomes a god unto himself, to satisfy his own appetites. Thus his famous words, "The horror! The horror!" And he dies before Marlow can return him to the world where the paradigm is "righted" to its accustomed "European" design.

Politics and sociology aside, thematically *Heart of Darkness* has much in common with *The Puttermesser Papers*. Both see civilization as a veneer, and human evil as irremediable, even using magic to fight it, or exploit it, in Kurtz's case. Puttermesser's New York is the dark continent, and finally she is brutally murdered there, just as she indulges in her highly "civilized" passion for reading – and after she has entered the heart of darkness seeking to redeem it.

*   *   *

George Orwell's *1984* is culturally neutral in terms of darkness and light, but it uses images of darkness to denote the triumph of evil. Oceania is everywhere dull and grey. Real human feeling is furtive or animal, something only the uneducated "proles" can experience freely, hidden from the light. More broadly, the novel is a template for the paradigm turned on its head. It is a sort of anti-romance in several respects – mainly, though, because the protagonist-resisters have only a peripheral interest in reforming the society. They act mostly in the name of personal freedom, clouded by pessimism that even this freedom will be short-lived and any wider reform or revolution is impossible. They have, never mind their rebellion, bought into the societal message that even Goldstein and his minions can't win (Goldstein being Big Brother's arch-enemy, and therefore, for reasons of agitprop, arch-enemy of the people). Winston Smith sees the proles as the only hope precisely because they are outside the society – they are the Unchosen, as it were, a sort of slave class, a parody of the Hebrews in Egypt. On the other hand, the ultimate Outsider is a Jewish intellectual, and in many ways the heart of the party – its raison d'etre as *pharmakos*, Trotsky to Big Brother's Stalin, and the scapegoat that helps the perverse society propagandize its oppressiveness as necessary to maintaining the rule of law. (This comports with the general, nightmarish theme of everything is its own opposite, highlighting Orwell's persistent contentions about the dangerous plasticity of language.) Ironically, what we now call "Orwellian" is more cynical than the communist line that the state is the people, and particularly the worker. In Orwell, the middle class, the local habitation of the reasonable person, is the machinery of its own oppression (harking back toward the old, corrupted paradigm, the world of Robin Hood, Kafka, and Ozick, as well as what Steiner says about the Kafkaesque victim participating in his own persecution). This, of course, makes it Hell: you, humankind, got yourself into this. Reason is twisted so that everything is a paradox: War is Peace. The Ministry of Love dispenses torture and death. Goodthink is denying your profoundest desires and needs. Freedom is Slavery. Ignorance is Strength, if not exactly bliss. Instability is stability, because it perpetuates the fear that keeps the masses obedient. As in Hell, history is erased. There is no yesterday, only the painful moment. Even Big Brother is more than a version of Stalin: he is a Beelzebubian parody of Yahweh – omniscient, omnipresent (via the telescreen), and capable of terrific ad hoc violence. To the modern eye, Oceania looks a lot like the East Germany of the film, *The Lives of Others*.

Insofar as the paradigm is inverted, the level just below the socio-pathic/Satanic is an anti-Paradise, a hell on earth. That is, it is the mirror image of Eden as the beginning and end of law. As Eden is pre-law, Hades is post-law. Its mirror-Adamic anti-hero is the unreasoning person. In Orwell, Winston Smith's neighbour Parsons is an exemplar:[14] he stupidly follows the party line, all the while aware that soon, in their own dumb loyalty to the perverse social system, his own children will betray him for crimes he never commits:

I   State of constant, hellish fear – Big Brother
II   Realm of party insiders – the neo-reasonable person (unreasoning from a democratic view)
III Outer party/Proles – world of experience
IV   Democracy redefined as Hell

Narratives on this paradigm are very frequently dystopic and set in the future, even if only just a few years from their writing. In each the reader is a sort of Dante hosted to his own tour of hell. The subtext is: "If we continue down the path we're on, this is where it will end." The exceptions to this, such as *Lord of the Flies*, imagine people returned to dystopia or an ungoverned state of nature – in a fallen world – because of some disaster. The "airborne toxic event" of Don DeLillo's *White Noise* does this by implication – as a metaphor for the more pervasive if less visible toxicity of modern life – and in the aftermath the narrator takes the law into his own hands, cathartic revenge that, but for his second thoughts and aid to the victim, would have been murder. That is, Jack Gladney exists at the transitional stage as a moral outlaw. He is Chair of Hitler Studies (a discipline he has invented as a career move) at the University-on-the-Hill (one way or another, a parody of earthly paradise), and friend to Murray Siskind, a sports-writer turned professor so obsessed with popular culture that everything he says is jargon, with its own lonely, idiosyncratic rationale. He is the anti-reasonable man. Gladney's everyday life is our own, but gives us a terrible chill because the volume is turned up just enough that we can hear the thrum of our daily fear over all the noise we make to try to hide it. Gladney's own fears for his family, his wife's seeming illness and paranoia, his son's fatalistic curiosity are symptomatic of modern human defence mechanisms that fail. We are only one "event" from a full-blown anxiety neurosis, or worse. The "event" breaches the scrim, revealing a veneer-culture that uses consumerism and the propaganda of "self-actualization" to distract it from its weapons of mass destruction, genocide, catastrophic climate change, psychotic global markets, and political terrorism. The inherent anarchy – this vision of a future where law cannot reach – might be our future, but we don't want to think about it.

Evil as Transitional: From Youth to Maturity, Evil to Redemption (or Not)

One task of literature, albeit a task that does not interest some very good writers, is to try to explain human evil. Many works which consider the problem take a sociological or psychological approach, showing bad behaviour as a product of a difficult social environment that can be redeemed. This, of course, follows the larger law-literature paradigm of fall (or of beginning in a fallen condition) and redemption. Sometimes, as in Dickens, the hero rises above his environment no matter its depredations. In one of his best-known works, a work (however) of sketchy literary merit, Anthony Burgess suggests that such behaviour is a stage of growth, and that maturity (time) brings redemption, just as – we would add – the paradigm symbolically mimics the movement from spring to winter back to spring, as in the stories of Moses and Christ, which reach their epiphany at the stage of death and redemption in spring with Passover and Easter.

A Clockwork Orange shows that, as to the imaginative paradigm, ontogeny begets or recapitulates phylogeny: the development of the young mimics the development of the species and culture. Again, we can chart this paradigmatically. The second column represents socialization and is imperfect as to category, given that ego begins to assert itself in early childhood (it is not all Id), as does the superego in later childhood, as the ego is domesticated.

Infancy/Innocence	Pre-consciousness	Pre-law
Childhood/Utopian, education	Id state/Ego	Minority/law affects/"not responsible"
Adulthood/Experience	Ego/Superego	Majority/affected & affects law/duty
Old Age/Death	Ego/Id	Subject to judgment

Burgess has said the point of the novel is that humans are not necessarily born good but that moral growth is possible; otherwise, we are clockwork in the hands of God, Satan, or state. He might have something darker to say, though, regarding certain conceptions of the

law-and-literature enterprise, a pessimism that seems to support Judge
Posner's view – as against those of Richard Weisberg and Robin West,
say – about whether literature can make us more empathetic and just.
Burgess in any event might accept Achebe's view of *Heart of Darkness*,
that while literature is not itself a moral universe, it exerts moral influence that could be corrosive. Toward the end of his life Burgess worried that misreadings of *A Clockwork Orange* (deliberate or otherwise)
might contribute to youth violence.[15] Ultra-violent Alex, with his taste
for classical music, himself laughs at the notion that art can be a force
for good.

Of course, some bad people are beyond redemption, at least in this
world, even if we catch them young. They never manage to climb up
from psychopathy. Graham Greene, foreshadowing Burgess in *A Clockwork,* suggests they remain stuck in childhood, never developing the
super-ego that permits socialization. Of his thoroughly nasty Pinkie,
the seventeen-year-old double murderer of *Brighton Rock*, Greene has
remarked:

> The Pinkies are the real Peter Pans – doomed to be juvenile for a
> lifetime. They have something of a fallen angel about them, a
> morality which once belonged to another place. The outlaw of
> justice always keeps in his heart the sense of justice outraged – his
> crimes have an excuse and yet he is pursued by the Others. The
> Others have committed worse crimes and flourish. The world is
> full of Others who wear the masks of Success, of a Happy Family.
> Whatever crime he may be driven to commit the child who does-
> n't grow up remains the great champion of justice. "An eye for an
> eye." "Give them a dose of their own medicine." As children we
> have all suffered punishments for faults we have not committed,
> but the wound has soon healed. With ... Pinkie the wound never
> heals.[16]

5

Humpty Dumpty in Wig and Gown:
Legalese as Dialect, or,
the Philology of Precedent

I. LEGALESE AS DIALECT

Looking at the big picture of law in and as literature, we have proposed an analytical framework that depends on the cultural or imaginative structures that literature shares with law. There remains the
rhetorical or, more precisely, the philological[1] – the similarities and
differences in how the two disciplines use language.

When litigation is reduced to a case report, there is movement from
oral to written narrative. The case report is very often novelistic, hon-
ing down the action (in both senses of the word) to its essentials. The
struggle is set out, the issues joined, the climax of decision reached,
the denouement of damages or sentencing announced. In the way of
a Faulkner novel, say, multiple judgments in a single case yield multiple narratives. The literary qualities of the case report reside partly
in this dynamic, the dialectic between good and evil (or right and
wrong), as well as in:

- the focus on defining or extreme moments in a life;
- a sort of fated outcome, based on received wisdom or principles
  (a resistance to chaos, an attempt to impose meaning on event);
- a resolution at the end that can be satisfactory or not.

Yet here we are concerned mostly but not exclusively with how
judges construe language, how they "make meaning." Our analysis will
have little if any application to cases straightforward on their facts –
where, say, someone kicks in a window to gain access to somebody
else's home. Though he takes nothing, on these bare facts it is clear

there has been a "breaking and entering," even if he pleads he was trying to save someone from a fire or he was in another city on the night
in question. Those defences of necessity and alibi don't change the fact
that someone broke into the dwelling. Of greater relevance for us is the
case where the accused was selling chocolates, knocked at a door that
proved to be ajar, and walked in calling, "Anybody home?" As Chief
Baron Pollock once said, "Judges are philologists of the highest order"
(*Ex parte Davis* (1857), 5 W.R. 522 at 523), and it will be up to them to
decide the threshold issue (pun intended): did the salesman remain an
invitee or was he a trespasser? Did he "break" before entering?

Such cases show us that, from without – from, that is, the perspective of language as it is generally understood by its everyday users –
legalese is often babble. But internally – in its limited universe – it
must be coherent and thereby capable of application and analysis. If
we add philological structures to our basic paradigm, they mirror the
scheme we set out regarding narrative duty:

Supreme authority/legislator	Law Creator/Language by fiat
Realm of judges/Legal fictions	Juristic/interpretive/mediative: language of justice
World of experience/lawyers	Advocacy: language of legalism
Underworld	Anti-legislative/Reversal of the legislative "mean": language in the mirror

Recall our main points about legal narrative:

- As "creators," legislators establish the regulatory mean or starting
  point.
- In their interpretive or "priestly" role, judges mediate between the
  legislators and their subjects, which latter are generally represented by advocates.
- In a democracy, the legislator is meant to act for the communal
  good. Usually the advocate acts in the specific, individual interests
  of his client. The central role of the judge is to balance these. That
  is, litigation is an exercise in dialectical materialism: the existing
  law (or "received wisdom") is the thesis; the challenging party's
  contentions (as plaintiff, applicant, etc.) comprise the antithesis;
  and the judgment is the synthesis.

- As the priest mediates between the language of God and the vulgate, so does the judge mediate between legalese and the vernacular. The judges' duty is to respect legislative supremacy, settled precedent, and by inference from those, the good of the larger society. They are meant to work justice in the broad sense – to mediate and synthesize.
- The scofflaw and the anarchist, the sociopath and the common criminal simply reject the socio-linguistic mean, or turn it on its head. Their language is anti-democratic along a continuum of selfishness, mirroring their place on the continuum of evil we identified earlier: where a poacher might say that he acts justly because he breaks the law to feed his family, a totalitarian dictator completely reverses the language of democracy in furtherance of oligarchy. As Big Brother puts it, "War is peace," "Love is hate," "Freedom is slavery." This is the language of parody and perversion.
- The archetype here is the narrative of the Tower of Babel. Mediating between the legislator's language and the interpretations proposed by the advocate-litigant, judges re-establish a single or "chosen" meaning that, for the time being, becomes common currency and, ideally, makes peace.

The Metaphorical Tendency

A few examples from the case law will help clarify what we might call the philology of *stare decisis*. Consider how, in all their priestly majesty, British judges have turned potatoes into meat. During the nineteenth century, British innkeepers and other purveyors of refreshment chafed against erosion of their profits by so-called "Lord's Day" acts. From 1677, the *Sunday Observance Act* had allowed only "inns, cook's shops, or victualling houses" to sell meat on the sabbath, on the breathtaking presumption, apparently, that God (through his parliamentary delegates) would exempt the better class of food retailer from proper religious observance, but no one else. Foodsellers providing more humble meals saw this – or their lawyers purported to see it, for the purposes of advocacy – as classist.

The Law Journal is poignant about the evidence in the case of Bullen,[2] a Blackburn "chipped potato dealer," or fish-and-chips restaurateur, prosecuted under the act in 1905:

It was proved that the appellant in the course of his business, cut up and cooked or fried potatoes, sometimes alone and sometimes with fish, and that these articles had become a popular food with the working classes. The fried potatoes and fish, together or separately, were served on the appellant's premises as well as off, and were always sold warm. The customers, when supplied off the premises, often brought their own receptacles for the food, but were sometimes supplied in paper bags belonging to the appellant. On Sunday, January 22, 1905, the appellant was carrying on his usual business, there being customers upon his premises eating the chipped potatoes, others who purchased articles of food and took them away in bags or basins, and some who ate the food in the street near the appellant's shop.

Bullen was convicted at trial: while the landed gentry were free to shop for their Sunday joint, those of more modest tea-time habits were accessories to a crime. On his appeal to the Court of King's Bench, Lord Alverstone, the chief justice, found that, come Sunday it "would be ridiculous to say that, although a man may cook mutton, he must not cook an eel pie." Even if some customers bought only French fries for their dinner, at common law, French fries were meat. As for fish, well, one bloke's meat, after all, is another man's *poisson* ...

But not his *crème glacée*. In 1915, a man named Slater attempted to stretch the metaphor to ice cream, and found it wouldn't reach. On Boxing Day (December 26, the day in Britain and parts of the Commonwealth traditionally set aside for packaging gifts for the poor), which also happened to be a Sunday, Slater had bought an ice cream sandwich from Berni, "a licensed refreshment house keeper," only to have his pleasure in consuming it interrupted by a constable, who charged him with "aiding and abetting" Berni in violating the *Sunday Observance Act*.

At trial, Slater argued, among other things, that ice cream was a "sweetmeat," and therefore a form of meat within the exemptions. But the justices decided that the definition of "ice cream" was irrelevant and convicted him.

On appeal, his lawyer re-emphasized the meat argument: the constituent elements of the ice cream, he said – milk, sugar, eggs, and egg powder, sandwiched between two biscuits – could each be described as "meat" under certain usages of that word in English. Indeed, *The Oxford English Dictionary* suggests this view: it gives Samuel Johnson's definition of meat as "food in general; anything used as nourishment for men or animals; usually, solid food, in contradistinction to drink," but adds that this usage had become "archaic and dialectical." It also makes special mention of "green meat": "grass or green vegetables used for food or fodder."

Justice Darling allowed that meat could be "anything that can be eaten," as in such expressions as "the meat of an egg," "meat and drink," and "one man's meat is another man's poison." And indeed, we read in Matthew III, 4 that John the Baptist's "meat was locusts and wild honey." But his lordship held that meat could not be ice cream. "Meat" in the *Sunday Observance Act* had nothing to do with proverbial usage. Justice Horridge tersely agreed, noting that he had already said that ice cream was not meat in *Amorette v. James*, in which James was found guilty of selling ice cream to six boys on "the Lord's day." "There is nothing in the term 'ice-cream,'" he added, "as there is in the term 'mutton chop,' which would make it necessary for us to say that ice cream fell within the exemptions."

Given modern developments in both England and North America, Justice Darling has had the last word. He concluded his opinion in *Slater* by cocking a snook at judicial, and philological, activism:

> I think it is plain that many judges, not liking this kind of legisla-
> tion – I do not like it myself – have tried to get out of the statute
> by holding or suggesting that all kinds of things might be "meat"
> although they were not. In my opinion, the best way to attain that
> object is to construe it strictly, in the way the Puritans who pro-
> cured it would have construed it; if that is done it will very soon
> be repealed.[3]

Rhetorically we construct from these rulings the following "dialectical materialism":

THESIS (APPELLANT)	ANTITHESIS (CROWN)	SYNTHESIS (COURT)
Potatoes are meat	Potatoes are potatoes	Potatoes can be meat, but ice cream cannot

Justice Darling was acknowledging parliamentary supremacy – the primacy of received wisdom – where some of his colleagues engaged in social engineering. Then again, maybe he was being too conserva-tive, an occupational hazard, of course, among priests: only activists err on the side of liberalism and risk angering the supreme authority. Legally, anyway, it remained reasonable that ice cream could have been meat under the law: if French fries could be meat, it's only a little stretch to say ice cream could be, too.

This is applied literature, if you will, and perhaps literature in the service of social engineering. Presumably all the judges involved were acting in the community interest: again, metaphor at the judicial level is, at least ideally, a matter not of special-interest advocacy but of judicial interpretation for the entire community. If you interpret the law conservatively, you might just barely see potatoes as meat; if you have a more liberal penchant, you might just stretch the definition to ice cream. Bullen and Slater were acting out of self-interest, though many others – business people, enthusiasts of fish and chips, the poor in general – stood to benefit from their advocacy. The Crown acted in the state interest, or at least formally so, presumptively aligning itself with statutory law but from a defined (presumptive) bias that the legislation itself was lawful and clear on its face:

Legislature	Parliament says sell only meat on Sunday.
Judicial, reasonable man	Presumptively, potatoes and ice cream are not meat.
World of Experience	Interpretively, potatoes and ice cream are meat because "meat" means sustaining food of any sort.
Underworld	I'll eat what I want, when I want.

There are two more things to say about this. First, that everyday language and legal language exist in separate but contingent universes: to help them decide law cases, judges look at dictionaries and "ordinary meaning," but ordinary usage is not decisive. There's a necessary, priestly, semantic or interpretive warp. Second, in creating a new or synthesized meaning, any judicial interpretation of established law creates a new semantic mean for that law. This is what we usually call a new precedent. Where yesterday meat was presumptively animal flesh, today it is also potatoes. Or, where yesterday meat was any kind of foodstuff, today it does not include sweets and popcorn. This is, like making golems or literature (be it poetry or case law), a creative act, or a recreative act, in the sense that it mimics but does not replace the Word. The Word is restored, if you will, to justice, or at least our contemporary view of it.

That is, these cases often seem to divide themselves into two categories of linguistic logic, one metaphysical or metaphorical – French fries are meat – the other concrete or anti-metaphorical – ice cream is not meat. This is not to insist, however, that judicial philology is always one or the other. We said before that the underlying structures here evolve with time, adapting to the cultural norms of the day and thereby engaging what some might see as social engineering. We noted that today the shifts in the paradigm reflect more democratic or inclusive, and more skeptical or scientific, premises. Rhetorically we see this in the judicial treatment of the word "person," for example. Notoriously, until fairly recently, corporations could be legal persons, metaphorically, but, save in a few defined circumstances, generally women could not: they were biological and social persons, but mostly did not have the same rights as legal persons. Obviously, that view has become widely unpopular in western societies,[4] and in 1929 it was dealt a decisive blow when the Privy Council of the House of Lords held that women were "qualified persons" such that they could be appointed to Canada's senate.[5]

To the non-lawyer, it is absurd beyond consideration that a woman is not a person. Outside legal definitions, there is no need to resort to metaphor to call a woman a person. The law frequently stimulates bemusement and often amusement in this way, seeming eccentric or lunatic if not "a ass," such that many volumes have been published compiling the dissonance between ordinary language and legalese. (Particularly notable are Robert Megarry's *Miscellany-at-Law*, and *A Second Miscellany-at-Law*.)[6] Where the dissonance arises from the judiciary (where it is interpretive), it is usually a matter of metaphor (potatoes are meat); where it arises from advocacy, usually it can be either metaphorical or not. For example, in *Jessin v. County of Shasta*, counsel for the municipality argued that vasectomies constitute mayhem (at common law, the disabling or amputation of a body part so as to make the victim less productive in the community). The county didn't want to pay for voluntary vasectomies, so it resorted to metaphor based on ancient British law saying that "disabling the testicles" amounted to mayhem. In this case, the district court was anti-metaphorical: county-funded vasectomies were reasonable family planning that did not "render the patient impotent or unable to fight for the king."[7]

But of course it is the metaphorical (or metaphysical) tendency that makes precedent. Usually the language involved is not the legal terms of art in any particular field of law, but how the authorial judges take everyday speech and turn it into a distinctive dialect.[8] Consider a line of recent cases drawn from automobile insurance litigation. The latest of them details how, upon leaving a variety store, Bonnie Lewis walked into a steel pole protruding on a truck parked in the street. She was knocked unconscious and the truck was gone before anyone could identify it. Lewis sued her own vehicle insurer, who refused to pay on the basis that, as stipulated in her policy, she was not "struck" or "hit by" a motor vehicle or even the pole. The Ontario Court of Appeal disagreed, ruling, in effect, that if you walk into a truck it hit you.[9]

This looks eccentric, and seems to be the first time Canadian courts have said that, for the purposes of automobile insurance, if you walk into something, it can be said to strike you – or, more precisely and bizarrely, if you walk into object A as it sits on object B, object B struck you. But it is part of a semantic drift of several years' standing. In the 1995 case of *McIntyre v. Ontario*,[10] a cyclist sued his motor-vehicle insurer, claiming that though a car hadn't crashed into him he thought it was going to and, in trying to avoid a collision, he hurt himself. Justice Granger refers there to an endorsement in an earlier case "wherein Justice Stayshyn held that even in the absence of actual physical striking, an insured will be found to have been struck within the meaning of the policy if there was a reasonable apprehension of being struck." That is, according to this doctrine of "notional striking,"[11] nothing even has to touch the plaintiff. In *Talbot v. Gan General Insurance Co.*,[12] another bicycle mishap after a near collision, this argument prevailed to defeat the insurer's motion for summary judgment.

In *Lewis*, the appeal court cites an Ontario case from 2009 in a way that seems to endorse this philology:

> In *Tucci v. Pugliese* (2009), 98 O.R. (3d) 151 (S.C.J.), Mrs. Tucci was seated at her breakfast table when the uninsured car of the defendant ran into the wall of her house. The resulting sudden loud bang and the violent shaking of the house caused Mrs. Tucci to suffer shock, as well as physical and psychological damage. On the insurer's motion to dismiss her claim, it argued that she was not "struck by" an automobile. The trial judge refused to strike the claim because Mrs. Tucci's "injuries arguably resulted from the proximate, sensory invasion, the notional equivalent of being struck."

Then there is a 1974 insurance case in which pedestrian Strum was at least hit by something, a street sign, which was bent into him when the defendant's car mounted the sidewalk near where Strum was standing and crashed into the sign. Ontario's High Court of Justice held that Strum was "struck by the described automobile."[13]

Just as literature criticizes the "real world" for its injustices, or attempts to redress them, judges reshape language in an alternative linguistic universe: they speak English there, but in a dialect called Legalese. They take an apparent absurdity and rationalize it to the ends of what they perceive as just. The plaintiff was as good as struck because she suffered injury, even if it was not physical. She was assaulted if not battered, and in our modern world we make little distinction between these because we are solicitous of the psychological and spiritual being.

Is *Lewis* a "high water-mark?" (As I say, judges are fond of metaphor.) A few years ago, Fred Wolfe went hunting with some friends, an annual outing. It was still dark and he thought he saw the flash of a deer tail, so he stopped his truck, got out, and took a shot. It turned out the putative deer was his hunting companion Harold Herbison. The Ontario Court of Appeal ordered Wolfe's auto insurer to pay Herbison $832,000 plus interest and costs. Herbison's injuries arose, it said, from the use or operation of the truck. On appeal, the Supreme Court of Canada held this was a little too much like Humpty Dumpty telling words what to mean.[14]

We might graph the synthetic result this way:

THESIS   The pole/car hit me
ANTITHESIS   You hit the pole/car
SYNTHESIS   In the linguistic universe of automobile-insurance law the pole/car
              hit you, but the mere presence of an automobile is not determinative
              of its insurer's duty to indemnify.

When we find in law that French fries are meat, amusement park rides are common carriers,[15] and you can be "struck" without being touched, law is using metaphor in an attempt to reach (Edenic) justice. It remakes language in the image of justice. As with poetry, it reconfigures the imperfect mortal world, sometimes to assist the otherwise oppressed or disadvantaged, other times to protect established interests. Here are some further bemusing examples, identified to the extent possible as metaphorical (setting precedent or a new linguistic mean) or anti-metaphorical (where the judiciary rejects the metaphor as advocated):

1. METAPHORICAL: AT LAW, YOU CAN BE ALIVE WHILE DEAD   At the beginning of the British "Enlightenment," the Old Bailey judges convicted Thomas Walcott of treason, sentencing him to be drawn (dragged through the streets, sometimes without the benefit of a hurdle), hanged, and disembowelled, after which his entrails were to be burned. Thomas's son John appealed, successfully, on the ground that the sentence was not in the conventional form. Because the judges had omitted the prescription that the entrails should be "burned while he was yet alive" – that Thomas was to watch the incineration, never mind the extreme unlikelihood that this was possible – the House of Lords ruled the judgment void. Their eccentric philology seems to have been a matter of deterrence *in terrorem*, ensuring that the *ultimum supplicium*, the ultimate sanction, would be imposed for high crimes against the state, even if such sanction were the equivalent of whipping a dead horse: *R. v. Walcott* (1694), 4 Mod. 395; aff'd (1696), Shaw P.C. 127. This of course correlates with our suggestion that, analytically, the judge's principal task is to interpret the law in the community interest, even if the result might seem metaphysical, at best, in individual cases.

2. METAPHORICAL: AN ACCIDENT CAN BE DELIBERATE   In the early part of the last century, a group of boys at a trade school attacked their assistant manager, killing him. This obliged the House of Lords to decide whether the incident amounted to an "accident" entitling the teacher's estate to worker's compensation. The law lords held that the assault was an accident, insofar as it was not "expected or designed" by the victim: *Board of Management of Trim Joint District School v. Kelly*, [1914] A.C. 667. In a situation subject to ordinary semantics, the question would be whether the attackers had expected or set out to injure the teacher so as to render him unfit for work. If so, the act would be deliberate, not accidental. But it is just reasonable enough to say that for the teacher this was a workplace accident – something unexpected happened to him, through no apparent fault of his own – to allow for sympathetic compensation.

3. METAPHORICAL THAT LOOKS LIKE ANTI-METAPHORICAL: SORT OF HAVE GUN, WILL TRAVEL   In *U.S. v. Foster*, 133 F.3d 704 (1998), the US Court of Appeals for the ninth district held that someone

transporting a gun in the back of a pick-up truck is not "carrying" the weapon, at least not for the purposes of 18 U.S.C. subsection 924(c)(1). Police stopped Foster's truck and found a bucket and a zippered bag in the truck bed, under a snapped-down tarp. The bucket contained small plastic bags, a set of scales, and some scribbles on paper about pricing. The bag contained a nine-millimetre semi-automatic pistol. The majority affirmed its earlier view that "in order for a defendant to be convicted of 'carrying' a gun in violation of section 924(c)(1), the defendant must have transported the firearm on or about his or her person.... This means the firearm must have been immediately available for use by the defendant." The gun was not "immediately available" in this case. In his stinging dissent, Judge Trott remarked,

> Only a person trained in an American law school under the Socratic method could postulate the formal but fanciful freeze-frame distinctions that animate the conclusion that a firearm transported in a drug trafficker's car on the way to a sale is not "carried" by him. The courts are supposed to interpret Congressional will, not contrive sterile artificial lines. The statute we interpret here on its face covers "carrying."

Usually, to say something is not something else (ice cream is not meat) is anti-metaphorical, but in such cases as this, where we say that something is not what it generally is, we seem to have meta-metaphor.

4. ANTI-METAPHORICAL: SOMETHING FISHY IN INSURANCE EXCLU-SIONS   In May 1990, independent truckers set up a road-block in Drummondville, Quebec, to protest taxes, international competition, and red tape. Rather than sit in the bottleneck of traffic, a couple of truckers for Midland Transport decided to wait for the blockage to clear. They were carrying fish, which spoiled. The cargo was insured, but not for "an act of God, the Queen's or public enemies, riots, strikes" and so on. The insurer relied on those exclusions and the trial judge found that, though the Midland truckers were not part of a union, they had been part of a strike and, at law, were the Queen's or public enemies. He defined this latter phrase to mean "illegal acts by a segment of the public against the interests and rights of the state," and held that this extended to anyone blocking a public highway. The Newfoundland Court of Appeal disagreed, holding that these interpretations of "strike" and "public enemies" were over-broad: *Fishery*

Products International Limited v. Midland Transport Limited (1994), 113 D.L.R. (4th) 651.

5. METAPHORICAL AND ANTI-METAPHORICAL: A PERSON MIGHT BE A PENIS, BUT NOT A BUTTOCK   So Justice Nosanchuk ruled in *The Queen v. Balazsy* (1980), 54 C.C.C. (2d) 346. To taunt some of his peers in a small town, a young man had "pulled his pants down and wiggled his naked buttocks in front of a restaurant window." Police charged him with indecency by exposing his private person. Justice Nosanchuk found that at common law the "private person" was an organ designed for procreation: it could be a penis or a vagina, but not a buttock or a breast. Still he found Balaszy had been "thumbing his nose" at his friends in an indecent fashion. Note, too, that at common law, eyes, tongues, arms, legs, and fingers can be "members" that, if disabled or severed, can found a prosecution for mayhem. The same is not true where the victim is disfigured by an attack on his ears or nose: Blackstone, *Commentaries on the Law of England*, IV, at 199, 205; *Sensobaugh v. State*, 244 S.W. 379 (C.C.A. Tex., 1922); *Cockroft v. Smith* (1705), 11 Mod. 43; *State v. Bass*, 120 S.E.2d (S.C.N.C., 1961).

6. METAPHORICAL (AND ANTI-METAPHORICAL): LESS (AND MORE) THAN THE DIFFERENCE OF ITS PARTS   British courts have held that an indictment is insufficient where it charges that the accused stole "three eggs of the goods and chattels" of the victim. A proper indictment specifies whether the eggs were those of a guinea hen but not those of an adder "or some other species of eggs which cannot be subject of larceny" (presumably because the latter are *ferae naturae*). The same court held, however, on the very next day, that where a man was charged with bestiality with a bitch, the indictment need not specify what kind of animal was involved: *R. v. Cox* (1844), 1 Car. and K., 494, 495. *R. v. Halloway* (1823), 1 C & P. 127, holds that one cannot be said to "steal a brass furnace" if the object had been broken into pieces of metal before it arrived in the prosecuting jurisdiction, and the accused was not guilty of stealing "two turkies" insofar as the indictment did not specify that the birds were dead. After all, an accused stealing a pair of socks cannot be convicted unless the socks match, and one does not "steal a duck" if the bird is a drake.

These cases are anti-metaphorical to the extent that they define what a word is not: the legal reasoning is so selfishly categorical or lit-

eral minded (ostensibly in the name of justice), a drake is not necessarily a duck, and objects are paired only if they are more or less iden-
tical, never mind that they are objectively the same as to category.

7. METAPHORICAL AND ANTI-METAPHORICAL: IT DOESN'T TAKE A
HEAP OF LIVIN' AFTER ALL According to the Ontario Court of
Appeal, an uncovered section of asphalt used for parking motor vehicles can be a common bawdy house. Bare pavement takes on that
homey (metaphorical) designation once the prosecution proves that
prostitution occurs within a "substantial" part of it. The Crown did so
in *R. v. Pierce and Goloher* (1982), 37 O.R. (2d) 721, but the court
acquitted the two accused women because there was no proof they
were "keepers" of the impugned household. Keepers, the court held,
could be trespassers, so long as they at least attempted to exercise control over the premises, but there was no evidence that the women
directed their customers to the lot or that they had the slightest interest in which space the customer used in it, much less a lease agreement with the lot's owner.

II. A NOTE ON LEGAL LANGUAGE IN LITERATURE

Does law add anything to the rhetorical and aesthetic qualities of
literature, as opposed to what law and literature share as narrative?
Serious readers read seriously, after all, not just for the story but for
how it is told, for the play of language.

A full discussion of this topic could comprise another book, perhaps, one beyond our analytic focus on the imaginative structures sup-
porting narrative. Speaking generally, and beyond uneven attempts to
depict legalese in its professional setting, literature often uses the language of law parodically, more broadly and obviously in works such as
Ian Frazier's "Coyote v. Acme" (the "opening statement" – which
sounds a good deal like a written complaint or statement of claim – by
counsel for Wile E. Coyote, much aggrieved in his cartoon attempts at
predation regarding The Roadrunner), William Gaddis's *A Frolic of His
Own*, Dickens's *Bleak House*, and Kafka's *The Trial*. Mortimer's Rumpole
delightfully applies pompous legalese to his household life and other
everyday intercourse. We see the precedent for this, albeit usually more
archly, subtly, or in passing, in Shakespeare particularly, and in other
Renaissance poets who of course pun regularly on legal language.[16]

6

Putting It All Together:
The Structures of Law and Literature –
Law as Revolution, Justice as Nostalgia

Here, in more or less point form, is a summary of the method proposed:

(1) Archetypal or "myth" literary criticism seems to provide the most productive spadework for law-and-literature studies. This is because law is integral to culture, and is central to how we make sense of our existence in the world. In creating culture, we at least unconsciously adhere to structures – hierarchies, paradigms, etc. – which frame how we regulate and understand our lives. We draw these structures from observing the cycle of life around us.

(2) The archetypes evolve in a revolutionary cycle, new legal structures and ideas of justice replacing the old. Secular law largely replaces sacred law but is informed by it, just as secular law evolves with and informs our developing technocracy and a steady movement from community survival to emphasis on individual development and expression. The symbols we create reflect this (inevitably, as spring moves to summer and so on), in a constant urge to renewal. When this movement is stymied or reversed, as when totalitarianism defeats democratic impulses, so is the archetypal paradigm.

(3) The archetype of a paradise is the beginning and end of law. In a paradisal state, reasonableness or obeisance is reflexive and justice is a given. We need positive law once we fall from a paradisal state. In that fallen state, we yearn for perfect, paradisal justice, which is never quite attainable outside of paradise, or paradise regained. The symbology of sacred law, which provides the foundation for secular law,

makes this clear. Unmitigated justice becomes a matter of nostalgia and, for some, faith. Where the paradigm is turned on its head, as with totalitarianism, everything is reversed, and the demonic takes precedence. It sets up a hell on earth, which is post-law. Myth criticism calls the paradisal model apocalyptic, and the hellish model demonic. We have adapted these for law-and-literature studies as, respectively, a rule-of-law or democratic model and a sociopathic or totalitarian model.

(4) The central animating principle of law and literature – and the central regulatory principle of democratic law – is the search for justice. The central animating feature of justice in law and literature is the notion of duty, the idea that our neighbour's interest is largely our own. It accepts that in more advanced, civilized societies, duty is outward looking, defining itself as oriented toward the common good. If the rule of law becomes corrupted, the duty undertaken might be to a smaller "revolutionary" group (as with Robin Hood or "alternative" societies or cults). If the notion of duty is corrupted, we move towards pure self-interest, evil, and totalitarianism.

(5) The narrative of duty, and therefore of justice, depends (obviously) on the storyteller. In the law-as-literature context, the judge is an interpretive, priest-like storyteller mediating between legislative fiat – which provides "received wisdom" and, ideally, is community oriented – and individual advocacy, which is more self-interested and middlebrow. In doing this, the law creates its own dialect, distinct from but contingent with everyday language.

(6) Once we identify the structural underlay of law and literature, we can use whatever supplementary form of analysis seems to promote our further understanding.

II. SOME FURTHER CASES IN POINT

Case One: After the Fall:
Resolving the Pisgah Perplex to Get Justice for Moses

As stories adumbrating the conundrum of reward and restitution, the stories of Moses and Job are the *ne plus ultra* narratives about justice in our culture. For here resides the vexing problem of what happens to the Lawgiver: yes, we can say that Yahweh rewards Moses's loyalty in manifold ways – chiefly by making him his primary biographer and the founder of a nation that so far has resisted every imaginable depredation. Yes, in this he has won immortality. But if he is to deserve such transcendent fame, an immortality denied all but the protagonists of the Bible, why punish him at all by forbidding him entrance to Canaan, the symbol of escape from the contingent world, the metaphor for the Day of Judgment, of ultimate justice on earth? Why make it a particular point that Joshua is to regain Eden and everybody else on the voyage is to die without meeting the goal personally?

Where, finally, is the justice?

MOSES' CRIME AND THE JUSTICE OF HIS SENTENCE   What is Moses charged with that the sentence is so harsh? His sister and counsellor Miriam has just died, the rabble is hounding him again for water and food, he is dog-tired and dejected. In a humanist reading, he would be entitled to ask with Christ, "Why hast thou forsaken me?" In the early days of leaving Egypt, in Rephidim, he has contended with a similar problem, on which occasion Yahweh ordered him to "smite" a rock with his shepherd's staff. At that time, the staff was just beginning to take on its magical possibilities. Now, in the desert of Zin, Yahweh has told him and Aaron to assemble the people and in their presence command the rock to bring forth water – to speak to it. It is not surprising that in his turbulent state of mind Moses reverts to the method that proved so effective, and impressive, in the past. In fact, it feels as though he has been set up for failure, not unlike Adam in Eden or, worse (and later), Job, the victim of a Practical Joke. As before in Rephidim, first Moses scolds the people, but taking more directly personal offence. In Rephidim, he asks, "Why chide ye with me? Wherefore do ye tempt the Lord?" Now, he shouts, clearly fed up to his sandblasted eye teeth, "Here now ye rebels: must we fetch you water out of this rock?" He makes no reference to Yahweh or Supreme Law. Then, for good measure, "You want water, *I'll* give you hooligans water," he strikes the rock, in direct disobedience to divine command, of *mandamus*. And he hits the rock not once, but, after seeing that this time hitting is not the preferred method, he strikes it again anyway. Moral philosophy and literary critics call this hubris. Mortal law calls it *mens rea* (aggravated *mens rea*, at that), the intention that makes an act criminal where it might otherwise attract excuse.

It is an act, apparently, of anger, contempt, even doubt, when, in the prosecution's view, Moses should have acted in faith or according to the received rule of Law. His crime is presumption, first that you hit a rock to get water out of it, second that you have the godlike power to do that. In this respect, Moses's behaviour recalls Donne's "a sin of fear" – doubt that God ultimately will redeem us. In his misfeasance, by this Hebrew Bible view, Moses has denied himself earthly redemption. He has soured his just desserts (to be left with just deserts!).

But for such a serious punishment, one would expect malfeasance, deliberate bad behaviour, something that could not be mitigated by provocation or even a sort of somnambulistic automatism, the temporary insanity that can excuse crime among humans. Given the enormity of the punishment, then, Buber's explanation is compelling: "The wonder-working staff in his hand does not transform him into a possessor of superhuman powers; when once he uses that staff unbidden he is subject to judgement." Moses has committed a felony. Arguably, he has broken the first commandment (or the second one, depending on how you read the relevant passages), the prime provision in Israel's constitution: "Thou shalt have no other gods before me." He has presumed to appropriate godly power for himself. In aggravation, he has shown this reckless defiance before the people in whom he is supposed to be inculcating absolute allegiance to Yahweh and their social contract with him as supreme legal authority. This is a failure of leadership as well as of delegated power. He has disobeyed divine *mandamus* before the entire body of the Chosen People. As Yahweh puts it in the indictment, which also serves as the reasons for sentence: "Because ye believed me not to sanctify me in the eyes of the children of Israel, therefore ye shall not bring the congregation into the land which I have given them" (Numbers 20:12). As a matter of general deterrence, the narrative requires that he be sacrificed, thereby setting up the Christ narrative. The cause is greater than the man.

Then again, to be effective at least by modern lights, sentencing is meant to be tempered with understanding, mercy. Where, finally, is the justice for Moses, who did so much more good than wrong, and intimates so in his "submissions to sentence"? The answer is implicit in the question: pure justice, not simply Law, is Moses's legacy.[1] Justice is not a matter of individual satisfaction but a model for human progress. Moses's story assures us that, under the law, no person, no matter that person's status or power in the community, no matter that fortune has chosen him for celebrity and honour, is better than any of the rest of us. This is pointedly true for those we have come to call role models. No man is a law unto himself, and no one is above the law. The commonwealth comes first.

In comparison, the stories of Job and Jesus are consolation prizes.

THE PISGAH PERPLEX AS A COMMENTARY ON INDIVIDUAL EXPERIENCE WITH THE RULE OF LAW   At an iconic level, the Pisgah Perplex is, in large part, the inability or disinclination to believe in an afterlife. It is supremely regulatory in positing that you cannot be a criminal in this life only to be redeemed in immortality. This is why Buber's explanation of the judgment against Moses seems legalistic but unjust. Moses repeats the sins of Eve and Prometheus, reaching for the gods' fire, introducing (and re-introducing) death into Paradise. As the serpent tells Eve in Genesis 3:5, "For God doth know that in the day ye eat thereof [i.e., of the Tree of Knowledge], then your eyes shall be opened, and ye shall be as gods, knowing good and evil." The suggestion is that God is unfairly jealous of omniscience, that knowledge is power, Eve's for the plucking. Milton shows this graphically by moving this scene into a foreshadowing dream of Eve's. As she sleeps, Satan tells her that the forbidden fruit seems

> only fit
> For gods, yet able to make gods of men; ...
> Taste this, and be henceforth among the gods
> Thyself a goddess; not to earth confin'd
> But sometimes in the air, as wee, sometimes
> Ascend to Heav'n by merit thine, and see
> What life the Gods live there, and so live thou.
>
> (*Paradise Lost*, V. 69–78)

What Eve ultimately goes for, and what Moses seeks blindly in his moment of terrible frustration, is the immortality – or at least unmortality, the godliness – otherwise denied them. They give way to temptation, where Christ will not. Thus is he "henceforth among the gods," ascending "to Heav'n by merit" more realized and graphic. And here lies the iconographic difference for law and literature: with the purportedly more "equitable" Christian version, the collective unconscious imports redemption to supply justice and make faith less difficult – in fact, almost too easy. (Recall our discussion of Coetzee's *Disgrace*.) Thus, as we have seen, does the Renaissance rigour of the British common law courts connote the sterner, Hebrew Bible view,

Deliberately unexpressed in the cult goal is the suggestion that acceptance of the fuzzy definition and loyalty to the "virtues" propounded in the totem's name will address material urges: milk and honey. Sustenance. Birds and bees. Warmth. Rivers flowing. Streets of gold. God will provide. Santa Claus is coming to town. Eventually if not now. So you better watch out and you'd better not cry. Here is the beginning and end of law.

In his prophets and messengers God is looking for a starry-eyed idealist, not a hard-headed realist – someone who accepts the immaterial and its narrative possibilities:[3] a Tevye, not a Donald Trump. While the realist might have some fuzzy belief in God out of superstition or some carefully hidden precaution, just in case He exists, the realist thinks the idealist is a fool. And, sure enough, plenty of fools tell us that they have found God. In fact, so many fools and lunatics claim to be messiahs or angels of the Lord, it is enough to make the ordinary agnostic-in-the-street a born-again atheist. So, if God's search for an idealist is to overcome our skepticism, we have to distinguish his discovery of a perfect idealist like Moses or Jesus from cases where fools claim they have found Him. Or, of course, we can decide that Moses and Jesus were fools – or narcissists, megalomaniacs, insane, and so on – themselves. Here, as modern literary theorists put it, the reader makes meaning.

The crux of this distinction has to reside in what the messenger/lawgiver purports to do in God's name. Is he mad, hearing voices in his head, as Moses heard the angel of God in the burning bush? Is he vulgarly hungry for power, like the typical plutocrat, masking his appetites for money, sex, and control with what he calls good works and community service? Is he, in fact, his own law (as with Allie Fox in *The Mosquito Coast*)? Or does he really do the Right Thing – act with legal authority?

The realist will immediately scoff, "What is the right thing?" If you say, feeding the poor, he will tell you that capitalism does that better than a purportedly more egalitarian system such as Marxism. If you reply that Marxism is basically a Judeo-Christian idea, and (with Steiner) it is the people within it, not the system, that are flawed, he will reply, inevitably, "Yes, but we have to be realistic. Marxism doesn't work because people won't do it."

This sounds absolutist – "Capital is God." But if suddenly the United States turned to Marxism, the realist would be an early apologist for it. The Mosaic view of the Right Thing is genuinely absolutist. The right thing is the right thing. If the system fails, the cause is never the system, it is always the people within it. They murmur. They hit rocks instead of speaking to them. They worship golden calves or Egyptian idols instead of Yahweh.

Case Two: Legal Versus Colloquial or Moral Reasonableness: Job, the Man on the Edom Ox-cart

When baseball manager Leo Durocher died in 1991, there was the sense that Judge Clarence Thomas died with him. As every obituary reminded us of Durocher's cynical motto, "Nice guys finish last," Judge Thomas was telling the Senate Judiciary Committee, as it vetted his appointment to the United States Supreme Court, "I've lost the belief that if I did my best, all would work out." Judge Thomas called his experience before the committee "Kafkaesque," meaning, apparently, that in Kafka unjust things seem to happen to ordinary people, "ordinarily reasonable persons," as lawyers say. Thomas's nemesis Anita Hill – the young lawyer who accused Thomas of sexually harassing her when she worked for him at the US Department of Education and the Equal Employment Opportunity Commission – had already made the same point, in a way many observers found easier to believe.

Northrop Frye has remarked that Kafka's oeuvre can be read as a series of commentaries on the Book of Job. But in Kafka, seldom does anyone make a concentrated moral choice the way Job does (can we even say "the hunger artist" does this, particularly as he admits at last that he starves himself not so much as performance art as because he doesn't like to eat?), and there finally is no consolation for suffering – no recompense when the Law's faithful are afflicted, for why there seems such a chasm between law and justice – beyond the most abstruse consolations of philosophy. Then again, where there is no pay-off in Kafka (dues are paid but to what end?; even the social order seems broken), odder still, the payoff for spiritual fidelity in the Book of Job is predominantly if not purely material: Job is rewarded twice the riches he lost. His dead children and the horrific sickness he endured – scraping at his boils and blackened skin with broken pottery – are mere bygones.

On first approaching the Book of Job, a poem written after the Five Books of Moses, we reasonably imagine that it will explicate apparent injustice on a transcendent level, resolve the Pisgah Perplex, explain why the Lawgiver was denied his ultimate earthly reward, the new

Eden, which by any sensitive accounting transcends the material. We expect that, to adapt Milton's majestic phrase in his own account of biblical, epic justice, Job will justify the ways of a putatively just God to men.

Rivers of ink have been consumed looking for justice in Job. Of course, the biblical version derives from a cautionary folk tale. So perhaps the material repayment is allegorical, to make it easy for ordinary people – the ordinarily reasonable man, such as Job himself – to understand that faith and respect for The Law really are repaid concretely, despite the sometimes heavy cost in social and moral order. (To the Israelites starving and sunburnt in the desert, Israel was the land of milk and honey, not the land of sublime poetry or perfect justice.) Perhaps implicit is the message that virtue is its own reward, that stuff is just stuff; there are rewards besides money and sex which respect for the law engenders in our daily lives, rewards that are unspectacular, like health and peace, until we lose them through neglect and bad behaviour. Job's entire universe, after all, from his personal body to his community, the body politic, is devastated in the lesson. Even non-lawyer Frye puts this resolution in hard-nosed legal terms: Job's ordeal "is not a punishment but a testing," such that "there is no breach of contract [between God and Job] to attract theological lawyers," and the righteous sufferer "is restored to his original state, with interest." While there is no contract, Job still gets contract remedy: he is returned to the position he would have occupied but for the breach – or at least for passing his final exam.

But tell this to the young mother who serves fourteen years in prison after being wrongfully convicted of murdering her infant child.[4] Proclaim "Virtue is its own reward" to the young working father in the food-bank line who wants to know why bad people often enjoy health and happy families and even peace of mind, on top of very fat bonuses, hot sex, and corporate boxes at the baseball park. In this he echoes Job, the archetypal reasonable person:

> If I speak of strength, lo, he [God] is strong; and if of judgment, who shall set me a time to plead? If I justify myself, mine own mouth shall condemn me: if I say, I am perfect, it shall also prove me perverse ... The earth is given into the hand of the wicked: he covereth the faces of the judges thereof; if not, where, and who is he ...
> Wherefore do the wicked live, become old, yea, are mighty in power? Their seed is established in their sight with them, and

their offspring before their eyes. Their houses are safe from fear, neither is the rod of God upon them" (21:7–9).

"Wherefor do the wicked live, become old, yea, are mighty in power?" Job asks this again and again, a man crying out to know the cause of his affliction, and never to get an answer. God "covereth the faces of the judges thereof."

Our exemplary young parents would like to plead their cases, but have no clue as to what they are accused of, who is their accuser, and where is their trier. Surely this is closer to Kafkaesque than what Justice Thomas experienced. That is, if there is a covenant of due process – a prototypical (metaphysical) constitution (natural justice which these parents have believed in as an act of faith and citizen of the social order) guaranteeing the rights to know the charges against you, confront your accuser, and a fair hearing before an objective trier – how will the parents sue for it? "Oh that I knew where I might find him, that I might come even to his seat! I would order my cause before him, and fill my mouth with arguments. I would know the words which he would answer me, and understand what he would say unto me ... But he is in one mind and who can turn him?" (Chapter 23). They plead anyway, of course, all the while wondering with Job how can justice be weighed in the balance when the trier seems to have his ponderous finger on one side, from the start: "Let me be weighed in an even balance, that God may know mine integrity" (31:6). "What is man that thou shouldest magnify him and that thou shouldest set thine heart upon him? And that thou shouldest visit him every morning, and try him every moment?" (7:17–18). The trial started long ago, without notice: a commentary on Kafka, indeed.

How do we explain to a Job in the darkest night of his soul, "It's true that despite your 'niceness', your refined sense of duty, your children are dead. But if people didn't respect the Law as you do, there would be anarchy; blood would flow in the roads. Nobody could take a step without looking over his shoulder. If people did things only for worldly reward, life would be vapour. We would be so busy just trying to get through the day, it wouldn't be worth the struggle. So really, you're not doing badly. It was all just a test, and now you're a good example, a solid citizen. Through all of this, you respected your duty to the Law, and thereby the community." His friends intimate some of this, while also voicing the "ordinary person's" prejudice that lies behind so many wrongful convictions in our justice systems: if Job is on trial, he must have done something wrong. Perhaps this is why even God, the trier, rejects their otherwise conventional religious arguments out of hand. But the Book of Job never actually explains this, making whatever justice there is seem, from our mortal point of view, all the more arbitrary.

Nor does it address perhaps that most vexing question: what doctrine of virtue rationalizes a parent's grief – even a criminal parent's grief – over the loss of a young child? After Rabbi Harold Kushner's fourteen-year-old son died of progeria, a congenital disease that causes people to age at something like seven or eight times the normal rate, he tried to make sense of his suffering by writing *When Bad Things Happen to Good People*. But the tragedy remains inexplicable. The best Kushner could do was speculate that perhaps the lesson of Job is that God – the Law – doesn't control everything that happens in the world. Fair enough, but why, then, has this perplexed us since Adam were a lad?

Considering the enormity of what God is otherwise said to be responsible for – from mayflies and pansies to dinosaurs (or, in the language of Job, the behemoth and leviathan), the rings around Saturn, consciousness, puppies, snake venom, the eye, clown fish, giraffes, the Milky Way, Venus flytraps, the Sahara, octopi, volcanoes, strawberries, amoebas, blowfish, nuclear fission, quantum mechanics, spider webs, the Grand Canyon, cinnamon, and chocolate – this reformulation of the doctrine of free will is not much consolation. If you believe in God, however, you can extrapolate from what Kushner says – that perhaps God does not or cannot control everything in the world – to a sort of resolution, if not consolation.

First, yes, what Rabbi Kushner seems to suggest does not differ much from what theologians since the Middle Ages have formulated about freedom of choice also being God-given. God, according to the so-called *Deus otiosus* proposition, made the world and then left it pretty well to its own devices. (Mind you, part of that grand scheme seems to have meant lions eating lambs, and only after terror and pain.) Suffering is a legacy of what Paul called Original Sin, the fall of Adam and Eve. There is no necessary explanation, at least not in human notions of justice, as to why a baby dies of cancer while a mass murderer lives to be eighty. A perhaps less cruel extrapolation is that in creating the earth (and perhaps the whole universe), God created a Frankenstein or a golem, stupidly, pathetically bent on its own destruction, broken free of its creator's control. The laws of nature strain toward anarchy. The history of the world is simply entropy run riot.

In this context, God is relieved of responsibility for why illiterate rock star hooligans seem pretty well remunerated when you, for all your virtue and thoughtfulness, feel a little cheated. It might even let him off the hook for Ted Bundy and Jack the Ripper. With millionaire rock-music, sports, and film stars, the question becomes not "Why do the not-so-righteous flourish while the righteous suffer?" but, "Why does society so often reward moral indifference while ignoring true goodness?" Free will takes justice into the secular legal arena. Free choice produces positive law.

You might say that, as with Moses and his five books, Job's higher reward for his piety is having his own book in the Bible, literary immortality, not to mention a monument in moral and legal history that has stood against the corrosive millennia. But in the story proper, his reward is the same as the rock star's, and has the same secular feel. The Bible never explains exactly how double recovery of material goods is supposed to make up for lost children, or why those innocents were sacrificed in a bet with the devil. It doesn't even make sense under our secular law (*pace* Frye), which does its best to put us in the position we would have been in if not for the damages we innocently suffered. Double recovery is viewed as unjust.

We mentioned earlier that after the American writer Peter De Vries lost his young teenage daughter to cancer, like Rabbi Kushner he wrote an autobiographical book, the novel *The Blood of the Lamb*. As his child is dying of cancer, the protagonist, Don Wanderhope, confronts the unyielding fact that fidelity to the rule of law is not mystical or transcendent, but a mere hedge against the injustice built into the world:

> I believe that man must learn to live without those consolations
> called religious, which his own intelligence must by now have
> told him belong to the childhood of the race. Philosophy can real-
> ly give us nothing permanent to believe either; it is too rich in
> answers, each canceling out the rest. The quest for Meaning is
> foredoomed. Human life 'means' nothing. But that is not to say
> that it is not worth living. What does a Debussy Arabesque 'mean,'
> or a rainbow or a rose? A man delights in all of these, knowing
> himself to be no more – a wisp of music and a haze of dreams dis-
> solving against the sun. Man has only his own two feet to stand

on, his own trinity to see him through: Reason, Courage, and Grace. And the first plus the second equals the third.

This is another way of saying the ordinarily reasonable person is not unlike Charlie Chaplin's little tramp, at sometimes absurd pains to maintain his dignity in an at best indifferent, and often apparently unjust, universe. And by putting Reason at the top of the trinity (as God does, coincidentally, in *Paradise Lost*), it presumes that a frequent response to the Book of Job, that "God works in mysterious ways," is no answer at all. From such a presumption, and more than even the Pisgah Perplex, the Book of Job seems to rub the reader's nose in the apparent arbitrariness of justice, and the futility of reason in the face of divine autocracy. But in the end, the Book cannot stand being "Kafkaesque," leaving us to take our consolation where we might, as in homilies. Job gets double his material loss. Chapter 28 tells us that wisdom "cannot be valued with gold" (28:15), but justice seems another matter. In one of its many ambiguous moments, the book (which probably is the work of many hands over many years, a committee and its redactors) tells us it is tantamount to sin – a breach of divine law – to "have made gold my hope ... or confidence," to have "rejoiced because my wealth was great, and because mine hand had gotten much" (31: 24–5). Yet chillingly, this is Job's only apparent recompense, precisely because life and legacy are priceless and once lost, incapable of restitution. Job's story leaves behind the more visceral, profounder injustices signified by his manifold loss, of his children, his reputation and friendships (if he is honest), his pious contentment. (We think inevitably of Iago's words, that have become a cliché of defamation law: "Who steals my purse steals trash; ... / But he that filches from me my good name / Robs me of that which not enriches him, And makes me poor indeed.") And perhaps most painful, he must live – to 140, twenty years longer, interestingly, than Moses – with the torment that his faith has been tested for a bet with Satan.

Then again, compromise is the lot of the reasonable person, doing his best in a fallen – imperfect – world. *The Fall and Rise of Reginald Perrin*, a novel by David Nobbs which is perhaps better known as the television comedy adapted from it, shows how Perrin, a marketing executive at a company called Sunshine Desserts, resolves a severe case of male menopause by faking suicide and starting life over as a pig swiller. Just before Perrin pretends to kill himself, while he's still the marketing manager at Sunshine, the British Fruit Growers Association invites him to speak at a luncheon. Stewing in his own juices, as well as in generous quantities of free table wine, Perrin lectures the fruit growers and dessert marketers on what the conventional or "reasonable" world sees as progress: "What has progress done for Me? One day I will die, and on my grave it will say, 'Here lies Reginald Iolanthe Perrin; he didn't know the names of the flowers and the trees, but he knew the rhubarb crumble sales for Schleswig-Holstein.'"

Now of course every fruit grower listening thinks reflexively that Perrin is a candidate for the Twinkie defence: obsession with desserts has crumbled *him*. But in the back of their minds they must be wondering about their own hold on reason.

Probably many reading this book can quote large sections of a criminal code or the local *Planning Act* or the Rule Against Perpetuities. Perhaps one or two even know the rhubarb crumble sales figures for Schleswig-Holstein. But most of us could not name many of the trees and flowers right outside our offices. Is this reasonable? What *are* we here for?

The law's answer seems fairly clear. When the law asks in a negligence or contract or sexual assault case whether a reasonable person would have acted in the same way as the defendant acted, the law is not talking about the old granola who knows the names of the flowers and the trees and the birds and the bees. The reasonable person of the law reports is not the sensitive, thoughtful fellow who will live longer and move more gently across the planet for eating tofu, instead of lamb or baby veal, and bicycling to the office where the thermostat is set at 26 degrees Celsius (79 Fahrenheit) all summer. With its fundamentalist approach to duty, really reasonable behaviour – pacifism, vegetarianism, cycling to work, even, God forbid, Marxism's redistribution of wealth – would usually be seen in our law courts as anti-establishment if not dangerous. At common law, duty is self-serving and "idealism" is a dirty word. When the law says "reasonable person" it is talking about the sensible fellow who knows the rhubarb crumble sales figures for Schleswig-Holstein.

As we have seen, this is frequently where law and literature collide and contend. Justice is poetry; law is prose. Until very recently, anyway, what type of person did our non-literary mind's eye see when it encountered "the reasonable or ordinarily prudent person?" Many of us probably saw a clerk at Acme Insurance Corp. White. Bad haircut. Loosely-knotted necktie that goes with nothing in anybody's wardrobe now that Liberace is dead. (Of course, the reasonable man was heterosexual, at least to all appearances.) And we say "guy" and "man" deliberately, although there is a pretence lately that the man on the Clapham omnibus has an equal partner in the woman driving her Toyota RAV 4 on Interstate 25. Reasonableness as the law defines it is still overwhelmingly, and unfairly, a male preserve, entrenched as it is from classical if not biblical times, with the male as the archetype of reason and the female as the archetype of feeling – as though all of us didn't have both attributes in our personalities, as though there is something unreasonable about reason tempered with passion.

Despite years of peripatetic effort, I have never been able to track down the first appearance in law of the Clapham omnibus character, although in a 1903 libel action Lord Justice Collins attributes the creation of this Adam in legal paradise to Lord Bowen.[5] The classic formulation that we all know is from a 1933 case called *Hall v. Brooklands Auto Racing Club*,[6] an action prosecuted after a car jumped the curb at Brooklands' race course and killed two spectators. The English Court of Appeal found that the plaintiffs did not have a claim in negligence. When the reasonable man paid the price of admission, they said, he would "quite understand that he was facing the risk of any such possible but improbable accident."

How times have changed, which itself is a signal thing about the reasonable man: in law as in literature, he is reasonable according to the lights of his time and place. Today the Hall family would probably get tens of thousands of pounds in damages. But in the era of *Hall v. Brooklands*, when the law was stricter about personal responsibility, the reasonable man, Lord Justice Greer found, "is sometimes described as the man in the street or the man on the Clapham omnibus or, as I recently read in an American author, the man who takes the magazines at home, and in the evening pushes the lawnmower in his shirtsleeves." In other words, this Norman Rockwellian hero is very definitely not the *objectively* reasonable man, the retrohippie who, as the cars roar their mindless, polluting, crashing-and-mutilating circuit at Brooklands, gently mows his lawn with a recycled push mower and hand rakes the maple keys onto his compost heap – instead of expending fossil fuels and waking the neighbour's baby while blowing the leaves into the gutter. The *reasonable* man is at the car races.

Mind you, in 1933 you wouldn't have expected the reasonable man to be out back in his Birkenstocks, hand-raising his own organic radicchio while humming "Give Peace a Chance." The world was considerably less packaged and automated. There were no motorized lawnmowers or leaf-blowers or atom bombs, nor was there television and the Internet to commercialize and sexualize and propagandize every waking moment. But given these momentous changes in the intervening eighty years, with the modern availability of information and education, has the reasonable person become all the more reasoning?

It used to be that the reasonable person was an excellent if odious creature, to use A.P. Herbert's wonderful phrase – someone rather inhuman, at least when he wasn't going to watch auto races. Lord Bramwell said that the reasonable man was an impossible combination of acrobat and Hebrew prophet (serious competition, it would seem, even for Job),[7] and Oliver Holmes suggested that he was virtually angelic – Adam in an unearthly paradise. Since then, however, the reasonable person has suffered a bad case of democracy – or rather, a case of bad democracy, in which freedom is taken as licence. "The Reasonable Man is always thinking of others," Herbert wrote in 1935,

> prudence is his guide, and 'Safety First' ... is his rule of life. All solid virtues are his, save only that peculiar quality by which the affection of other men is won. ... He is one who invariably looks where he is going, and is careful to examine the immediate foreground before he executes a leap or bound; who neither star-gazes nor is lost in meditation when approaching trap-doors or the margin of a dock; ... who never mounts a moving omnibus, and does not alight from any car while the train is in motion; who investigates the *bona fides* of every mendicant before distributing alms, and will inform himself of the history and habits of a dog before administering a caress; ... who never swears, gambles, or loses his temper; who uses nothing except in moderation, and even while he flogs his child is meditating only on the golden mean.[8]

Granted, even in the 1930s it would have been difficult to find a person living anywhere near this standard. But were this the law's reasonable person of today, everyone in town would either be in jail or bankrupt because of judgment debts. Instead, self-assertiveness is rampant, and prized. The community interest is secondary to individual expression. Perhaps we're killing ourselves with tolerance – or is it ambivalence? It is very hard to determine what is reasonable amid some incoherent consensus that democracy means *every* individual action is reasonable, that freedom is commensurate with licence. With cultural relativism in the ascendant, no one is on the same wavelength as his neighbour, both the subject and object of legal duty. In this atmosphere, an atmosphere in which all kinds of competing desires and urges and fanaticisms are at full boil just under the surface of entrenched convention, it can be hard to say what is reasonable, and very easy for trouble to erupt on Main Street.[9]

Confronted with this problem in notorious cases like *D.P.P. v. Morgan*[10] and *R. v. Pappajohn*,[11] the highest courts in Britain and Canada threw up their hands over the question of what a reasonable person would do. They said intercourse was not rape if the accused honestly believed the complainant consented, even if only the most thoughtless, slathering troglodyte would have believed consent existed. Narrative perspective trumped principle. Where previously the reasonable person was at least reasonable on paper, it had become impossible to define reasonableness even as a legal fiction. You could actually see the reasonable man of the tort and contracts cases of the 1930s and -40s – the man on the Clapham omnibus, the ordinarily prudent person – breathe his last in those cases. The judges refused even to think about what "reasonable" could mean. Despite legislative attempts to redress this, we are left with the increasing philosophical difficulty of what objective reasonableness means in a society that otherwise strains to say reasonableness is relative. But as we saw when we looked at the concept of duty, law and literature meet at this crossroads. Where literature does not dramatize or satirize or bemoan this state of affairs, it attempts to redress it.

As our biblical analysis has shown, the problem of finding a standard of reasonableness is as old as our civilization. You would think that the law would regard one man in particular as the pre-eminent reasonable person, even though he's been dead for 2,400 years. I was taught several areas of law according to his "method," and in the hands of a competent teacher it remains not a bad method. But you might say (to end more or less where I began) that Socrates was the pinko Tilley-hat-type granola-eater of his day – the really reasonable person, as opposed to the reasonable person as legal fiction, that law report paragon who is too good to be true but not quite good enough to be desirable.

At least as a mythic or literary figure, Socrates was too good to be attractive to vested interests, those that today find it more amenable to use migrant labour to turn the planet into a toilet than to clean up their act and pay living wages. Not surprisingly, he faced capital punishment for such eminent reasonableness.

Some will answer that all this means that (like Moses v. Donald Trump) the law's reasonable person is a realist who has to live in the real world of mortgages and telephone bills. Socrates and Mohandas Gandhi and Mother Teresa are not reasonable, some will say; they are ideologues, the stuff of poetry not prose, of literature, not law, and they must expect to suffer in the real world. Certainly not many of us would want Gandhi or Mother Teresa to be managing partner in our real estate and tax practice, or to act as an investment advisor. But the more important question is, who would we rather have model the environment in which our children will live? Who would we rather have shaping the vision of your country and culture? Donald Trump? Mick Jagger?

The upshot of all this seems to be that at law a reasonable person is not necessarily reasonable to ordinarily reasonable persons – to, that is, the "person in the street." He is truly fictive. As we discussed in Chapter Five, law has its own dialect or linguistic universe, intimately related to the rest of our cultural life, but distinct. While sometimes sharing terrain with poetry and metaphor, its tropes are different. When lawyers say a something or someone is reasonable, they mean something different from what ordinary (reasonable) novelists mean, as well as what ordinary people mean in everyday, colloquial speech.

In 1997, the Supreme Court of Canada made this sharply clear regarding reasonableness of doubt, in *R. v. Lifchus*. They did not trust ordinary people to rely on their native sense of reasonableness. Ordinarily reasonable persons (in the universe of legalese, people are rarely people; they are persons), they seemed to say, do not necessarily have reasonable doubts. A judge must explain to them what such a doubt is.

William Lifchus was a Manitoba stockbroker on trial for fraud and theft. The trial judge charged the jury that,

When I use the words "proof beyond a reasonable doubt," I use those words in their ordinary, natural everyday sense. There isn't one of you who hasn't said, Gosh I've got a doubt about such and so. Perfectly everyday word. There isn't one of you who doesn't have a notion of reasonable. That, too, is a perfectly ordinary concept ... The words "doubt," the words "reasonable" are ordinary, everyday words that I am sure you understand.

On these instructions, the jury convicted Lifchus of fraud only, a result that suggests they had considered doubt as instructed, on whatever standard, and they doubted the accused had committed theft. Lifchus appealed the fraud conviction, attacking the judge's charge. When the case reached the Supreme Court, Justice Peter Cory, for the entire bench, admitted that

> in some jurisdictions, most notably the United Kingdom, the position appears to be that there is no need to define "reasonable doubt" beyond telling jurors that they cannot convict unless they are "sure" that the accused is guilty. Indeed, some very eminent jurists have espoused the view that, because the words "reasonable doubt" are readily understood by jurors, it may even be unwise to attempt a definition.

However, Justice Cory cited with approval Justice Ginsburg's words in *Victor v. Nebraska*, (127 L Ed 2d 583 (1994)) that: "While judges and lawyers are familiar with the reasonable doubt standard, the words 'beyond a reasonable doubt' are not self-defining for jurors ... Thus, even if definitions of reasonable doubt are necessarily imperfect, the alternative – refusing to define the concept at all – is not obviously preferable." Justice Cory then noted: "The phrase 'beyond a reasonable doubt' is composed of words which are commonly used in everyday speech. Yet, these words have a specific meaning in the legal context. This special meaning of the words 'reasonable doubt' may not correspond precisely to the meaning ordinarily attributed to them."

Even where judges tried to define reasonableness, Justice Cory worried about paraphrasing. Describing "beyond a reasonable doubt" as amounting "to a moral certainty" dangerously tempted jurors to act on feeling instead of evidence. Providing metaphorical interpretations, such as "beyond a haunting or substantial or serious doubt" invited adjudication on subjective standards of what was haunting, substantial, or serious. (It invited fiction.) Even to say a reasonable doubt is one for which you can give a reason might smother inarticulable doubt – which, paradoxically, sounds as though the poor juror should rely, at some inarticulable time or other, on nerves and feeling, after all.

In his model charge, however, Justice Cory seems to suggest that a reasonable doubt is something only a reasonable person would have: "A reasonable doubt is not an imaginary or frivolous doubt. It must not be based upon sympathy or prejudice. Rather, it is based on reason and common sense. It is logically derived from the evidence or absence of evidence."

"Rather, it is based on reason and common sense." This would seem to be the sort of reason and common sense only a "reasonable person" in the *legal* (versus colloquial) sense would have; a truly "ordinary reasonable person" – like many jurors off the street, presumably – might be moved by some sympathy or other emotion, while still judging from the evidence of his senses. And generally, what a reasonable person would think is, by definition, not defined by judges or law.

So we have a model charge that is no model of reason. While I am aware of no judge so brave as to label reasonable doubt a legal fiction, it remains ambiguous whether the reasonable person of civil litigation would know intuitively what is meant by "reasonable doubt" in criminal cases. But it seems that he would have a better chance at it than a flesh-and-blood mortal.

What remains clear, however, is that, with both the reasonable person and reasonable doubt, we remain in a paradisal, not-quite-human realm, the realm of *fiction*. More worrisome is whether the judgment in *Lifchus* suggests that as a society we can no longer be trusted to have a communal sense of justice, and are prone to act idiosyncratically, defining from our own self-centres – our personal biases, sub-cultures, and predilections versus community standards – what is reasonable in the larger culture. We already have walked the dark pathways our novelists, dramatists, and poets tell us this sort of subjective reasonableness can lead, particularly when that subjective view seems most fundamentally, well, reasonable.

As we suggested earlier, at the level of archetype there is an easier reply to the problems of justice and evil as they arise in the stories of Moses, Job, and Christ: the moment you are "chosen," the moment you are Heaven's darling, a leader, by definition you are no longer a reasonable person. Nor then is your fate reasonable, let alone ordinary. Fictively, the reasonable person is ordinary, the community-minded Joe or Jane in the street. At the level of archetype he loses his status of truly ordinary reasonableness precisely because he is to be made an example of what happens when we drift from that standard, toward excessive individualism, social Darwinism.

As a legal fiction, the reasonable person is not physically heroic. He, in fact, avoids heroics at all costs. He does not stand out, and for that reason does not enjoy the immortality (on a secular level) of Moses or Job or Jesus. Personifying the social contract, his very being is community. Which bring us, finally, to God's speech, which concludes the Book of Job.

Cynthia Ozick has called the Book of Job "comfortless."[12] Probably not everyone reads Job this way, though the book does little to address the problem it sets of justice against evil. Ozick herself is left to fall back on an interpretation that perhaps gives comfort to some, the cold, cliché comfort of Job's realization in the end, "I have uttered what I did not understand, things too wonderful for me, which I did not know." Translation, God works in mysterious ways. "His new knowledge is this," Ozick concludes: "that a transcendent God denies us a god of our own devising ... The ways of the true God cannot be penetrated. The false comforters cannot decipher them." The problem with this is not just a matter of comfortlessness, but a difficulty of faith and leadership: all we have is our own understanding, limited though it might be. How do we show allegiance to – keep the faith with – a system of law that seems unjust? If justice is indecipherable, how are we not stuck in a Kafka fiction? If all there is to a justice system is deterrence, it is, as Job has complained until this point, not simply punishment without process, but punishment without reason, or rhyme. If a parable is meant to instruct, what lesson is there in inscrutability?

While God's speech provides little by way of answer to Job's racked questions, it does tell us something about evil, equated biblically with sin and secularly with crime. There is no getting around the fact that evil is of this world, a fallen world, as signified by God's pointed description of the land and sea monsters, behemoth and leviathan. In fact, as Frye notes, the latter "is a creature of whom God seems to be rather proud."[13] God boasts graphically of both, actually, but as the true symbol of the underworld, the prototype of the dragon slain by God at the end of days, and by knights in the name of Christianity, leviathan – the evolutionary cousin of Eden's serpent – gets the Bible's more vivid descriptions, appearing also in the Psalms, Daniel, Isaiah and, finally, in Revelations as the seven-headed, ten-horned dragon of the sea, an analogue of other such evil incarnations as Islam's Bhamat and the Sirens of Greco-Roman mythology. In Job, God announces at some bullying length – as though describing the newest video game he's mastered – that his thinking, soulful creature man is no match for his awful, and highly picturesque, dumb sea monster. The profounder message is perhaps that no amount of reasonable behaviour will erad- icate evil, a companion to man in Creation post-Eden. But legal rea- sonableness can keep it at bay.

Otherwise, the appearance of the monsters seems tacked-on and beside the point, as if everything Job suffered is scarcely worth com- ment: "Yeah, but look what I made!" Frye says the monsters make God's speech make sense, demonstrating that, while the bet with Satan placed Job in the belly of the beast (in a hell on earth, like Jonah in the whale, the place of trial), he has now emerged, where the beast is visible. This certainly makes sense in terms of legal iconography, as a final metaphor in the Jobian message that even when the very worst happens to us, even when we find ourselves in hell's entrails, we will survive under the rule of law if only we maintain faith with it. After the Fall, earth is no paradise. The best we can do is to make evil itself a monstrous outlaw: if it is to remain literally outside our law as a community, then we must keep it outside us as individuals, as a mat- ter of what we now call enlightened self-interest, a matter of survival as a civilized society.

Case Three: What the Sirens Sang: A Law-and-Literature Answer

In his *Lives of the Caesars*, the Roman historian Suetonius tells us that Tiberias "loved most affectionately" the "liberal sciences." In particular, the emperor (42 BC–37 AD) enjoyed quizzing professors on matters such as "who was Hecuba's mother? What name Achilles had among the Virgins? What it was that the mermaids were wont to sing?"[14] Suetonius suggests that such questions might be pure ivory-tower, "mere fooleries and matters ridiculous." Yet the Siren-song question invokes the original source of law in western societies, and thereby the well-spring of law and literature here. Again we find its answer in that first illegal act in our cultural imagination: Adam's tasting of the forbidden fruit in the Garden of Eden.

On this view, the Pentateuch's depiction of Eve – and to a certain extent, the snake-eyed Satan of Eden and The Book of Job – is an archetypal development of the Sirens. Recall again that in Eden there is only one legal requirement, a leasehold covenant that the tenants are not to eat of the Tree of Knowledge of Good and Evil. The covenant's breach brings on the Fall, a descent from earthly paradise to the world of contention and death, where positive law becomes necessary. Human law begins and ends in Paradise, with the desire to be godlike – omniscient – which provides the key, symbolically if not musically, to Sirensong.

SIRENSONG: A CONCISE LITERARY BIOGRAPHY In this fallen world where sin and crime blur, squad-car sirens are, like Eden's serpent, scary and seductive all at once, their namesake being the fantastical ocean nymphs, half-woman, half-bird, that writers later confounded with fishy mermaids.[15] The literal-minded have said that siren-mermaids are nothing more than hideous sea-cows which love-starved sailors took for magical women.[16] Of course birds are renowned for their singing where fish and dugongs are not. Then, too, literature and the visual arts associate birds with incorporeal freedom and the soul, and it is sometimes said of the Sirens that, having dined on their victims' flesh, they wing away their "imprisoned" souls.[17] In any event, the relevant history first documents them in Homer's *Odyssey*,[18] the hero's crew binding him to the mast after he's stopped their ears with beeswax. Like a sybarite devoted to erotic asphyxia, he wants to hear the Sirensong while avoiding the lethal consequences of the listening – a watery end, throwing himself helplessly toward the song's source, or starving himself dead pining over its beauties; a navigational hazard if ever there was one, often symbolized by the sea-bleached bones piled around the Sirens' Edenic island setting.

When Odysseus docks at Circe's island for what turns out to be fantastically hazardous rest and recreation, the sorceress – having herself seduced half his crew with wine and song before changing them into pigs – warns him that any man who hears the Sirensong will be tempted by it to his death. His curiosity piqued, and never one to shirk a challenge, the great adventurer orders his crew to lash him to the mast. So does Odysseus hear the Oceanides flatter him about his fame, and then brag of their own: "No seaman ever sailed his black ship past this spot," T.E. Lawrence's translation has it, "without listening to the sweet tones that flow from our lips." Robert Fitzgerald pictures the Sirens as teasing braggarts, making them nah-nah-nah like children about how no sailor can resist the pull of their "green mirror." These, by themselves, are not very compelling assertions. Next, however, and significantly for our purposes here, no matter whose translation you read, the lethal maidens promise to bestow on Odysseus knowledge of all earthly events past, present, and future. It is at this point that he becomes desperate for his crew to release him, against strict orders. Here is George Chapman's felicitous translation from 1614:

> Come here, thou, worthy of a world of praise,
> That dost so high the Grecian glory raise.
> Ulysses! stay thy ship, and that song heare
> That none past ever but it bent his eare,
> But left him ravisht and instructed more
> By us than any ever heard before.
> For we know all things whatsover were
> In wide Troy labour'd, whatsoever there
> The Grecians and the Troyans both sustain'd
> By those high issues that the Gods ordain'd:
> And whatsoever all the earth can show
> T'inform a knowledge of desert, we know.
>
> This they gave accent in the sweetest straine
> That ever open'd an enammor'd vaine –
> When mine constrain'd heart needs would have mine eare
> Yet more delighted, force way forth, and heare.
> To which end I commanded with all signe
> Sterne looks could make (for not a joynt of mine
> Had powre to stirre) my friends to rise, and give
> My limbs free way.

Already we hear that archetypal theme, echoed in the biblical narrative of the Fall: giving in to the temptation of the song is like eating of the Tree of Knowledge, breaching Paradise's single covenant. *Surrender and I will tell you what I know, the very formulae and meaning of Creation.* If the Sirens, archetypally, are Eve, the sailors are Adam. The snake is the sexual allure between them, like sea-slime. The algae-green mirror is what one falls into, like Narcissus into the watery looking-glass. Death enters the world, consequentially on sin and eventually crime.

Christian iconography redeems the archetype, legally providing pardon by redemption, still with related imagery: Odysseus is lashed to the mast as Christ is nailed to the cross. Indeed, in his translation of *The Odyssey* (Oxford: 1932), T.E. Shaw has Odysseus say "they tied me stiffly upright to the tabernacle," a synonym for mast-socket which of course reverberates with sacred-law overtones – the Hebrews' portable home for the Ark of the Covenant during their deliverance from Egypt, the Jewish Temple, and in Christianity the box that holds the communion wine and wafer that signify the body of Christ.

Symbolically, Odysseus as Logos, the Word as Law, resists the temptation of its demonic opposite. With monotheism, the heroic adventurer evolves into the deity, the son of man now permitted omniscience as Supreme Ruler, the "one greater Man" at the opening of Milton's *Paradise Lost*, who will restore us to immortality in a more perfect paradise than that from which we fell, a paradise where law is unnecessary – indeed, unknown:

> Of man's first disobedience and the fruit
> Of that forbidden tree, whose mortal taste
> Brought Death into the world, and all our woe,
> With loss of Eden, till one greater Man
> Restore us, and regain the blissful Seat,
> Sing Heav'nly Muse, that on the secret top
> of Oreb, or of Sinai, didst inspire
> That Shepherd, who first taught the chosen see,
> In the beginning how the Heav'ns and Earth
> Rose out of Chaos,

natural law being, through "right reason," an answer to chaos.[19]

Samuel Daniel, a contemporary of Shakespeare, proposed a Siren-song that has a Hegelian, or even Marxist, ring today. In "Ulysses and the Siren" (1605) he sets up a duet between sailor and temptress, a dialectic between the glories of labour on the high seas against the bourgeois torpor of eternally cavorting with sea-dwelling nymphomaniacs. Ulysses (Odysseus's Roman name) allows that the siren is a "delicious nymph," but turns her offer down:

> Fair nymph, if fame or honour were
> To be attained with ease,
> Then would I come and rest me there,

And leave such toils as these.

The Siren persists, invoking natural law to urge Ulysses to cast aside his bourgeois conventionalism:

That doth opinion only cause
That's out of custom bred,
Which makes us many other laws
Than ever nature did.

In his *Purgatorio*, Dante had used a Siren to make a similar point, although for him the supreme good was divine love against the dim-sighted carnality represented by the sea-nymph. In a dream he encounters a cross-eyed woman who at first is maimed and homely, but his lust makes her whole and beautiful. She sings to him beguilingly about how she is a Siren. "I can show you such a good time, as I showed Ulysses," she tells him, "you'll never want to leave me." A vision of the Virgin appears at her side, and at the same moment, Virgil comes to tear away the siren's clothes to expose her breasts and foul belly – or, rather, Dante's foul mind. And if there is any doubt about what is foul, what fair, Dante awakes to find Virgil scolding him that he has called him three times – presumably just as God had to call Moses more than once to get his attention away from worldly matters. Pagan superstition evolves into monotheistic law, and eventually Christian mercy or leavening "equity."

With Kafka, we reach the modernist, ironic development of the Homeric Sirens. Now their song is irresistible even if the sailor deafens himself, and "the longing of those they seduced would have broken far stronger bonds than chains and masts." Ulysses (here called, as in the Daniel poem) stops up his ears anyway, perhaps because the Sirens have yet "a more fatal weapon," silence. This Kafkaesque variation is predictably ambiguous about the author's anti-Homeric motives: the author first tells us that Ulysses does not hear the Sirens' silence because he believes they are singing – "he saw their throats rising and falling, their breasts lifting, their eyes filled with tears, their lips half-parted." Very quickly Ulysses manages, in fact, to ignore the nymphs altogether, sailing blissfully out of earshot and view. Yet Ulysses is "such a fox," Kafka concludes, perhaps he is only pretending not to hear the silence, showing his sanguine resistance to the gods as "a sort of shield."[20]

In the Siren "episode" of *Ulysses*,[21] James Joyce's irony is sardonic in a different way: the Sirens are inarticulate barmaids, more or less world-weary and cynical about the men they flirtatiously serve for their living. All nerves, feelings, and sexual entropy, they giggle and pant and sigh until breathless over their tea, to the extent that Lydia Douce ends by saying, "I feel all wet," gossiping about men, whom lust makes "frightful idiots." The barmaids' attraction has little or nothing to do with anything they vocalize:

> Miss Douce reached high to take a flagon, stretching her satin arm, her bust, that all but burst, so high.
> – O! O! jerked Lenehan, gasping at each stretch. O!
> But easily she seized her prey and led it low in triumph ...
> Lenehan still drank and grinned at his tilted ale and at Miss Douce's lips that all but hummed, not shut, the oceansong her lips had trilled. Idolores. The eastern seas.

The rest is small-talk and snatches of pop balladry. The barmaids share in the bird imagery of the episode (for example, Douce ruffles her "nosewings"), but the really beautiful music is asexual and made by men, particularly the blind piano-tuner and Ben Dollard, evoking Irish sentimentality – dosed with nationalism – that can drown you (protagonist Bloom seems to find) if you let it. Cynical and calculating, the barmaids sing snatches of popular tunes as they work, including that "Idolores [I'm Dolores] queen of the eastern seas," associating Douce with *douleur*, pain, dolour, but (again) vulgarly: to the punters' fevered request, *Sonnez la cloche!*, she wordlessly lifts her skirt and slaps her garter belt to her thigh, suggesting her French is all of the visceral variety:

> – Go on! Do! *Sonnez!*
> Bending, she nipped a peak of skirt above her knee.
> Delayed. Taunted them still, bending, suspending, with wilful eyes.
> – *Sonnez!*
> Smack. She let free sudden in rebound her nipped elastic

garter smackwarm against her smackable woman's
warmhosed thigh.

   – *La cloche!* cried gleeful Lenehan.

Having inarticulately "rung the bell," Douce "smilesmirks," but
nothing comes from her lips until the show is over and she teases
Blazes Boylan (flirting with him, not Lenehan) that he is "the essence
of vulgarity." Never mind that her surname is French for "sweet," she
goes sour when Boylan leaves the pub immediately thereafter, for an
assignation with Bloom's wife Molly. If there is a point about the
Sirensong here, could it be that its lure is subjective, all in your head:
the Sirensong is what you tell yourself about it? We make our own
prisons. Bloom, after all, feels nothing for the barmaids, though shortly before he arrives at the pub he has seen an advertising poster of
mermaids smoking tobacco: wordless, the seduction in your head. As
he thinks (dolorously) of Boylan on his way to make love to his wife,
he recalls his own attraction to Molly, and she to him, on their first
meeting: "Spanishy eyes. Under a peartree alone patio this hour in old
Madrid one side in shadow Dolores shedolores. At me. Luring. Ah,
alluring." The allure is wordless, the song all in his head. Indeed, as he
dines now in the pub with lawyer Richie and listens to him whistle
"All Is Lost Now," he incorporates the tune's sentiment into this train
of thought about Molly, surrender during later life that has become
more like giving up – and the thought-train more like a train *wreck*,
the fall from innocence mythic, now mimicking the Fall, which itself
mimics the fall of Narcissus (from air to water) and Echo, plummet-
ing from innocence:

> All most too new call is lost in all. Echo. How sweet the answer.
> How is that done? All lost now. Mournful he whistled. Fall, sur-
> render, lost ... In sleep she went to him. Innocence in the moon ...
> Call name. Touch water ... Too late. She longed to go. That's why.
> Woman. As easy stop the sea. Yes: all is lost.

Finally, speaking of mooning, in *The White Goddess*, Robert Graves's
1946 treatise on poetry and the moon goddess as muse, the Sirens
adopt the yet more modern habit of laying it on the line in every
sense, forthrightly promising limitless sex, eternal bliss ("No grief nor
gloom, sickness nor death / Disturbs our long tranquility") and ample
snacks fit for a demi-god –

A starry crown awaits your head
A hero feast is spread for you:
Swineflesh, milk and mead[22]

– snacks, in fact, to die for:[23] the rub being, who is feast, who fed, who "inspires" whom? Again, connection literally is made between Siren and archetypal muse.[24] They are first principles, like Eve, our first and prime muse, the female side of the eternal principle, seeking wholeness by union (or harmony) with the male side, just as sailors pine for union with them and the poet is lovesick for his inspiration. Fatal attraction. As Graves notes, "A poet cannot continue to be a poet if he feels that he has made a permanent conquest of the Muse, that she is always his for the asking."[25] Conquering one's muse becomes the ultimate paradox: it, finally, is impossible because it destroys you. It stops the music, a sanction that reverberates deeply into and out of our legal culture. The "little death" becomes Death *simpliciter.*

NOSTALGIA FOR LAWLESSNESS: EDEN, ELYSIUM, AND THE IDEA OF PARADISE   Like Kafka, in *Comus*, a defence of chastity, Milton speaks of the Sirens' fatal attraction but does not guess at what they sing. His lyrical description of the song's power, though, seems itself meant to echo it, or at least to have succumbed to its rhythmic seduction. In the words of Comus, son of Bacchus, we hear the hypnotic susurrus of the sea, just when, significantly enough, he is enraptured by the singing of the poem's chaste heroine, the "Lady" on whom Comus has lecherous designs:

I have oft heard
My mother Circe with the Sirens three,
Amidst the flowry-kirtl'd Naiades
Culling their potent herbs and baleful drugs,
Who as they sung, would take the prison'd soul,
And lap it in Elysium; Scylla wept,
And chid her barking waves into attention,
And fell Charybdis murmur'd soft applause:
Yet they in pleasing slumber lull'd the sense,
And in sweet madness robb'd[26] it of itself.
But such a sacred and home-felt delight,
Such sober certainty of waking bliss,
I never heard 'til now.

The Sirensong induces such longing that tears spring even from the six barking heads of the sea-monster Scylla, and it elicits watery applause from Charybdis, the monstrous whirlpool so powerful that it swallowed the entire sea twice each day. More significantly for our analysis, having imprisoned the listener's soul, the Sirens "lap it in Elysium," in Homer an island where the weather is always temperate, and the chosen – mortal heroes – attain an earthly immortality amid warm ocean breezes. Were Milton using Judaeo-Christian typology, he might of course have said "lap it in Eden."

And so does law meet literature, on the primary ground that was our point of departure: we long for Paradise where there is no need for positive law. Peaceful coexistence, the social contract, is tacit, presumed. Each of us knows our legal duty instinctively. The need for mortal law – broadly defined duty – begins with our fall from paradise, as we lose our pure natural-law state, individually and as a society. The individualized metaphor for this is the departure from carefree childhood for duty-bound adulthood: we trade intimations of immortality for anxiety over entropy. (As we have seen, John Updike's "Here Come the Maples," about a couple's slow descent from the innocence of young honeymooners – on the cusp of real adulthood – to their allegedly no-fault divorce hearing in middle age, constitutes the perfect law-and-lit morality play on this idea. In this – not coincidentally – final story of the Maples series, Joan and Richard Maple devolve from Adam and Eve to Hänsel and Gretel, lovers to arthritic sibling-strangers, standing before the witch's cottage made of pastries and sweets.) Earthly justice can never achieve the perfection of Heaven's, so we mortals long to return at least to that pre-law state, an earthly paradise, perfect justice being achievable only upon redemption to some better world. The substance of the Sirensong preys on that nostalgia, encapsulating the longing:

(1) This nostalgia for the prelaw is, commensurately, nostalgia for the infantile, the irresponsibility of childhood. Again, as Frye remarks of Adam and Eve in *Paradise Lost* (and as Updike echoes in his story), just after they breach their tenancy covenant and are evicted from the Garden, they "remain dramatically in the position of children baffled by their first contact with an adult situation. ... 'Henceforth I learn that to obey is best,' Adam says, as he and Eve go hand in hand out to the world before them."[27] Temptation teaches us legal duty. Again, Eve is of course both our first mother and first lover. She meets all needs and, as love object, knows everything one needs to know. The sailors'

overwhelming attraction to the Sirens reflects this darkly: there is the hypnotic, sexual longing for the mother, for the return to amniotic slumber in the lapping, timeless sea. A large part of the Sirensong's power is that it pushes Oedipal (forbidden, illegal) buttons. As long as we are protected inside the womb, we are in earthly paradise. Immortal, we can breathe while living, fully nourished and at peace, safe underwater, out of the direct sunlight, where nothing is required of us but blissful slumber.

(2) As in the Eden story, and in the stories of Moses unlawfully beating the rock and his messianic development in Christ, temptation is necessary to prove – test, put on trial – our sense of legal duty. Christ resists temptation where his prototype, Moses, fails. Odysseus is Christlike insofar as he defeats the Sirens.

(3) As temptresses, the Sirens are all about forbidden things (again, innocence tempted), the things of sin under sacred law and crime under secular; in particular:

(a) Trying to be like the gods, knowing (omnisciently) what they know. (In *Paradise Lost*, the thrust of Satan's argument to Eve is, what is the harm in that? In the Pentateuch, God tells Moses to speak to the rock for water, but in anger he strikes it with his staff, taking on the supernatural power of gods to himself.) This breaches the second (first?) Commandment, a prime constitutional (and dictatorial) requirement in Judaeo-Christian law;

(b) That incestuous, Oedipal element; permission to know not just everything but, as it were, everyone; this, too, is a pre-law, pre-societal view; who were Cain and Abel to take as wives but blood relations?;

(c) Conglomerately among the various versions of the Siren myth, all the deadly sins, with particular reference to (more or less in this order) lust, avarice (regarding knowledge), envy, gluttony, pride, and sloth.

Unless we are tempted, we cannot prove (give evidence of) our fealty to the Law, or the law. As legal standard-bearer, the reasonable person of our law reports passes this test. (Though tempted to stay in bed, he rises early to shovel the snow from his sidewalk; though tempted to wait for payday to address the spongy brake on his hybrid automobile, he immediately visits the garage for an expensive repair.) Adam begins his life in that "excellent but odious creature's"[28] epiphanic sphere, up on the mountain in the garden, and Moses makes his way up there (having been chosen by the Supreme Legislator as lawgiver for his reasonableness) but ultimately they fail the test (that Christ at last passes). Wordsworth, in his "Ode to Duty," calls upon the title goddess, "Stern Daughter of the Voice of God ... Stern Lawgiver," to put him to the test, the trials of thoughtful maturity being more fulfilling than the carelessness of youth. The allegedly mature Ogden Nash, in his Wordsworth take-off, abdicates – "O Duty, / Why hast thou not the visage of a sweetie or a cutie? / ... Why art thou so different from Venus / And why do thou and I have so few interests mutually in common between us? / ... When Duty / whispers low, Thou must, this erstwhile youth replies / I just can't" – and Eliot's anxious Prufrock lacks the gumption even to try:

> Shall I part my hair behind? Do I dare to eat a peach?
> I shall wear white flannel trousers, and walk upon the beach.
> I have heard the mermaids singing, each to each.
>
> I do not think they will sing to me.
>
> I have seen them riding seaward on the waves
> Combing the white hair of the waves blown back
> When the wind blows the water white and black.
>
> We have lingered in the chambers of the sea
> By sea-girls wreathed with seaweed red and brown
> Till human voices wake us, and we drown.

He is imprisoned by his fearful mortality: "And I have seen the eternal Footman hold my coat, and snicker / and in short, I was afraid." He is no hero; for as long as he lives he will be a hangashore: "And indeed there will be time / To wonder, 'Do I dare?' and, 'Do I dare?' / Time to turn back and descend the stair." He will hear only human voices, the mundane trumped up as knowing: "In the room the women come and go / Talking of Michelangelo."

The Sirensong, in other words, is the demonic manifestation of the Logos, the Word that pre-empts human legal constructs and contains all life, all law, all poetry, promising godlike knowledge of these, entire, and the purported absolute peace that comes with omniscience, never mind the temper tantrums of Yahweh. It is the call of a power beyond all human law. That wailing we hear in the night – the one that fills our bars and prisons and mental hospitals – is the call of our nature.

Case Four: Justice by Golem:
Playing God with the Rule of Law

We said above that when the rule of law has gone perverse, imagination supplies moral outlaws like Robin Hood, revolutionaries like Winston Smith of George Orwell's *1984*, super-heroes like Superman, Batman, and guardian angels, all of whom intervene on behalf of the oppressed. Ultimately, as creations of a mortal world, of a Creation itself fallen, these fail as well. Adam's gravity pulls our heroes from the heights, back to earth and entropy.

Evolving in literature from the plaything of religious mystics to a flawed narrative champion of the persecuted, the golem has come to signify both the redemptive as well as the cataclysmic power of the Word at the heart of the Law – the power of creation, of men doing all that the gods can. One way or another, the golem brings down judgment, on persecutor or on his own creator. This defining trait has brought him and his simulacra to feature in their own sub-category of narrative works, with a resurgence of such appearances in the last 125 years or so, as both champion and mortally dangerous artifact for those who would play God and thereby offend his primary, constitutional Law. And perhaps symptomatic of especially anxious times, in which our only hope of deliverance from ourselves and our degraded environments seems to lie in magic, the last dozen years have produced a mini-boom in literary treatments of the golem and his dual justice aspect.

A BRIEF HISTORY, FROM MYSTICAL CONJURATION TO ROBOTIC CHAMPION   Originally, the golem had nothing to do with justice; rather, it was an experiment in mysticism or numerology, precursor to modern scientific creation of life in the test-tube – a relationship at the core of Harry Mulisch's 1998 novel, *The Procedure*. According to the Talmud (commentaries on Mosaic law, 200–500 AD), before he was a man with a human soul, Adam was golem (גאלם), mere matter.[29] The Talmud credits the first man-made golem to Rava (299–353 AD, "founder of the Babylonian academy in Mechuza"):[30] "For Rava created a man and sent him to Rabbi Zera. The rabbi spoke to him and he did not answer. Then he said: 'You must have been made by the companions [of the academy]; return to dust.'"[31] Note already the important points that, like Adam, the golem is made of earth and, unlike Adam, he is mute. "In the Talmud this passage is immediately followed by another story: 'Rav Hanina and Rav Oshaya busied themselves on the eve of every Sabbath with the *Book of Creation* ... They made a calf one-third the natural size and ate it."[32]

At this manifoldly nascent stage, golems are something a devout man skilled in white magic can conjure up. Through intimate knowledge of the godhead and the Law's mysteries, he can mimic creation and invest his handiwork with an animating soul (*nefesh*), an animal spirit if not a *ruakh*, the immortal soul that Yahweh blew into Adam's nostrils.[33] Jewish tradition says that once kabbalists mastered the *Book of Creation* – the *Sefer Yetzirah*, a little manual, headache-making in its cryptic nature, on numerology and the mystical or magical uses of the names of God – they were able (sometimes with further instruction from manuscripts now lost) to make a golem. As Chapter Two of these "rules of procedure" puts it, "It comes out that all that is formed and all that is spoken emanates from one Name."[34] The *Book* facilitated humankind's closest approach to the Word. Thus the suggested etymology of "abracadabra," from the Hebrew for 'I will create as I speak.'"[35] Golem-making was a celebration, or proof, of the acolytes' mastery of the *Sefer Yetzirah*.[36] Then again, some scholars say this triumphal act of "creation" was immaterial, accomplished all at the spiritual level and evincing mastery of the *Book* as a manual of religious meditation.[37]

This of course answers the prime legal question: if mortals create living beings, aren't they breaking the Law, breaching central, constitutional prescriptions against taking the godhead's power unto oneself and against idolatry? In producing a version of Adam, aren't they also repeating Adam's sin that brought death into the world and produced "all our woe," co-opting to themselves godlike knowledge of good and evil? (In some golem narratives, the creator actually breathes into the creature's nostrils to animate him, just as God breathed life into Adam. And Gershom Scholem notes that "Jesus demonstrated his claim to be the son of God by making birds of clay and uttering the name of God over them, whereupon they lived, stood up, and flew off into the air.")[38] Are they not committing the spiritual equivalent of sedition? In "The Golem," Borges writes of this "criminality":

So, composed of consonants and vowels,
there must exist one awe-inspiring word
that God inheres in – that, when spoken, holds
Almightiness in syllables unslurred.

Adam knew it in the Garden, so did the stars.
The rusty work of sin, so the cabbalists say,
obliterated it completely;
no generation has found it to this day.[39]

(Yet the poet himself goes on to talk about later legends of golem-making that rely on the Name.) There are other legalistic or theological responses, central among them that holy men are welcome to participate in God's secrets, to the extent he wishes to reveal these to them.[40] These *tzaddiks* can at least approach Edenic meta-consciousness. Medieval Kabbalists speculated in this way that God himself handed Abraham the *Book of Creation*, and that after "meditating on it" for three years with Noah's son Shem, the men "knew how to create a world."[41] While these legalities of golem creation will play a part in our discussion, our greater interest here is the fact of such creation as a way of providing retributive, and thereby dangerous, justice – poetic or narrative justice, if not the real-world variety.

The danger of playing God, in any event – the risk of disobeying the primary prescription of sacred law – is very often evident. In at least one narrative, from the thirteenth century, the golem itself warns its pious creators that "God alone made Adam" and that they should kill him in the way God killed Adam "and not create another man, lest the world succumb to idolatry."[42] Jakob Grimm's golem tale of 1808 marks a sort of bridge, showing the transition from mysticism to legend, with this risk factor – and other typical legendary elements that persist, including one way to kill a golem – firmly entrenched:

After saying certain prayers and observing certain fast days, the Polish Jews make the figure of a man from clay or mud, and when they pronounce the miraculous *Shemhamphoras* [apparently Grimm means the Name] over him, he must come to life. He cannot speak, but he understands fairly well what is said or commanded. They call him *golem* and use him as a servant to do all sorts of housework. But he must never leave the house. On his forehead is written *emet* [Hebrew for "truth"]; every day he gains in weight and becomes somewhat larger and stronger than all the others in the house ... For fear of him, they therefore erase the first letter, so that nothing remains but *met* ["dead"], whereupon he collapses and turns to clay again. But one man's golem grew so tall ... that the man could no longer reach his forehead. In terror, he ordered the servant to take off his boots, thinking that when he bent down he could reach his forehead. So it happened, and the Jew successfully erased the first letter, but the whole heap of clay fell on him and crushed him.⁴³

At this intermediate stage, the golem is a domestic Frankenstein, and he is mute. This latter factor goes again to the legalities: if creation is Word and language separates man from animal (in older, non-scientific belief, at least), only God-created man may speak. Not until the late nineteenth century does the golem move firmly across the bridge, from the world of religious mysticism – and creation for its own sake – to narrative or ethnic legend marrying championship with justice. The best-known of these earliest champion narratives is I.L. Peretz's "The Golem," 1893. Peretz tells us, originally in Yiddish, that the Jewish ghetto of Prague was under attack by mobs who "were about to rape the women, roast the children, and slaughter the rest." Rabbi Judah Loew, the (genuine, historical) chief rabbi of Prague in the late sixteenth century (here called "Rabbi Loeb"), goes "into the street in front of the teacher's house" and melds a golem of clay. The rabbi blows into its nose to animate it and when he whispers "the Name into its ear" it departs and assails "our enemies, threshing them as with flails." With the sabbath approaching, the ghetto's mayor comes to the rabbi complaining that "there will not be a gentile left to light the sabbath fires" (work forbidden to religious Jews). Rabbi Loew sings a sabbath prayer and the golem returns to him in the synagogue – later usually identified as Prague's Altneue Shul. To restore the golem to soulless clay, the rabbi again whispers into its ear, then stores it in the synagogue's attic. "No living creature may look at it, particularly women in pregnancy." Anyone who touches the cobwebs covering the inanimate golem dies. And here Peretz hints at the primary legal conundrum that crops up in kabbalistic commentary: he relates that a Prague *tzaddik* wonders, "May such a golem be included in a congregation of worshippers?"; that is, may an animated golem compose part of the quorum needed for daily prayers?⁴⁴ This, and related questions, as whether a golem is "unclean" when it dies (such that priests cannot come near) or whether killing a golem is homicide, beg the larger, central question: is the golem a man in law? He clearly is a legal person, the way a corporation is, but it seems generally he is not an individual. (Again, his usual muteness is a telling detail.) Historically he lacks a *ruakh*, that defining characteristic separating human from animal in Jewish law.

In his *In the Pale: Stories and Legends of the Russian Jews*, published a few years after the Peretz *conte*, Henry Iliowizi includes "The Baal-Shem and His Golem," a quirky golem story that is altogether ignored in scholarly histories and later narratives – perhaps for its quirkiness. Of all the "modern" versions, this is the only one where the golem is forged from iron instead of clay, and by angels, not mortals. Here, uniquely, it looks nothing like a man, and very much like a comic-book avenger, an aspect of the character that itself develops with time.

Also uniquely, while subsequent "champion" versions are concerned with addressing murderous anti-semitism, this golem's job is to redress an aggravation of chronic petty racism in an obscure village in Moghlieff: the local magistrate has forbidden the local Chassidim – the mystic sect – to pray above a whisper, and when they defy him he turns fire hoses on them, breaking out the windows of their synagogue and turning its floor to muck. But the golem awaits no escalation of violence to justify his own. Deliberately choosing the day of the magistrate's wedding to the mayor's Jew-hating daughter, and having consulted the *Book of Creation*, the *Zohar*, and other mystical treatises, the Baal-Shem (a rabbi-mystic) instructs the local smithy on how to conjure and command the avenging angels.[45] Uniquely again, the religious leader has no direct participation in the golem's creation. He is not even present:

> Strange shapes will emerge from the invisible vast to do as thou wilt command. They will vanish at the crowing of the cock, but the thing will be done. Fear them not; they have no power over thee; thou hast power over them. Make them forge for me a horror of black iron. It shall be as awe-inspiring as Death, as terrible as the Plague, gigantic as the Anak who followed Noah's Ark through the waters of the deluge, implacable as Satan the Beast and Lilith the Harlot. Hissing serpents shall be its hair; its eyes shall glow like the fire of hell; from its mouth shall shoot forth a live dragon as tongue; its claws shall be like those of the tiger, and its tail a venomous hydra. The Golem's hands shall reach to the soles of its feet. Dress it in a garb of feathers as black as Abaddon. It shall stride forth with wings outspread, shall breathe fire and vomit flame; a hellish roar shall issue from its throat; and I shall cause it to move and act as a power possessed of reason and will ...

Useless to say that the Golem had been despatched on its bloody way. Its mission was that of the destructive power that

visited every first-born in ancient Egypt. Unspeakable was the horror that seized the people at the sight of the fiendish apparition ...
Toward the Mayor's residence the Golem advanced, rending the
air with infernal notes; therein it disappeared. A minute's dreadful
silence was broken by a tremendous explosion, like the eruption
of a volcano. Showers of flying debris filled the neighborhood,
hurting hundreds of people, who fell prostrate to save their lives.
The convulsion was followed by an outburst of fire and the total
annihilation of the festive dwelling and all therein. As if to complete the desolation, a thunder-storm broke over the city, giving
the ruins an air of Sodom and Gomorrah.[46]

The response seems disproportionate to the evil, the golem skirting
the boundaries of amok and Iliowizi himself characterizing it as "a
gorgon."[47]

Twelve years later saw the publication of a collection of golem stories that have most influenced literary iterations since. While the
Peretz and Iliowizi narratives adumbrate a precedent for the literary
golem as champion, Yudl Rosenberg's *The Golem and the Wondrous
Deeds of the Maharal of Prague* is the beginning and true source of the
narrative's modern era – a model of preventive, retributive, and perhaps redemptive justice that looks forward but also back to its mystical origins.

THE "BLOOD LIBEL" AS THE NARRATIVE'S MOTIVE FORCE   Rosenberg's collection, originally composed in Hebrew and translated into
Yiddish, purports to be a manuscript written by Rabbi Loew's son-in-
law, recounting the creation of a golem to perform domestic chores
and protect Prague's Jews against "blood libels" – accusations, detailed
in Chapter Three, that Jews used the blood of Christians, often children (the blood of the lamb, so to say), in making Passover matzohs.
Although Rosenberg's cumulative narrative reads like a collection
of folk tales, it is sophisticated insofar as at first it shows the rabbi
(the "Maharal," an acronym formed from *Morenu Ha-Rav Loew*, "Our
teacher, Rabbi Loew") successfully refuting the accusations before the
cardinal of Prague and regional priests, thereby winning a promise
from King Rudolf to protect his community.[48] As well, Rosenberg's
stories depict the local rule of law as occasionally functional even for
Jews, who now and again successfully defend secular court prosecutions for ritual murder. In other words, reason precedes violence. But

then the anti-semites prove so persistent and formidable, as led by the obsessively anti-Jewish cleric, Father Thaddeus, that Rabbi Loew must resort to counter-ruses to catch them out, and eventually must rely on the golem and his supernatural powers even for this private detective work. Sometimes the rabbi disguises the golem for this purpose, as a poor deaf mute, in the way that Superman would later disguise himself as Clark Kent, "mild-mannered reporter," when he wasn't fighting for "truth, justice, and the American way."

In his essay, "The Recipe for Life," Michael Chabon provides a neat summary of golem chemistry:

> A golem is brought to life by means of magic formulae, one word at a time. In some accounts, the animating Name of God is inscribed on the golem's forehead, in others, the Name is written on a tablet, and tucked under the blank gray tongue of the golem. Sometimes the magical word is the Hebrew word for truth, *emet*.[49]

(And sure enough, speaking of golem recipes, as Rabbi Loew answers a call to visit King Rudolf in Mulisch's *The Procedure*, he walks down Golden Street, where he views the monarch's "second-rate" alchemists busy in their laboratories pushing past the laws of the physical world. Ever curious Rudolf, it turns out, wants to "order" a golem, with consequences I outline below.) Chabon's "one word at a time" is usually the scheme proposed in the *Book of Creation*. Using that formula and other arcana, Rosenberg's Rabbi Loew, the rabbi's assistant, and his son-in-law make a golem from the mud of the Moldau. "Most of all," Rosenberg tells us, "Rabbi Loew used the golem to fight against the blood libel," generally during the days leading up to Passover. While this golem – named Yossele (a Yiddish diminutive of Yoseyf, Joseph) – was susceptible to mortal injury at the hands of men, he had superhuman strength and when the rabbi "had to send the golem to a place of great danger ... he placed an amulet written on deerskin upon the golem, which made him invisible."[50]

In discussing Cynthia Ozick's use of the golem narratives, we saw how the blood libel begins in the iconography of sacred law, rendering an entire race a scapegoat. That is, Rosenberg's motivation for the action of his stories is canny. Apparently subscribing to the maxim that turnabout is fair play (and thereby justice), one of his stories – "A Very Amazing Tale About a Blood Libel by the Priest Thaddeus Which Caused His Final Downfall and His Banishment from Prague"

– twists the Sir Hugh narrative[51] back on its perpetrators. Passover is two weeks away. The evil priest kidnaps his servant's son as the child plays outside Thaddeus's home. He murders the boy and bottles his blood, contriving matters so that it looks like it is to be sold to prominent Prague Jews, including Rabbi Loew, for baking in matzohs. Thaddeus hides the bottles, labelled with their "buyers'" names, in a derelict pentagonal castle, used as a "squat" by poor Jewish artists, artisans, and vagrants. From various events, paranormal and conventional, Rabbi Loew deduces that some harm is to come to his community by way of the castle. Because of the structural and demonic evils of the deteriorating building, the rabbi sends his golem inside alone to investigate, so that the creature finds the bottles and the child's body. On the rabbi's instructions, the golem moves the body to Thaddeus's cellar, whereupon the priest's scheme is discovered by the police.

THE PRAGUE GOLEM AS A LEADING PRECEDENT OF MODERN, AND MODERNIST, CHAMPIONS OF JUSTICE   The popularity of Rosenberg's stories, particularly as they were translated from Hebrew into Yiddish, spurred a cottage industry in contemporary golem narratives. In 1917, Chayim Bloch published a German version of Rosenberg's golem book, a work that in some literary details is more vivid than Rosenberg's – which is perhaps one way that Bloch rationalized not crediting Rosenberg as its originator.[52] Gustav Meyrink's 1914 novel in German, *The Golem*, ranks with H. Leivick's 1921 Yiddish play of the same name as an expressionist classic of golem lit., a moody, creepy rendering picked up in part in Mulisch's *The Procedure* and, to a lesser extent, in S. Bastomski's brief golem narrative in his *Yiddish Folktales and Legends of Old Prague*, 1923. Meyrink is all gothic, emphasizing the danger of golem creation: his Prague is mostly nightmarish, seemingly that of his own post-World War I era, the setting for a hash of mystical themes, mostly half-digested kabbalism and Blavatsky Rosicrucianism. The golem – which is not necessarily anything manifest beyond the manic-depressive narrator's hallucination – stands at the gateway to the black and white arts, and (harking back to the Peretz narrative) people have died by looking at it in the attic. A spectre, it has no championship role.

Leivick, too, uses the golem as highlight in an atmosphere of insidious racist violence. Yet this not-quite-man, a miserable creature beset by sexual desire and loneliness, capable of speech but lacking the vocabulary to rationalize his own strange existence in the oppressive darkness, has as his main purpose saving the Jews of Prague. The play often feels like free associations on the benighted nature of mankind, tribalism, and violence (the principal and culminating action of Leivick's drama occurs in the frightening pentagonal castle – here called the fifth tower – familiar from Rosenberg), making manifest what is occasionally only suggested in the other narratives of the day (Dovid Frishman's, discussed below, being a notable exception) – a sense of cruelty in his creation as the plaything of show-off mystics: the golem is the ultimate stranger in a strange land, and in that way he embodies all Jewish suffering. Like Adam after the Fall, he has free will, but constantly is brow-beaten to ignore it.

Bastomski's version has no championship theme: the golem is merely a domestic servant, a Frankenstein's monster that must be destroyed after he runs amok, killing animals and uprooting a tree. But as discussed earlier, this danger element has significant legal relevance, inculcating the central constitutional principle of Hebraic society: there is one God and man shall not attempt to steal his thunder in any sense, even to the extent of "making graven images." Chabon and Mulisch add the gloss, implicitly, that creators of narratives share this risk. "The idea of the novelist as the little God of his creation," Chabon writes in his "Recipe" essay

> – *present partout et visible nulle part* – is a key tenet of the traditional novelist .... But what gripped me, as I read and re-read Scholem's essay ["The Idea of the Golem," as quoted above], was not the metaphor or allegory of the *nature* of making golems and novels, but that of the *consequences* thereof.
>
> "Golem-making is dangerous," Scholem writes, "like all major creation it endangers the life of the creator – the source of danger, however, is not the golem ... but the man himself." From the golem that grew so large that it collapsed, killing a certain Rabbi Elijah in Poland, to Frankenstein's monster, golems frequently end by threatening or even taking the lives of their creators.
>
> When I read these words I saw at once a connection to my own work. Anything good that I have written has, at some point during its composition, left me feeling uneasy and afraid. It has seemed, for a moment at least, to put me at risk.

Dovid Frishman's "The Golem," a short story of 1922, is a sort of *conte morale* on the legal and mortal dangers, as well as a dialogue – a dialectic, really – on materialism versus metaphysics. Frishman's man-from-clay is "able to destroy the entire world,"[53] but agonizes between the gravitational poles of his existence – the carnal (or earthly-material) versus the spiritual, immediate gratification versus supposed eternal fulfillment, with the two extremes represented by Rabbi Loew's granddaughter, pointedly called Eve, and the rabbi himself. Eve, as persistent temptress, makes the golem "human" by kissing him, as a princess would a talking frog in a pagan fairy tale. With her raging hormones she is frequently more Lilith than Eve – Lilith being, in Jewish folklore, Adam's first wife, who broke with him over his refusal to see her as an equal, such that she blasphemed by uttering the Name (in a forbidden, destructive instead of meditative/communing/creative context) and took up on her own as a succubus.[54] Overcome with lust for the golem, this modernized Eve promises, "I will be God's name" to him, and in his arms decides that "evidently a human created by human hands is a thousand times more perfect and more beautiful than a figure created by God."[55] She makes love with the golem (apparently) in a churchyard and mortuary, such that the creative "crimes" become mingled with carnality verging on the Dantesque, or perhaps Blakean – blasphemy, fornication, perversity, all of it arising from the innocence of youthful empiricism,[56] doubt, and sexuality. In the mortal world, creation is ineluctably related to sex. This golem, torn between desire and the Law (arguably, between the law and why we need it in a fallen world), has dignity, but partly for that reason, he is no champion. He has free will that resists the Law and the primary prescription that he is to obey his maker.

Thereafter, the golem seldom appears in significant literary works until 1982, when Cynthia Ozick published "Puttermesser and Xanthippe" in the literary magazine *Salmagundi*, as an instalment in the saga[57] of Ruth Puttermesser. Recall that she creates Xanthippe more or less in the manner of Rabbi Loew, extending the archetypology: God makes Adam, Rabbi Loew creates the golem, Frankenstein creates his homemade man-child, Puttermesser constructs the mute child Xanthippe. We noted how Ozick parodies the archetypal pattern of creation myths, constructing a "daughter of woman" where the Jewish Bible gives us a supreme being creating a foredoomed mortal and Christianity supplies the balm, a "son of man" who promises redemption and immortality in Paradise. The animistic root-stalk is obvious – the cycle of creation mimicking the cycle of nature, just as spring and creation or birth gives way to summer's maturity which leads to autumn's ageing and ends in winter's death – until Christ redeems time and the entropy that defines it. Characterizing this sort of motif as "polytheistic confusion,"[58] Scholem recalls the Jewish legend that Adam's grandson, Enoch, asked his father Seth about the family ancestry. Advised that God had created Grandpa straight from the earth, Enoch sought to replicate the experiment. He made a mud-man, but then complained to his father that it just lay there. Seth explained that to give Adam life, God had breathed into his nostrils. Seth tried this on his golem. "Satan came and slipped into the figure and so gave it an appearance of life. So the name of God was desecrated, and idolatry began ..."[59] Here the *Et in Arcadia ego* theme is made manifest, evil being instrumental in the golem's "birth" from the dust to which it returns, or at least animating the creature as it had Adam and Eve in the Garden. In each case, the creation becomes wilful and spurns the control of its creator, such that, one way or another, it fashions the conditions of its own destruction.

Such magical justice as the golem might provide is nostalgic, a hankering after a time when the weight of responsibility sat lightly upon us. Typically, of course, it is memoir nostalgia, looking backward through the lens of our childhood innocence, so that the world itself seems to have been, if not happier, at least imbued with the promise of perfection, a worldly Adam-and Eve paradise. Such is the atmosphere of Michael Chabon's *The Amazing Adventures of Kavalier and Clay* (2000), never mind that its backdrop is the Jewish Holocaust. Its central theme, in fact, is manifold escapism, even for Rabbi Loew's golem of Prague, whose story Chabon picks up.

As a young teenager, Josef Kavalier escapes from Prague to Lithuania in a coffin *with* the inanimate golem (returned to Moldavian clay), which he has helped spirit out of Czechoslovakia so as to protect it from Nazi depredations. He continues on to Manhattan, where, to fund his dream of bringing his family as refugees to the United States, he creates highly successful comic books with his cousin, Sammy Clay (né Klayman).[60] As Kavalier is a talented pencil artist but also has trained as a magician and amateur escape artist with a Czech master, the cousins build their comics enterprise on a character called The Escapist, a Houdini-like figure and all-around Nazi-whipper.

In writing the adventures that Kavalier brings to life as ironic magician, Clay provides the material for this modern Rabbi Loew: hence Sammy's surname, which of course could as easily have been Word (or perhaps Wortman). The team's comic-book plots feature their super-hero champions despatching Nazi leaders and minions as horribly as possible. (The boys' struggle with their publisher to maintain that theme mirrors the resistance of the American public to enter the second world war, Chabon depicting this reluctance as an offence against natural justice.) Kavalier saves enough money and lobbies persistently to bring his younger brother and other child-refugees to New York in a ship commissioned for the purpose, only to see it sunk by a U-boat. He abandons the comics business and joins the Navy, evidently so that he can take direct revenge on Germany, but finds himself stationed in the Antarctic ... where, as sole survivor in his platoon, he shoots (by misadventure) a similarly lonesome, equally pathetic German geologist, while trying to befriend the man.

When Kavalier returns to New York and emerges from seclusion to begin rebuilding his life – again, more or less rescued by Clay – the golem's coffin itself makes its way to join him in the New World. Inside, the golem has crumbled to dust, like the cousins' other childish ideas of magic, escape, earthly justice, and championship. Chabon gives us a "happy" ending, but it is heavily mitigated by a pervasive air of loss, mortality, and Clay's benighted life: where continental Kavalier is tall, brave, handsome, bright, athletic, the better artist, Clay is runty, earnest, lonely, and a self-denying homosexual; for the brief time that he is partly "out of the closet," his lover is *treyf* – unkosher – even in name: Bacon, an indulgence of assimilation in the New World. Clay's business interests fail, he is ambivalent father to Kavalier's son and miserable husband to his cousin's former lover (during Kavalier's long and silent absence); he is for all intents and purposes impotent, even to the extent that his artistic creations all falter and die out. The Old World has died with the golem, the Holocaust, and the idea that we can escape back to some earthly paradise. In the fallen world, evil persists and death has the last word. Magic is all artifice, and true justice is a fiction, pure only when it is poetic, metaphorical.

In Mulisch's *The Procedure* – written in 1998 but published in English a year after *Kavalier* – the champion theme is oblique and the most thoroughly modern in its self-conscious ironies. Rabbi Loew makes the golem because King Rudolf wants one. Loew is reluctant, but extracts a royal promise that Rudolf will protect Prague's Jews to the best of his ability. In other words, Rudolf is the actual (and correspondingly reluctant or at least dubious and ironic) champion.

Mulisch's interest in the golem legends concerns not justice by championship but what they tell us about creation and the Word, and particularly – again – the dangers (sins or crimes against nature) of playing God. The first part of the book is metafictional in this way, proposing, like Chabon in his "Recipe" essay, that writing novels is a form of golem-making. Like Ozick's Puttermesser, Mulisch's Loew creates a "Lilith, not an Adam, " if not deliberately: his son-in-law has made an error in reciting the meditative formulae and the creature's penis remains caked mud that comes free in the rabbi's hand. As with most versions of golem creation in the manner of God with Adam, the danger is made palpable. Mulisch explores the two sides of Lilith (herself an invention of kabbalists), as the benign first wife of Adam (created at the same time as Adam), but also as the succubus who rages in jealousy against Eve. In Mulisch's telling, Loew destroys the golem after it runs wild and murders (and perhaps rapes) his son-in-law, whose wife, Esther (the namesake of another famous champion for justice against anti-semites), has left him with the couple's triplet sons. This plot is mirrored in the larger, contemporary story of Victor Werker, a brilliant scientist who creates a monocellular life form (a crystal) from inorganic matter. (Here, the triplets become strangers whom Werker's mother nursed at the same time she was nursing him.) Yet the parallel between Werker and Loew is everywhere blurred: Werker remains impotent otherwise than in his work, with a daughter (Aurora, she that brings the sun or light) having been still-born, possibly as part of the judgment on his attempts to usurp godly powers. The "milk-uncles" are a sort of male version of the judgmental Furies of classical mythology, and Werker's accuser (and perhaps executioner) is the same art expert, Netter, who nominates him as "the greatest surrogate child-maker in the visual arts in the twentieth century," before an international committee. The committee is one of several struck by a consortium of European television networks producing a series called "The Verdict," and tasked with choosing the most important achievers of the past millennium. Netter compares Werker to Pygmalion and, allusively, one supposes, to the maker of Lilith-golems: "The misogynist carved the figure of a naked woman from ivory, with which he fell in love and which came to life. Through the intervention of Aphrodite the ivory turned to flesh and blood. Well, that's what I call creation. He has abolished the boundary between art and reality."[61] In doing the same, Werker is heroic within the scientific and technological communities, but suffers ironic judgment in the sphere of metaphor and the spirit: he is subject to poetic justice. A page later, Werker wonders: "Nietzsche's Zarathustra had a vision of God being dead – had he Victor, himself, actually perhaps eliminated God a hundred years later by creating life? Is the soul of the commandment that thou shalt not kill perhaps the commandment that thou shalt not create life?" That, after all, is the legacy of Adam and Eve. Werker flees from the broadcast venue, to his own godlike death – stabbed, apparently by Netter, after passing "by the Altneuschul, beneath the clock of the Jewish town hall whose hands move in the opposite direction, [where he stops] in a sweat and with his heart pounding [to] take a deep breath." Time cycles back and forth. Like Adam, like Rabbi Loew's golem, his creation of life has brought death into the world.

While golem stories are often compared to *Frankenstein*, Mulisch's version is perhaps the most direct parallel in modern literature: the back-firing creation is a matter of pure science, not an instrument of justice or the result of total surrender to a higher power. It seeks, in fact, to beat that power at its own game, and therein lies its crime.

Case Five: Magical Realism Revisited:
The Magical Legalism of Marcel Aymé

If we view a justice system as irremediably broken, one literary recourse is magic realism. This is the use Cynthia Ozick makes of golem narratives – albeit to tell us that, as human creations in a fallen world, the justice achieved even through them ultimately fails. Then again, there are the stories of Marcel Aymé,[62] where metaphysical powers alter the law though it is not necessarily viewed as corrupt. Aymé's characters often align themselves with what we have called charming rogues, as opposed to moral outlaws who seek revolutionary change.

Some such rogues are more charming than others. A prime, and delightful, example is M. Duperrier in the celebrated story "Grace."[63] Duperrier is the best Christian not just on his street, but in all of Montmartre of 1939. He is so "just and charitable," in fact, that one day he finds a halo hovering rakishly about his forehead on a slant, like a beret. He cannot dislodge this luminous distinction no matter how hard his wife tries to wrench it off. She, it turns out, finds the halo profoundly embarrassing. What will the neighbours think? Cousin Leopold, with his fancy car and villa? What will the local shopkeepers say?

Too embarrassed to leave the house with her husband in his cocked, over-sized and slightly luminescent head-covering, unable to sleep because of the heavenly glow by which Duperrier reads the Bible in bed, the devout Mme. Duperrier hits on a plan: "It's simple," she tells her pious spouse. "All you have to do is sin." Duperrier prays to God. These were the days before the law – or conventional (arguably male-dominated) wisdom – knew reasonable persons; there were only reasonable men.[64] Women, rightly or wrongly, were generally viewed as ruled by impulse and passion more than by reason. "You know women," Duperrier tells God. "My wife is losing the will to live. Worse, the day is coming that her hatred of my halo will cause her to curse the heaven which has given it to me." Duperrier decides that it is his "duty of Christian charity" to take his wife's advice.

He outdoes himself in envy, sloth, and anger – when Mme. Duperrier complains that the halo just keeps hanging on, he howls, "'You wallow in sin as a favour to women, and here's the thanks you get'" – but, given the price of lobster and fine wine, he struggles with the conflict between avarice and gluttony, never mind that he economizes by donating buttons from his underpants in the parish charity box. By 1944 he resolves the ambiguities sufficiently to maintain his new-found obesity, no longer envisioning Paradise as "a symphony of souls in diaphanous robes" but as "a vast dining room." Though he occasionally beats Mme. Duperrier when not rounding on her to "shut her face," she decides that a husband who is "an atheist, playboy, and potty-mouth like cousin Leopold was preferable to a haloed one. At least he didn't embarrass her in front of the milkman."

Though Duperrier and his wife have avoided lust as the most satanic of the deadly sins, at last the desperate Mme. buys her husband a sex manual and he ends up a pimp, "kicking the arse" of his twenty-five-year-old *putain* to "reinvigorate her flagging ardour" in the streets. The young woman, whose earnings Duperrier tots up by the light of his halo, had come to Montmartre to serve as maid to a municipal councillor. But he turned out to be a socialist and atheist, and she could not stand to work for "godless people." By contrast, Duperrier and his halo "could not help but make a strong impression on this little pious soul," who sees him as "the equal" of Saint Ives – patron saint of lawyers – and Saint Ronan. Indeed, while Mme. Duperrier has suggested it would be more economical to practice the sin of lust in the marriage bed, as "a loyal husband" Duperrier has "courageously" determined that he should take his appetites elsewhere so as not to risk his wife's salvation.

And what of that persisting halo? As Frye puts it, Duperrier's "motive in doing all this was so fundamentally innocent that the halo stayed firmly in place."[65] "But from the depths of his failures and abjection," Aymé recounts in the story's final sentence, "throughout the dark night of his conscience, a murmur of thanks sometimes passes his lips, to God, that His gifts are absolutely unconditional."[66] By Heaven's judgment, Duperrier, steadfast in his faith in a higher rule of law, has acted reasonably.

An earlier Aymé story makes the same point by the more conventional and direct route. In "L'Huissier," "The Bailiff," the title character – sporting the Dickensian surname of Malicorne ("Badhorn") – arrives at Heaven's Gate to be cross-examined by St. Peter. The Gatekeeper shows blatant bias against those of Malicorne's profession and is further offended that Malicorne lists in his favour that, not only did he leave no debts of his own, but he did his job of enforcing against widows and orphans cheerfully and efficiently. Malicorne appeals to God, who is loath to admit him directly to Heaven but cannot send him straight to Hell because St. Peter has denied him natural, procedural justice. So God gives Malicorne another chance on earth to redeem himself – a new trial, as it were.

Resurrected, Malicorne becomes an obsessive donor to the poor and oppressed, and spontaneously offers pay-raises to his assistant and maid, never mind – as he earnestly remarks on his ledger of good and bad deeds – that they don't deserve them, and that, in particular, his maid is a slut. He approaches his redemption as literally and assiduously as he does his job, so that the "bad" column (by his own reckoning) remains nearly spotless. Finally, he visits a building owned by his biggest client, a slum landlord, where Malicorne gives a poor seamstress some money and dandles her little son on his knee. In his former life, he would have been at the flat, of course, but to seize the single mother's meagre belongings in lieu of unpaid rent. Sure enough, the landlord arrives and tells the seamstress that she is out of chances to pay her arrears of rent. Spontaneously, Malicorne intervenes and tells the landlord to get lost. The landlord shoots him dead.

Back before St. Peter and God, Malicorne tries to enumerate all the donations totted up in his moral accounts book. But, beaming at him, they don't want to hear of these supposed good deeds. "You have only one to your credit," St. Peter says – the fact that in Malicorne's final confrontation with the landlord he yelled "Down with landlords!" "Absolutely beautiful," God agrees. "He yelled it twice," St. Peter elaborates with pride, "and he died the very moment he was defending a poor woman against the rapaciousness of her landlord."[67] Where motive is generally irrelevant to crime under mortal positive law, it is crucial in the world of sacred law. And where the law might side with landlords, Heaven mitigates for the poor.

In this world below we are governed by shadows of Heaven (real or perceived); the secular godhead is the legislature and common law. Our secular priests – the interpreters of mortal law – are judges. And they tell us that the negligent or self-absorbed – not to mention gluttons and leches, the covetous, and slothful – are by definition unreasonable, more often than not blots on the rule of law. For this reason, we have classed reason as epiphanic, or emblematic of our nostalgia for perfect justice.

"Grace" makes graphic our earlier point that, though crime is the paradigmatic equivalent of sin, they are not always commensurate. In most of western society, adultery, atheism, and even promoting nonviolent anarchy are not crimes under secular law. While the seven deadly sins can lead to crime, they are not criminal in themselves. Otherwise, our prisons would be even more crowded with the greedy, overfed, and oversexed. At the same time, it is true that in secular law a reasonable person is probably not an anarchist or a welfare bum or a glutton, and generally he does not let sexual desire interfere with his better judgment. If he covets his neighbour's wife, he probably thinks better of seducing her. Reasonableness, in other words, often tracks morality: while all sins are not crimes, sin can almost always correspond with legal unreasonableness.

In his essay on crime and sin in the Bible, Northrop Frye remarks that the

> original Christian distinction between sin and crime was a part of the revolutionary aspect of Christianity, and the progressive blurring of the distinction was the result of the revolutionary impulse being smothered under new forms of entrenched privilege ... Christianity holds that Jesus was without sin, yet he was put to death as a criminal.[68]

We have seen that justice lies in the interstices, or at least that is how our literary narratives see it: to be just, law must have a moral component. Thus arises what Frye calls "the relativity of crime," the situation where a Robin Hood or Winston Smith (or Nelson Mandela or a resistance fighter in Vichy France) becomes a reasonable man. Frye then notes, "Whether the relativity of crime could also apply to sin or not is a more difficult question," and he proffers "Grace" as an example. The point is, while a man might remain pious when he sins for the right reasons, it is generally no legal excuse that to feed his family X robs banks politely or that he kills rival gang member Y while Y sleeps in his bed to stop Y doing the same to X at some unknown future date. The relativity that Frye mentions is one of social-political perception: crime and tort are what a given society defines them to be, such that Nazism or Jim Crow laws or apartheid can be "legal" in a given time and place. Sin, on the other hand, always retains its character as sin. Even if sometimes it is forgivable, it is absolute.

In other words, what differs in sacred narratives about sin and secular narratives about crime is the law's reaction. In being favoured by intangible, unearthly forces, Duperrier has one foot in the realm of metaphor. He is, by Heaven's lights, an irrevocably reasonable man, above we mere mortals, halfway to Paradise. He is subject to grace, forgiveness, redemption. But stuck here on Earth, we have no empirical proof of this: grace is all narrative, an imagining of received law and wisdom, stretching from classical myth through the Hebrew and Christian Bibles to Marcel Aymé's writing desk in the 1940s.

It must be said, however, that while Aymé writes often about piety and sin, his conception of religious justice can be inconsistent. In his "Poldéve Legend" (collected in the same volume as "Grace"), a woman who has lived a long, pious life dies a virgin. But at Heaven's gate she is made to wait in a long line behind the legions of soldiers dying in World War II, all comers on both sides admitted without question. Both factions, after all, claim God on their side. Outraged, the woman bends an attending angel's ear about her long years of devotion to God and the church – "Morning prayers, thanksgiving, six hours of mass every day. After mass, special prayers to St. Joseph and of thanks to the Virgin" – and she is about to be waved through the gate when St. Peter's attention is distracted by the spring offensive beginning on the Poldevian front. At last the woman is able to jump the queue, dubiously accepting a ride on a horse with her soldier-nephew, a ruthless thief and rapist she previously has disowned. When St. Peter challenges the nephew about "that woman" behind him on his saddle, the nephew replies that she is the regimental whore. "Oh, okay, then," St. Peter says, "go on in." Is this poetic justice encapsulated? (For Aymé, at least here and in "The Bailiff," apparently St. Peter can be cavalier as a supreme judge.)

Insofar as mortal law is irredeemably imperfect, there is no redemption for completely earthbound mortals, at least outside poetic justice – some sort of ending contrived by the author of his narrative (the ultimate Lawgiver in the context) that makes what they do all right. Again, this is where law and literature generally meet, to bridge the gap between law and justice. Where the law by itself cannot forgive the studiously unreasonable or anti-social man, literature, like sacred law, can grant him grace. Literature permits reperfected justice, pure justice that stretches back towards Eden, if often ironically these days.

This is the central analytical point one can make about the story "Dermuche."[69] The title character is an idiot – an apish, mostly docile simpleton who kills three pensioners simply so that he can have one of their phonograph records for his own unimpeded use. He just cannot get enough of the tune (a "ritornello," Aymé says) they listened to every Sunday. He is sentenced to the guillotine but doesn't mind, insofar as he is confident of spending eternity with Jesus. But the prison chaplain despairs of getting him to feel enough remorse for redemption or at least suspension of the death penalty. In matters of religious feeling, Dermuche can't get beyond what the chaplain tells him about Christ's birth – that the saviour was born in a stable between a cow and an ass to show us mortals that he is a friend of the dispossessed, including prisoners. Dermuche takes this to mean that Christ could as easily have been born in a prison, but not among "*les rentiers*" (the pensioners). Nothing else in the narrative of Christ's life makes sense to him, not literally let alone metaphorically. Oblivious to the social harm he has done, he writes a letter to Jesus in which he describes the *rentiers* as bastards and asks that, after he is guillotined, the lord provide him the beloved phonograph record in Heaven. Doubting that simple-minded Dermuche could have formed the requisite intent to commit capital murder, the chaplain prays for him and deposits the letter in a crèche. On December 24, the day scheduled for Dermuche's beheading (Aymé lays it on a bit thick here), the chaplain and prison officials discover that, overnight in his prison cot, Dermuche has time-travelled back to infancy. Anxious that their careers will be compromised should Dermuche use any ruse to escape the guillotine, the prison officials guillotine the infant. He's not as innocent as the baby Jesus (in their view), he's Dermuche the murdering simpleton, and still has the tattoos to prove it. After the execution, it occurs to Dermuche's lawyer that, if God has wiped out his client's first go at life, then by the same magic the murders never happened. He verifies that the *rentiers* are alive and that their neighbours are unaware of any recent crime in Nogent-sur-Marne. However, the *rentiers* complain that, the previous night, someone stole their phonograph record, which was sitting on the dining room table. Where mortal law is weak and subject to human materialism, sacred law provides perfect, poetic justice. Born innocent into a world of sin and crime, everybody gets that second chance. Dermuche has died for our (and his own) sins.

In Aymé magic is often a diversion from bourgeois, materialist experience. His "fantastic" stories sometimes share with golem narratives the yearning for better justice, and also those narrative's "wisdom" that such justice cannot be permanently achieved in the mundane physical world. While proudly capable of breaking in and out of prison at will, and greedy of the celebrity it brings him, Dutilleul, protagonist of "The Man Who Could Walk Through Walls," ends up encased in a courtyard wall, outside his married lover's home. Although he has become a folk hero whose powers have allowed him to drive his obnoxious boss mad, amass a fortune through burglary, and win over a beautiful mistress, they fail him at last, horrifically, as in an Edgar Allan Poe story. His mortality defeats his vanity of godliness, punishing him capitally for his sin-crimes not of burglary or even adultery, but of pride and taking onto himself the trappings of ultimate authority – sedition and idolatry all wrapped up, as in biblical times. This in itself is characteristic of Aymé, who likes to confound physical and metaphysical, sacred and profane, perhaps as a product of a profoundly Catholic culture coming to grips with the harsh realities of wartime Europe.

The story can also be seen as an extended parody of the archetypal symbol that Frye calls the *hortus conclusus* or enclosed garden "derived from the Song of Songs," where the bridegroom says of his bride, "A garden enclosed is my sister, my love; a spring shut up, a fountain sealed." The symbol, of conquering barriers to earthly (commonly sexual) Paradise, "derives," Frye says, "from the body of the Virgin" Mary.[70] It recurs in tales where suitors attempt to scale walls and towers or cross moats, etc., to tryst with captive or reluctant lovers (as in "Rapunzel," for example). Here, the symbolic narrative takes an ironic turn when the tryst kills the suitor. For Dutilleul, Paradise is not only inside various enclosures, but without, insofar as he is able to move in or out of anywhere, even the securest prison, at will. But this gift is also his entrapment – his Hell on Earth, where practising godlike magic is suicidal.

In "The Ration Card" and "The Decree," law – now itself a form of human vanity – is used to alter the passage of time. In the former, set in wartime, non-productive citizens are permitted to exist only a certain number of days per month. But human nature is such that the system fails – a black market develops for extra days and the rich and useless (including writers) find their way around the law. Scalpers defeat its purpose. In "The Decree," arrogant governments attempt to avoid the depredations of war by moving time ahead by seventeen years. Law becomes an opiate, imposing a sleep and a forgetting; the causes and horrors of war remain unaddressed. The narrator finds that by fiat, he has lost seventeen years of his life without living them – never mind that he has fathered two more children and lost his youth. He is like the Cumean sybil, who forgot to ask for eternal youth when the gods granted her eternal life.

(By contrast, the time-travel magic in "Dermuche" is a product of divine law, in reparation for the failings of mortal law. In "The Decree," time travel is forward, attempting by government fiat to wipe out the interim, which it does only in consciousness: it is law as denial of material truth and human immorality. In "Dermuche," there is no denial but redemption from a failure of mortal law and order, not to mention morality and justice.)

We find a similar if particularly creepy fatalism in *Les Sabines*. To rationalize her magical ability to commit adultery across the planet, with 67,000 lovers simultaneously, Sabine Lemurier tries to finesse both morality and law intellectually: she has broken neither sacred nor secular law, she reasons, insofar as marriage is not a union of bodies but of souls, and anyway secular law has not considered the question of ubiquity. "But she had too refined a conscience to take advantage of such lawyerly reasoning," Aymé tells us. Sabine's adulteries are "perfectly damnable." There follows the horrific come-uppance, beyond Dantesque, suffered at first by a scapegoat iteration (every community needs a goat, after all, to mitigate the harshness of the law), Louise Mégnin, but ultimately by the Sabines worldwide. The scapegoat lives in a hovel, where she is regularly raped by a stinking apeman, and the torture is all the harder for the reader to bear given the otherwise bemused charm – typically Aymesque – of the narrative. When Louise-Sabine dies, so does her worldwide cohort: as with Duperrier and his halo, as with wall-walker Dutilleul – and as with the fragile, pre-law immortality of Adam and Eve in Eden – Sabine's gift is her curse.

Analytically, these stories conjoin to show us the dark heart of Aymé's unique blend of charm and sadism (or at least fatalism): his magic realism is, finally, deeply cynical, about human nature and also its attempts to civilize itself under law. The childlike magic, playful and jokey in context, ends up, at best, childish illusion, mirroring the egocentric and wilful innocence of his protagonists. It doesn't achieve anything permanent, let alone perfect justice, because its metaphysics are firmly bound to the physical, fallen world. In this sense the stories are also deeply entrenched in the underlying Judeo-Christian narrative: the protagonists are punished for sin more than for crime – pride throughout, plus murder (and all the other sins of war) and playing at God in "The Decree," greed and playing at God in "The Ration Card," adultery and lust in *The Sabines*. Everywhere there is a religious or moral tension between carnality and guilt: sin is beyond commensurate with crime; as subject to a higher law, it is worse, yet often excusable as inevitably human.

Glossary of Some Terms
Used in This Book

ARCHETYPE   In literature, a "communicable unit ... a typical or recurring image ... a symbol which connects one [work] with another and thereby helps to unify and integrate our literary experience. And as the archetype is the communicable symbol, archetypal criticism is primarily concerned with literature as a social fact and as a mode of communication. By the study of conventions and genres, it attempts to fit poems [or literary works] into the body of poetry [literature] as a whole." Northrop Frye, *Anatomy of Criticism* (Princeton University Press, 1957), 99.

COMEDY   I use a technical definition of "comedy," drawn from literary criticism. It is based on the ending of the narrative in question, and depends on the stark dichotomy of comedy v. tragedy, with no middle ground. By "comedy," we mean a narrative that is not necessarily funny, but in which there is a renewal at the end – in which there is a happy ending, a new order. In this sense Shakespeare's *Measure for Measure* is a comedy (although it provides only the occasional chuckle), as are (surprisingly enough) the Book of Job and the narrative of the life of Christ. (You can see how this stark contrast works when you compare Christ's biography to its tragic analogue, the story of Moses.) Henry James put it wonderfully, describing the literary comic as "a distribution at the last of prizes, pensions, husbands, wives, babies, millions, appended paragraphs, and cheerful remarks." Think not just of Shakespeare, but of Dickens, or even Harry Potter. Despite horrific events and injustices, as the action concludes, there is a sense that a transcendent (or higher) justice prevails.

FICTION   See "myth."

JUSTICE   For the purposes of this book, I am not using "justice" in any complex philosophical sense. When I say "justice," I mean what the ordinary, reasonable person in our society would say is fair in the circumstances. Generally, because the law by itself often does not provide what we feel to be true justice, this amounts to grafting some moral principle onto the law as we know it. (This vernacular "definition" comes close to what the legal philosopher John Rawls means by "justice," but with an everyday conception of fairness, a conception that does not necessarily envision restructuring Western society. It is perhaps most like what legal theorists call "intuitional" justice.)

LEGAL FICTION   A metaphysical or imaginary state or person peculiar to legal discourse; e.g., the reasonable person (who is too nearly perfect to be real), the now extinct rule in family law that husband and wife were "one flesh" (a single person), the similarly outmoded concept that women were not "persons," the persisting idea that corporations *are* persons, the aged rule in estates law that, where it appears that people die simultaneously, or nearly so, their order of dying is determined by their ages, the oldest having died first, the youngest last ... See *supra* (at 47–8) regarding Empson's poetic consideration of such matters, and particularly how they reflect what he sees as human vanity – or perhaps arrogance.

MORAL (HEROIC) OUTLAW   In our "structural" context, fictional personages like Robin Hood, who though technically outlaws (in his case, literally outside the law's protection), perceive the rule of law to have become corrupted and therefore act against authority so as to restore the ideal legal order, and thereby favour justice (or at least their notion of it) over law as enforced in the society.

MYTH   In archetypal or myth criticism, a myth is something a group of people have believed to be true but is not provable by everyday experience or science. For instance, before and during the classical period some believed that life on earth arose when a sky father (a sun god) sprinkled his seed (rain and light) on an earth mother, who was receptive to this in the spring and summer. In the sense that it is non-empirical, myth is imaginative, like fiction. However, while the term includes religious narratives, it does not confirm, deny, or criticize religious belief. It merely signifies that we are looking at the literary, not the religious, aspects of the narrative – as, for example, in the story of Job: whether we believe it is factual is irrelevant to law-and-literature studies; we are looking at it as a story that forms a central part of our imaginative life as a community. (Religious writing often uses narrative, even where it speaks of law.) A *fiction* is something imagined ("made up") but that no one has taken to be real. Nevertheless, it remains pertinent, if trite, that fiction is often "truer than reality," just as myths are.

NATURAL JUSTICE Usually, this refers to procedural rights in administrative hearings, and, when used precisely, does not encompass the more general concepts of justice we discuss here. This book sometimes uses the term more broadly, in which cases it is less distinct from "justice" and from "natural law."

NATURAL LAW To the legal historian, this can have various shades of meaning. See, for example, the definition in *Black's Law Dictionary*. Generally, though, when we speak of natural law we mean (as the *Canadian Oxford Dictionary* or *COD* puts it), "unchanging moral principles common to all people by virtue of their nature as human beings" – the basic "rights" we are born with, as with the rights to life, liberty, self-determination, etc. Non-lawyers, including Prof. Frye, often confuse this with "the law of nature," which of course is animalistic and Darwinian (and therefore not the same thing at all). *Black's* defines our law's use of "natural" as "proceeding from or determined by physical causes or conditions, as distinguished from positive enactments of law, or attributable to the nature of man rather than to the commands of law, or based upon moral rather than legal considerations or sanctions." Compare, then, "natural law" to "positive law," *infra*.

PARADIGM *COD*: "1 an example or pattern followed ... 2 a mode of viewing the world which underlies the theories and methodology of science etc. in a particular period of history." A repeating structure, framework.

POETIC JUSTICE This book uses an expansive notion of the concept, which the *COD* defines as "well-deserved unforeseen retribution or reward," as where *Hamlet* speaks of a traitorous assassin being killed by his own bomb ("hoist with his own petard"), or where a nasty blabber-mouth at the office loses his voice when he's supposed to give an important presentation. I use the term poetically (as it were), to signify how literature redresses the gap between law and justice. Consider, for example, the circumstances of Allie Fox at the end of *The Mosquito Coast*. (Thus a motto for my law-and-literature course, "Law is prose, justice is poetry.")

POSITIVE LAW   "Law actually and specifically enacted or adopted by proper authority for the government of an organized jural society." (*Black's Law Dictionary*, fifth ed., which defines "jural society" as "the synonym of 'state' or 'organized political community.'")

(THE) RULE OF LAW usually refers to circumstances where a society is governed by set laws and principles. In democratic countries, we tend to assume that this is a good thing, but of course not all law is benign or respects natural law and justice. In Nazi Germany, Jim Crow America, and apartheid-era South Africa, for example, racism was completely legal and institutionalized.

Notes

CHAPTER ONE

1 Posner, *Law and Literature*.
2 Frye, *Anatomy of Criticism*, 96–104.
3 Who often have some illuminating things to say. I think.
4 His learning was awesome in the original sense of that word, but it is sometimes clear that it did not extend to jurisprudence. He makes some basic mistakes when he talks about law, and I think he is just wrong when he remarks near the end of his life that the Ten Commandments are perhaps not meant as law but to signify an unearthly standard of perfection, "auguries of innocence" (*Biblical and Classical Myths*, 214, hereinafter *BCM*). This misses their constitutional aspect, as a founding document of Israel's monotheism (though Frye is correct, of course, that they are different from the other Deuteronomic law, which is basically regulatory), and when he says two pages later that attempts to "incorporate" the more positive morality of "the gospel in legislation" is doomed because obedience would be impossible, he confuses law with perfected justice, which is law tempered with morality and hope. See my discussion of the works of Marcel Aymé in Chapter Six.
5 Probably the best known arguments along these lines are those of Judge Richard Posner in *Law and Literature*, and Julie Stone-Peters, in "Law, Literature and the Vanishing Real: On the Future of an Interdisciplinary Illusion."
6 In this context, I am constantly reminded of Eric Nicol, explaining in his introduction to *Shall We Join the Ladies* why he had to write his own introduction: lately, the professors who used to do it for free, or a desk copy, "have become aware of money – God knows how," and besides, "[a]ll the critics, including the minor ones, are busy writing books and see no reason

why they should waste time giving you praise in your book when they can
be giving you hell in their own."

7 As a reviewer of the manuscript has commented, it is only fair to add that
while many writers in law-literature studies have no literary theory, it is even
more evident, lately, that many "liberal arts" academics publishing in the field
are not legally literate. As the reviewer put it: "The point, I suppose, is that true
interdisciplinarity is not about dabbling in other people's pools. It's about
reading across the disciplines thoughtfully and over a long period of time."

8 Weisberg, *Poethics and Other Strategies of Law and Literature.*

9 August 8, 2011, 64.

10 I take it this is Julie Stone-Peters's main point.

11 See my *Where There's Life, There's Lawsuits: Not Altogether Serious Ruminations
on Law and Life* (Toronto: ECW Press 2003), 139–44.

CHAPTER TWO

1 Rilke, *Der Tod Moses*, 1915, trans. J.B. Leishman, in *Poems 1906–26* (New
York: New Directions, 1957).

2 Freud, *Moses and Monotheism.*

3 For the purposes of this analysis, I am not using "justice" in any complex
philosophical sense. When I say "justice," I mean what the ordinary, reasonable person in our society would say is fair in the circumstances, more or
less what legal theorists call "common-sense intuitive" justice. Usually,
because the law by itself often does not provide what we feel to be true justice, this amounts to grafting some moral principle onto the law as we
know it. (This vernacular "definition" comes close to what the legal philosopher John Rawls means by "justice," but with an everyday conception of
fairness, a conception that does not necessarily envision restructuring western society.)

4 Reik, *Mystery on the Mountain: The Drama of the Sinai Revelation*, 52–3.

5 See Frye, *Anatomy of Criticism*, 152.

6 I am assuming most readers would agree that Joshua's entrance into
Canaan in place of Moses is *anti*-climax, and, again, this all has reverberating implications for the legal-literary scholar.

7 Buber, *Moses: The Revelation and the Covenant*, 17.

8 1990, in *The Observer* (London).

9 For a closer examination of this, see Chapter Six, "Case One: After the Fall,
Resolving the Pisgah Perplex to Get Justice for Moses."

10 Class notes, "Principles of Literary Symbolism," Victoria College, University
of Toronto, 1973–74.

11 Most of Frye's published work is in this area, but see particularly *Anatomy of Criticism*. Regarding the apocalyptic paradigm, see especially pages 141ff. of the paperback edition (1971), and note that in lectures comprising his portion of *BCM*, when Frye opposes *apocalyptic* to *demonic*, he defines the former as "the ideal, the one that's associated with the garden of Eden, with the Promised Land, with Jerusalem and the temple, with Jesus' spiritual kingdom" (at 41). As I shall discuss, these are all versions of paradise, where positive law becomes unnecessary, or almost so, and justice is perfected. In this sense, they are legal fictions.

12 Class notes, *supra* note 10.

13 Ibid. and Frye, *Anatomy*, 147 and 238.

14 Class notes, *supra*, note 10.

15 Frye, *Anatomy*, 131-239.

16 Ibid., 205.

17 Graves, *The White Goddess*, 159. Graves writes, "The story of Moses in *The Pentateuch* was the familiar one of Canopic Hercules – the god who was cradled in an ark on the river Nile, performed great feats, died mysteriously on a mountain-top, and afterwards became a hero and a judge."

18 See, e.g., Marshall, "*Paradise Lost: Felix Culpa* and the Problem of Structure," 15–20; Madsen, "The Fortunate Fall in *Paradise Lost*," 1185–7.

19 Frye, *Anatomy*, 205.

20 Daiches, *Moses: Man in the Wilderness*, 207, 232. The Mosaic tradition, Daiches claims, rejects the notion of vicarious atonement, the blood of the lamb. But this is true only among the Israelites themselves (as with Abraham and the near-sacrifice of his son Isaac), insofar as it ignores the sacrifice of the Egyptian first born, and the blood sacrifice of animals and other innocents in Jewish tradition. It also overlooks Moses's own gloss on his tragic fate in Deuteronomy, that when he beseeched Yahweh to "let me go over ... and see the good land that is beyond the Jordan," God told him the subject was closed. "Yahweh was angry with me for your sakes, saying, 'Thou shalt not go thither.'" At least in the moment, the poor fellow seems more human than heroic, to feel scapegoated in "the rigid satisfaction" of death for death.

(Defending his view on vicarious atonement as "not Mosaic at all," Daiches says that the suggestion of vicarious atonement here amounts to an incipient move toward the Christian view of a messiah dying for the sins of his people. Then, too, Moses could simply be using "for your sakes" in the broad sense of, "You angered me, and in turn my impatience angered Yahweh.")

As tragedy (and as I adumbrate later in this book), the Moses story is austere, difficult to reconcile with human (and humane) notions of justice. It favours communal fate over individualism and individualized mercy when so much in the Christian myth depends on Christ the individual and individualized salvation and forgiveness. A compelling modern, comforting (and perhaps feminist) view (which Daiches quotes, at 254, from Lawrence Langner, in his play *Moses*, 1924) has it that Moses "the primitive moralist sees law as opposed to beauty," while his sister Miriam might take the enlightened view that "worship of the golden calf" is preferable to "killing animals in sacrifice." This has an aesthetic appeal, particularly in an age that celebrates individual expression and animal rights, but Buber's contrary view is more rational from the legal, communal view. The Pentateuch, after all, is famously (or notoriously) legalistic; its aesthetic requires the sort of archaeology we are attempting here. In forbidding images of deity, Moses did not "fight against art" but sought to "subject the revolt of fantasy against faith." The human tendency is to try to concretize things, to make them more readily understandable. But the rule of law permeates everything, like smoke from the sacrificial lamb, seamlessly. As God's highest priest, Moses had to resist "that natural and powerful tendency which can be found in all religions ... to reduce the divinity to a form available for and identifiable by the senses" – to make the sublime superior common currency, you might say in the law-and-literature context, malleable personally, and therefore vulgar.

21 This scheme suggested itself to me following a discussion with Anna Larsson, and other Scandinavian law students in my law-and-literature course, about the comparative law equivalency of our "reasonable person." The *pater familias* is of course a development from Roman law. Regarding that figure as a standard of reasonable behaviour, see, e.g., Widmer, *Unification of Tort Law: Fault*, 348. We will see that some literary figures negotiate or mediate between some of the levels. You could say, for example, that, during the course of *The Mosquito Coast,* Allie Fox inhabits or attempts to inhabit each of the four.

22 See, e.g., Frye, *BCM*, 100.

23 At 108.

24 I explore this distinction more fully in the section on Marcel Aymé, in Chapter Six, *infra*.

25 Buber, *Moses: The Revelation and the Covenant*, 124.

26 See *infra* at 28–31.

27 See *infra* at 108–14.

28 See *infra* at 90–7.

29 This comports with Frye's notion of the "action of comedy." See *infra*, notes 36, 64.

30 Austin, *Lectures on Jurisprudence*, 1832.

31 Although the Hebrew Bible pre-dates literature we conventionally call classical, the latter embodies polytheistic conceptions that pre-date them both,
and of course early Christianity co-existed with persisting polytheism. That
is why I place classical literature first on the chart.

32 Whether Christianity is in fact more merciful in application is a bitterly
fraught topic, of course, often challenged in the breach, and nothing to do
with this analysis beyond the following. Some (more knowledgeable in
theology and mythology than this author) argue that it backslides not just
to a sort of polytheism (with its Trinity, its Virgin Mother cults, etc.), but to
a "paganistic" tolerance for human sacrifice. That is, it gives the highest legal
encouragement to human martyrdom. This view compares the Christ
narrative, particularly as depicted in Christian litugy and ritual recreations –
"he died for our sins," "he is the Lamb," "this is the body, this the blood of
our Lord" (the Eucharist) – to that of Abraham and his willingness to
sacrifice his first-born son, where God asserts his absolute authority while
turning His back on human sacrifice. For more detail on this, see section
III, *infra*, "The mock execution of Isaac." I should note here, as well, that in
BCM, 215, Frye remarks, "nowhere in the New Testament is the legalism
which it condemns identified with Judaism." That is, the legalism is just
one interpretation by some theologians.

In an effort to explicate the several names of God in the Hebrew Bible,
Jewish tradition distinguishes among several of his "faces." *Adonay* is more
or less a personalized God; *Elohim* is Creator and source of Law. As one
translation of the Midrash has it, regarding this latter divine aspect, "Thus
spake the Holy One ... 'If I create the world by Mercy alone, sin will
abound; if by Justice alone, how can the world endure? I will create it by
both.'" If by "Justice" the Midrash signifies (more precisely) "Law," the
dichotomy makes sense. For isn't justice, even here, the law tempered with
mercy?

33 In the chassidic tradition of Torah, the feminine reasserts itself, as in the
belief that the glow of Moses' face when he comes down from Sinai with
the Law results from a sort of intercourse – as with the Muse – with the
Shekhina, God's female aspect.

34 See *infra*, regarding Astraea/Virgo, who perhaps has links with the cult of
the Virgin Mary.

35 See Frye, *Anatomy, passim* and particularly 40–9.

36 Ibid., 181: "The action of comedy, like the action of the Christian Bible,
moves from law to liberty. In the law there is an element of ritual bondage
which is abolished, and an element of habit or convention which is ful-

filled. The intolerable qualities of the *senex* [angry old man, in full *senex iratus*] represent the former..." Again, we think of Jesus, who says in the Sermon on the Mount that he does not destroy the Mosaic law, but fulfills it.

37 Richard Lattimore, "Introduction," in Aeschylus, *Oresteia*, (Chicago: University of Chicago Press 1953), 30.

38 See *supra*, note 33.

39 Bulfinch, *Bulfinch's Mythology of Greece and Rome with Eastern and Norse Legends*, 26 n1.

40 Ibid., 25–6.

41 Hanley, *Thoor Ballylee*, 10.

42 From a lecture on literary symbolism, October 30, 1973, at Victoria College, University of Toronto.

43 Yeats, *The Tower*, IV, l. 7.

44 Jeffares, *The Circus Animals*, 46.

45 See, *e.g.*, Graves, *The White Goddess, passim*.

46 Yeats, *The Tower*, II., 103–04.

47 With its "quiet revolution" – a movement away from theocratic Catholicism towards a secular order – Quebec has experienced this nostalgia on the local level, while in some cases nostalgically seeking a separatist counter-(r)evolution. This sort of nationalism is of course markedly utopian, envisioning a restoration of some paradisal order, even if through positive law.

48 Frye, *Anatomy*, 220.

49 See "Justice by Golem" in Chapter Six, *infra*.

50 As Frye notes, "In the third book of *Paradise Lost*, Milton represents God as arguing that he made man 'Sufficient to have stood though free to fall.' God knew that Adam would fall, but did not compel him to do so, and on that basis he disclaims legal responsibility. This argument is so bad that Milton ... did well to ascribe it to God ... Hence the passage is another example of existential projection: the real basis of the relation of Milton's God to Adam is the relation of the tragic poet to his hero." Frye, *Anatomy*, 211. I of course argue here that you can say the same thing about God and Moses.

51 All the more so given that today's young reader can have a starkly different perception of it. In teaching the story during 2010, in a law-and-literature seminar composed of upper-year law students aged about twenty-three to thirty, I jocularly asked, "Okay, who cried?" The students looked at me quizzically until a young woman finally said, "I found the divorce liberating." "Liberating," I fairly shrieked (twice, I fear), but this seemed to be the general consensus – no climax, as it were, all denouement. Mind you, in the years after Updike wrote the story, no-fault and other reforms have helped normalize if not institutionalize divorce, such that I imagine several of my

students came from "broken homes." Realizing this impelled me to gloss our discussion with a short history of divorce in Anglo-Canadian society, noting particularly how, "not all that long ago, you needed an act of Parliament to get one." Then I realized that, in a sense, this made their point. Then, too, the story is told from the viewpoint of a middle-aged man in crisis. Perhaps if we had his wife's point of view, we would find at least a measure of liberation.

52 See *infra*, Chapter Three, section IV.

53 Aristotle, *Poetics*, V, XVII, XVIII.

54 As we become more conscious of such stereotypes, they naturally change.

55 Ozick, *The Puttermesser Papers*, 54.

56 Child, ed., *The English and Scottish Popular Ballads*, verses 427–9.

57 See *infra*, at 91.

58 Robert Cover and Richard Weisberg both note that, as chief judge of the Massachusetts Supreme Court, Melville's father-in-law "tried some difficult cases," as Weisberg puts it, "under the conscience-jarring provisions of the *Fugitive Slave Act* ... Shaw may have been the model for Captain Vere, another adjudicator who seems forced to apply a given statute to morally innocent defendants." *The Failure of the Word*, 134.

59 This is confirmed in I Kings 16:34. See also Frye, *The Great Code*, 183–5.

60 The Isaac narrative is also incomplete as a prototype insofar as the temptation is put at the feet of the father – to disobey Yahweh's command – whereas with Moses and Christ the temptation to disobedience is the sons'.

61 At 261.

62 Comment to a law student as recorded by him in *Obiter Dicta*, the student newspaper at Osgoode Hall Law School, 1994.

63 Lubet, "Reconstructing Atticus Finch," 1344.

64 See Frye, *Anatomy*, 166.

65 Lévi-Strauss, *Structural Anthropology*, vol. I, 172 ff. Lévi-Strauss says the facts of the story were collected by "an admirable field-worker, M.C. Stevenson" in *The Zuni Indians, Twenty-third Annual Report of the Bureau of American Ethology*, 1905.

66 I use the words of the Canadian constitution here as perhaps more directly apt than the American "life, liberty, and the pursuit of happiness," although the point applies in the latter case, as well.

67 The introductory essay on Byron in the *Norton Anthology of English Literature*, Eighth ed., 2006, vol. II at 703, subheaded "The Satanic and Byronic Hero," might substantially describe Lurie as much as it does mad, bad, dangerous-to-know George Gordon: "He harbors an inner demon, a torturing memory of an enormous though nameless guilt, which drives him restlessly

toward an inevitable doom. He lives according to a simple and rigid code of his own ... He is absolutely self-reliant, inflexibly pursuing his own ends against any opposition, human or superhuman ...".

68 See, e.g., Coetzee, *The Lives of Animals*.

69 At 205.

CHAPTER THREE

1 *Donoghue v. Stevenson*, [1932] A.C. 562 (H.L.) at 599.

2 See for example Ward, *Law and Literature*, 5.

3 *The Norton Anthology of English Literature*, vol. II, 154.

4 *Areopagitica, A speech of Mr. John Milton for the liberty of unlicensed printing to the Parliament of England* (1644).

5 Milton, *Paradise Lost*, III, 106–16. This, of course, is the argument Frye finds patently unworthy of the Supreme Being. (See note 50 to Chapter Two.)

6 [1973] Q.B. 100.

7 J.C. Smith and Brian Hogan, *Criminal Law*, Butterworths, 1983 (5th ed.), 558, quoting Odgers, [1927A] 30 C.L.J. 196.

8 See, for example, Doniger, *The Bedtrick*. Doniger credits the first usage to William Lawrence, in *Shakespeare's Problem Comedies* (New York: Frederick Ungar, 1960; originally published in 1931).

9 In the golem's champion-of-justice iteration, its truth counters the anti-semitic lie of the blood libel. See *infra* at 185–98.

10 For more detail on the golem narrative, see Chapter Six: "Case Two: Justice by Golem: Playing God with the Rule of Law."

11 Ozick seems to confirm this interpretation in correspondence with me: "Marlowe's Doctor Faustus said it first (unless Job and Koheleth implied it even earlier): 'Hell hath no limits, nor is circumscrib'd one self place; *for where we are is hell*, and where hell is, there must we ever be.' Perhaps the operative phrase here may, more applicably, be altered to '*Who* we are is hell.' As Popeye is wont to declare (and also God, as has been frequently noted), 'I yam wot I yam,' and since all us higher mammals is wot we yam too, this may be why no purported trip to Pardes will allow us escape from Self. All of life is an Appointment in Samarra, no? – since we carry Samarra in our DNA? Puttermesser's dreams dissolve, just like ours; otherwise we would never wake to the morning's truth. You remember the Chinese philosopher's question: 'Am I a man dreaming I am a butterfly, or am I a butterfly dreaming I am a man?'" The boldface is Ozick's.

12 In Chapter Six, we will discuss another sort of magical realism, common in the works of Marcel Aymé, which alters existing laws or legal effect without

seeking any wider change. Unlike the magic used by champions (as with the golem), it does not assume a breakdown in a rule of law, and it is not necessarily revolutionary. While the champion model posits a community benefit of the magic, this other variety focusses on individual advantage or pleasure. It breaks laws roguishly, more or less, and sometimes maliciously. Their respective narratives view both varieties of magic as dangerous, with humans courting risk by flirting with godliness.

13 "Three days and nights she did sit by him, / And her poor heart was filled with woe. / 'Til cruel hunger crept upon her, / And home she was obliged to go." http://www.broadside.org/music/lyrics/bruton.html, last accessed May 10, 2011. The ballad is also known as "The Bramble Briar" and "The Constant Farmer's Son." The latter emphasizes the classism at play, as the girl is a Londoner infatuated with a farmer. See Mackenzie, *Ballads and Sea Songs from Nova Scotia*.

14 See Blackstone, *Chronicles of the Laws of England*, III, 337 ff.

15 Frye, *Anatomy*, 222.

16 In *Piers Plowman*, circa 1377, Sloth admits that he cannot recite the *paternoster* very well, but he knows the "rymes of Robyn Hood and Randolf erle of Chestre." (The fact that a deadly sin prefers outlawry to the Law suggests Robin's popular appeal.) Scholars have taken the latter to be Rannulf, who was Earl of Chester from 1181 to 1232. See Child, *The English and Scottish Popular Ballads*, vol. III, 40.

17 Frye, *Anatomy*, 156–7.

18 Rembar, *The Law of the Land: The Evolution of Our Legal System*, Simon and Schuster, 98.

19 Note that the Cain narrative is but one indication that Yahweh can be merciful, and that proponents of the Christian Bible sometimes protest too much to the contrary.

20 Child, *English and Scottish Popular Ballads*, vol. III, 52.

21 I have adapted Lewelyn's translation (see *infra*) from the Law French.

22 Child, *English and Scottish Popular Ballads*, vol. III, 240.

23 Hardin Craig, *Shakespeare: A Historical and Critical Study with Annotated Texts of Twenty-One Plays* (Chicago: Scott Foresman, 1958), at 293.

24 Child, *English and Scottish Popular Ballads*, vol. III, 241–2.

25 Leach, *The Ballad Book*, 425ff.

26 *Child, English and Scottish Popular Ballads*, vol. III, 239.

27 Frye says the Tower of Babel is the demonic counterpart to the body of Christ as the new Temple. See, for example, *The Great Code*, 158.

28 Theroux makes the connection direct, in a moment of black comedy at the novel's end. Seeking (literal) salvation from their father's messianic totalitar-

ianism, his sons come upon a missionary settlement, (ironically) the devil to Fox's industrialized neo-paganism, with all the modern conveniences. Mistaking the boys for "savages" (personifying Fox's "vision"), the missionary preacher offers them Kool-aid and a shower.

29 *Mosquito Coast* is also, of course, a coming-of-age novel. It begins when Charlie is thirteen; by the time he reaches fourteen, he has begun to understand that his father is not omnipotent, omnisicent, and perfect. Ultimately, he becomes "the man" of the family, orchestrating its return to conventional American life. Again, the motif is one of youth and renewal or rebirth, as with the god sacrifice in springtime – a "law" of nature. Here, Allie is sacrificed so that the family might be reborn.

30 Frye, *The Great Code*, 16.

31 Frye, *Anatomy*, 169.

CHAPTER FOUR

1 See, e.g., "V.S. Naipaul, James Kelman nominated for Man Booker International Prize," http://www.telegraph.co.uk/culture/books/bookprizes/5011645/V-S-Naipaul-James-Kelman-nominated-for-Man-Booker-International-Prize.html, March, 2009.

2 It's true that under the "old commandant" the colony in "In the Penal Colony" has gone beyond Kafkaesque, so to speak: the idiosyncracy of the officer and his undue process have become the norm, such that the justice paradigm is turned upside-down, with the underworld or world of psychopathy at the top. Insofar as the story is about how evil destroys itself – eats itself alive – it preserves the paradigm rightside-up.

3 Steiner, "K," reprinted in *Language and Silence*, 121.

4 The version I quote was collected by Andy Irvine and peformed by his band, Planxty, on their album *The Woman I Loved So Well*, Tara Records, 1992.

5 Kennedy, ed., *Folksongs of Britain and Ireland*, 26.

6 The French *sensible* works better here, really, incorporating sensitivity into reasonableness.

7 From W.K. McNeill, *Southern Folk Ballads*, as reproduced at http://mudcat.org/@displaysong.cfm?SongID=4412, accessed Apr. 19, 2011.

8 From *MacEdward Leach and the Songs of Atlantic Canada*, "Songs of Newfoundland," as provided at http://www.mun.ca/folklore/leach/songs/NFLD2/6-06_51.htm, accessed Apr. 19, 2011. More fully fledged, this version perhaps better merits the classification of ballad, where Mudcat wisely labels "Old Judge Duffy" a "comic song."

9 See Rawls, *A Theory of Justice* and *Justice as Fairness*.

10 In the volume *Le Passe-muraille* (Paris: Gallimard edition, 1992), collecting *Le Nain – Derrère chez Martin – Le Passe-muraille – Le Vin de Paris – En arrière*. The translation is mine.

11 In Sayles, *The Anarchists' Convention*, 23ff.

12 See, for example, Frye, *The Educated Imagination*.

13 See, especially, M.B.E. Smith, "Is There a Prima Facie Obligation to Obey the Law?" *Yale Law Journal*, 82:5, 1973.

14 Could it be that Orwell is cocking a Robin Hoodish snook here at Establishment religion?

15 See Blake Morrison's introduction to the Penguin Classics 2000 edition of the novel.

16 Greene, *Ways of Escape*, reprinted in *Fragments of Autobiography*, 210.

CHAPTER FIVE

1 Again, I don't give this word any special significance. I mean it in its usual sense of the study of how language develops, and of its internal relationships.

2 *Bullen v. Ward* (1905), 74 L.J. (K.B.).

3 *Slater v. Evans*, [1916] 2 K.B. 124.

4 It must be said, though, that until lately this discrimination was not seen as malicious, but rather as protective of the "weaker" and child-bearing sex, a point made in *Edwards v. Canada* (see next note).

5 *Edwards v. A.G. of Canada*, [1930] A.C. 124.

6 Stevens, 1955 and 1973 respectively.

7 79 Cal. Rprtr. 359 (1969), and see Blackstone, *Commentaries*, IV, 205.

8 "*dialect:* 1 a form of speech peculiar to a particular region. 2 a subordinate variety of a language with non-standard vocabulary, pronunciation, or grammar." *Canadian Oxford Dictionary*, 1998. Both definitions apply to law. (Consider the law's idiosyncratic pronunciations of *feoffment, sine die, nisi, laches, sub judice*, etc.)

9 *Lewis v. Economical Insurance Group*, [2010] O.J. No. 3158, where the philological strain and selectivity are apparent: "Second, in ordinary parlance, the words 'struck by' or 'hit by' generally connote simply 'coming into contact with,' and do not specifically ascribe movement to either object involved. For example, the *Canadian Oxford Dictionary*, 2nd ed., defines 'strike' as 'subject to an impact' and defines 'hit' as 'strike against, crash into, collide with.' Accordingly, we do not normally differentiate between 'Ms. Lewis was struck by the pole;' 'Ms. Lewis struck her head on a pole;' and, 'the pole struck Ms. Lewis above her right eye.'"

Examples of this linguistic dissonance in other areas of litigation are rife. For a summary of some of the more bemusing I have found, see the end of this chapter.

10 [1995] O.J. No. 491.

11 *Tucci v. Pugliese* (2009), 98 O.R. (3d) 151 (S.C.J.).

12 (1999), 44 O.R. (3d) 252 (S.C.J.).

13 *Re Strum and Cooperators Insurance Assn.* (1974), 2 O.R. (2d) 70.

14 *Lumbermens Mutual Casualty Co. v. Herbison*, [2007] 3 S.C.R. 393, holding that driving and hunting were here distinct. Compare *Ball v. Donais* (1993), Ontario Court of Appeal, file no. C10164 (unreported), where the court seems to maintain the vernacular distinction between driving and sailing. Ball was driving a snowmobile on the Thames River (in London, Ont.), which had frozen. He contended that Donais was doing the same, with his automobile. The two vehicles collided and Ball (the snowmobiler) sued Donais (the car-driver) in negligence. Donais argued that under Ontario's *Highway Traffic Act* Ball's action was out of time. On a pre-trial motion Ball replied, in part, by raising what the court called "a novel constitutional argument," namely (as the court put it an endorsement): "Because the accident took place on the frozen waters of the Thames River, the provisions of the provincial *Highway Traffic Act* cannot apply to the case because the constitutional authority over navigation and shipping rests in [the federal] Parliament. That argument, though amusing, we find to be otherwise without merit."

15 See *Mallais v. D.A. Campbell Amusements Ltd.* (2007), 277 D.L.R. (4th) 210 (Ont. C.A.), which holds they are not, but cites American authority to the contrary.

16 The examples have been heavily collected, of course. For a particularly arch and lawyerly example, see John Lord Campbell, *Shakespeare's Legal Acquirements Considered* (London: John Murray, 1859; reprinted by Kessinger Publishing, 2004).

CHAPTER SIX

1 And so, as we mentioned above, does the Torah-reading in Jewish practice move immediately from the story of Moses's death at the end of his five books directly back to Genesis and the establishment of earthly paradise.

2 Buber, *Moses*, 59.

3 In *BCM*, Frye says the "sacrifice" of Moses is part of a biblical pattern of sacrificing the eldest son (as with Isaac, Christ). The Israelites' forty years in the desert signifies that their first generation is sacrificed so the second might enter the Promised Land. At 117 and following.

4 In June, 2011, the appeal court in my own jurisdiction freed a woman in just such a case, the conviction having been based on the shoddy work of a forensic pathologist (who has proved to be a chronic offender in that regard.)

5 *McQuire v. Western Morning News Co. Ltd.*, [1903] 2 K.B. 205 at 216.

6 [1933] 1 K.B. 205.

7 See Megarry, *Miscellany-at-Law*, 260.

8 "*Fardel v. Potts*: The Reasonable Man," collected in *Uncommon Law*, 3-4.

9 You could say that in modern world any person of principle is in Job's shoes. What should be but isn't "the law," perfect civil, moral, and ethical, behaviour, is often scoffed at (or resisted) as the worldview of the weak, of losers – again, because individual material gain is made superior to the common good, and we revert to the animal in us, as though civilization is unnatural. (Which is why we need law.) Civilization serves individual interests because we need to exploit the community to survive; but it is not itself a life strategy for an animal, including humans. The current economic crisis shows this: the securities industry exploited oblivious investors/mortgagors, against the industry's own long-term self-interest. Still, many in the industry walked away rich and insulated from the crisis, having seen the risk as one calculated to work to their individual advantage.

10 [1976] AC 182.

11 [1980] 2 S.C.R. 120.

12 Ozick, "The Impious Impatience of Job," in *Quarrel and Quandary*, 71-3.

13 Frye, *The Great Code*, 194-5.

14 Suetonius, *The Historie of Twelve Caesars*, 226.

15 Milton distinguishes between them in *Comus*, at 878 ff.:

> And the Songs of Sirens sweet,
> By dead Parthenope's dear tomb,
> And fair Ligea's golden comb,
> Wherewith she sits on diamond rocks
> Sleeking her soft alluring locks ...

Parthenope is sometimes said to be a Siren who drowned herself when Odysseus resisted her advances. In typical mermaid fashion, Ligea holds a comb. (Mirrors are another typical mermaid accessory – Venus' symbol – and sometimes a lyre or other musical instrument.)

16 One critic of this theory remarks, "I have seen many plain women in my time, but never one with so plain a face as a dugong": Maple, *Old Wives Tales*, 131.

17 See, for example, the discussion of Milton's *Comus*, *infra*.

18 Book XII. There is some evidence, apparently, that they were imported into Greece, possibly from Egypt. See, e.g., Douglas, *Siren Land*.

19 This is, of course, the undercurrent of *Comus* and *Paradise Lost*, among other of his works. See, e.g., *Paradise Lost*, XII, 83 ff.

20 Trans. Willa and Edwin Muir, in *The Complete Short Stories*, 430.

21 In the Random House edition (1934), 252–86.

22 Graves, *The White Goddess*, 418–19.

23 Imagine the boon for an advertising agency to discover the Sirensong: "You must buy this, even if it kills you" – which only attests (again) to the visceral power of human weakness, perversity as against "right reason" under natural law.

24 It is perhaps important to distinguish such a muse from the Muses, per se, the latter sometimes being seen as opponents of the Sirens, whom they defeat (and destroy) in their comparative arts. That is, the literature sometimes makes the Sirens the demonic anti-type of the Muses.

25 Graves, *The White Goddess*, 444.

26 Milton's manuscripts give this as "rob'd," possibly suggesting "robed" or a deliberate ambiguity between "robbed" and "robed."

27 Frye, *Anatomy* 220.

28 "*Fardel v. Potts*: The Reasonable Man," collected in *Uncommon Law* (Bibliophile Books, London 1984), at 4.

29 Scholem, "The Idea of the Golem," in *On the Kabbalah and Its Symbolism*, 161.

30 Kaplan (ed.), *Sefer Yetzirah: The Book of Creation*, xxi.

31 Sanhedrin 65b, as quoted in Scholem, note 29 above, 166.

32 Ibid.

33 Genesis II, 7.

34 *Sefer Yetzirah*, 124.

35 Ibid., xxi.

36 See, e.g., Scholem, note 29, 177.

37 Ibid., 184, 188.

38 Ibid., 173n.

39 Jorge-Luis Borges, in *Selected Poems*, Alexander Coleman, ed., trans. Alan S. Trueblood, Penguin, 1999, at 193.

40 See, *e.g.*, Scholem, note 29, 173.

41 Ibid., 176–8.

42 Ibid., 179, quoting *Sefer Gematrioth*.

43 I have adapted this from Scholem, note 29, 159.

44 See, e.g., *A Treasury of Yiddish Stories*, 1973, at 245–6.

45 Later, the police flog a Jewish wine merchant who presents a bill for merchandise supplied at the wedding, but this succeeds the Baal-Shem's decision to strike back by golem.

46 Iliowizi, *In the Pale*, 169–71.

47 Ibid., 70.

48 Curt Leviant has provided a recent translation directly from Hebrew. A credulous few, including Gershon Winkler in his enthusiastic version of the "manuscript" (*The Golem of Prague* (Judaica Press, 1980), have taken it to be the real thing, as created circa 1580.

49 Chabon, *Maps and Legends*.

50 Rosenberg, *The Golem and the Wondrous Deeds of the Maharal of Prague*, 44.

51 *Supra*, page 102.

52 Leviant, at xxii, calls the Bloch "pirated," but it is not exactly a plagiarism. Then again, it is not anywhere an original work, even allowing for its folk elements.

53 See Neugroschel, trans., *The Golem*, 89.

54 Scholem, note 29, 163.

55 Neugroschel (ed.) *The Golem*, 100, 92. A page before Eve claims to be God's name, she is briefly saddened by the commandment not to make graven images, but, flushed with youthful hormones, shrugs the thought away.

56 At 104 Eve tells the golem that Heaven is all pie in the sky, but, putting the golem's hand on her breast, "I truly exist."

57 Ozick told the Puttermesser story in fits and starts over a period of thirty years. I use the word saga because, though the narrative insistently seems to be linked short stories, she says she always envisioned them as a forming a novel (see, e.g., the transcribed interview at http://www.yiddishbookcenter .org/node/359), and they are collected as *The Puttermesser Papers: A Novel*.

58 Frye would see it as an archetypal pattern?

59 Note 29 above, Scholem, 181.

60 In several respects, Chabon seems to have modeled the cousins on the creators of Superman, Jerome Siegel and Joseph Shuster.

61 Mulisch, *The Procedure*, 220.

62 Here I look at stories collected in *Le vin de Paris* ("La Grâce" and "Dermuche"), 1947, and *Le Passe-muraille* (all others), 1943, in which volumes there is a particular concentration of magic realism. Everything I quote here is my own translation from the original texts.

63 At 604 in the Gallimard collection, *Le Nain – Derrère chez Martin – Le Passe-muraille – Le Vin de Paris – En arrière*, Gallimard, 1992.

64 See, for example, Megarry, *Miscellany-at-Law*, 261.

65 Frye, "Crime and Sin in the Bible," 12.

66 Aymé, Gallimard collection (note 64), 617. I have translated *gratuité* as "unconditional," but it perhaps is pertinent that it also means gratuitousness.

67 This story appears in the volume *Le passe-muraille*.
68 Frye, "Crime and Sin in the Bible," 11.
69 Collected in *Le vin du Paris*.
70 Frye, *Anatomy*, 152.

Select Bibliography

Aeschylus. *Oresteia*. Chicago: University of Chicago Press, 1953.

Alighieri, Dante. *Purgatorio*. Translated by Jean and Robert Hollander. New York: Anchor, 2004.

Aristotle. *Poetics*. New York: Penguin, 2003.

Atwood, Margaret. *Alias Grace*. Toronto: McLelland & Stewart, 1996.

– *The Handmaid's Tale*. Toronto: Seal, 1998.

Austin, John. *Lectures on Jurisprudence*. London: J. Murry, 1832.

Aymé, Marcel. *Le confort intellectuel*. Paris: Flammarion, 1949.

– *Le Nain – Derrère chez Martin – Le Passe-muraille – Le Vin de Paris – En arrière*. Paris: Gallimard, 1992.

Ball v. Donais (1993), Ontario Court of Appeal, file no. C10164 (unreported).

Baron, Jane B. "Interdisciplinary Scholarship as Guilty Pleasure: The Case of Law and Literature," in Freeman & Lewis, eds. *Law and Literature*. London: Oxford University Press (1999): 21–45.

– "Law, Literature and the Problems of Interdisciplinarity." *Yale Law Journal* 108 (1999): 1059–85.

Binder, Guyora and Weisberg, Robert. *Literary Criticisms of Law*. Princeton: Princeton University Press, 2000.

Black, Henry Campbell. *Black's Law Dictionary*, fifth ed. Edited by Joseph Nolan and M.J. Conolly. St. Paul: West, 1979.

Blackstone, William. *Commentaries on the Laws of England: A Facsimile of the First Edition of 1765–1769*. Chicago: University of Chicago Press, 1979.

Bloch, Chayim. *Golem: Legends of the Ghetto of Prague*. Whitefish (Montana): Kessinger (undated).

Board of Management of Trim Joint District School v. Kelly, [1914] A.C. 667.

Bourget-Pailleron, Robert. "Quelques Romans de la Saison." *La revue des deux mondes* (Apr. 1, 1938): 686.

Bowers, Maggie Ann. *Magic(al) Realism*. London: Routledge, 2004.

Boyd-White, James. *Heracle's Bow: Essays on the Rhetoric and Poetics of Law*. Madison: University of Wisconsin Press, 1985.

– *The Legal Imagination*. Chicago: University of Chicago Press, 1973, 1985.

Buber, Martin. *Moses: The Revelation and the Covenant*. New York: Harper, 1958.

Bulfinch, Thomas. *Bulfinch's Mythology of Greece and Rome with Eastern and Norse Legends*. New York: Collier, 1962.

Bullen v. Ward (1905), 74 K.B. 916.

Burgess, Anthony. *A Clockwork Orange*. New York: Penguin, 2000.

Calabresi, Guido. "Introductory Letter." *Yale Journal of Law & the Humanities*, vol. 1, no. 1 (1988): vii.

Camus, Albert. *The Fall*. Translated by Justin O'Brien. New York: Vintage, 1991, 1965.

– *The Outsider*. Translated by Joseph Laredo. New York: Penguin, 1982.

Cardozo, Benjamin. *Law and Literature*. New York: Harcourt Brace, 1934.

Caudwell, Sara. *What the Sirens Sang*. New York: Dell, 1990.

Chabon, Michael. *The Amazing Adventures of Kavalier and Klay*. New York: Picador, 2001.

– *Maps and Legends*. San Francisco: McSweeney's, 2008.

Chaucer, Geoffrey. *A Chaucer Reader*. New York: Harcourt, Brace, 1952.

Child, Francis James (ed.). *The English and Scottish Popular Ballads*. New York: Dover Publications, 1965.

Cockroft v. Smith (1705), 11 Mod. 43.

Coetzee, J.M. *Disgrace*. London: Secker & Warburg, 1999.

– *The Lives of Animals*. Princeton: Princeton University Press, 2001.

– *Waiting for the Barbarians*. New York: Penguin, 1981.

Conrad, Joseph. "Heart of Darkness." New York: Modern Library, 1999.

Crane, Gregg. "The Path of Law and Literature." *American Literary History* 9 (1997): 758–74.

Daiches, David. *Moses: Man in the Wilderness*. London: Weidenfeld and Nicolson, 1975.

Daniel, Samuel. *Ulysses and the Siren. The Oxford Book of English Verse*. Oxford: Oxford University Press, 1990.

DeLillo, Don. *White Noise*. New York: Picador, 1986.

De Vries, Peter. *The Blood of the Lamb*. New York: Little Brown, 1961.

Dickens, Charles. *Bleak House*. London: Penguin, 1971.

Doniger, Wendy. *The Bedtrick*. Chicago: University of Chicago Press, 2005.

Donne, John. *The Complete Poetry and Selected Prose*. New York: Modern Library, 2001.

Donoghue v. Stevenson, [1932] A.C. 562 (H.L.).

Dostoevski, Fyodor. *Crime and Punishment*. London: Penguin, 1951.

Douglas, Norman. *Siren Land*. London: Penguin, 1983 (1911).

D.P.P. v. Morgan, [1976] AC 182.

Dreidger, Elmer. *Construction of Statutes*, 2nd ed. Toronto: Butterworths, 1983.

Dunlop, C.R.B. "Literature Studies in Law Schools." *Cardozo Studies in Law and Literature*, vol. 3, no. 1 (Spring/Summer 1991) 63–110.

Dworkin, Ronald. *Law's Empire*. Cambridge: Belknap Press, 1986.

Edwards v. A.G. of Canada, [1930] A.C. 124.

Eliot, T.S. *The Lovesong of J. Alfred Prufrock. The Norton Anthology of English Literature*, vol. II. New York: Norton, 1968 (1962), 1773.

Emerson, Ralph Waldo. *Collected Poems and Translations*. New York: Library of America, 1994.

Empson, William. *Collected Poems*. London: Chatto & Windus, 1955.

– *Milton's God*. San Franciso: New Directions, 1961.

Ex parte Davis (1857), 5 W.R. 522.

Fish, Stanley. *There's No Such Thing as Free Speech and It's a Good Thing Too*. Oxford: Oxford University Press, 1994.

– *Doing What Comes Naturally: Change, Rhetoric, and the Practice of Theory in Literary and Legal Studies*. Oxford: Oxford University Press, 1991.

– *Is There a Text in This Class? The Authority of Interpretive Communities*. Cambridge, Mass.: Harvard University Press, 1980.

Fishery Products International Limited v. Midland Transport Limited (1994), 113 D.L.R. (4th) 651.

Fiss, Owen M. "The Challenge Ahead." *Yale Journal of Law & the Humanities*, vol. 1, no. 1 (1988): viii–xi.

Fluck, Winfried. "Fiction and Justice." *New Literary History* 34 (2003): 19–42.

Forster, E.M. *A Passage to India*. New York: Harcourt Brace, 1952.

Fraser, J.G. *The Golden Bough*. Various editions 1922.

Frazier, Ian. *Coyote v. Acme*. Vancouver: Douglas & McIntyre, 1996.

Freud, Sigmund. *Moses and Monotheism*. New York: Vintage, 1939.

Frye, Northrop. *Anatomy of Critcism*. Princeton: Princeton University Press, 1957.

– (with Jay MacPherson), *Biblical and Classical Myths: The Mythological Framework of Western Culture*. Toronto: University of Toronto Press, 2004.

– "Crime and Sin in the Bible." *Rough Justice*. Edited by Martin L. Friedland. Toronto: University of Toronto Press, 1991.

– *The Educated Imagination*. Toronto: CBC Enterprises, 1986.

– *The Great Code*. New York: Harcourt Brace, 1983.

Gaddis, William. *A Frolic of His Own*. New York: Poseidon, 1994.

Golding, William. *Lord of the Flies.* London: Faber & Faber, 1963.

Goodrich, Peter. "Screening Law." *Law & Literature*, vol. 21, issue 1 (1999): 1–23.

Gordimer, Nadine. *The House Gun.* New York: Farar, Strauss and Giroux, 1998.

Graves, Robert. *The White Goddess.* London: Faber and Faber, 1948.

Greene, Graham. *Brighton Rock.* London: Penguin, 1964.

– *Fragments of Autobiography*, London: Penguin, 1991.

– *Our Man in Havana.* New York: Vintage, 2001 (1958).

Grey, Thomas C. *The Wallace Stevens Case: Law and the Practice of Poetry.* Cambridge: Harvard University Press, 1991.

Grisham, John. *The Rainmaker.* New York: Delta, 2005.

Hanley, Mary. *Thoor Ballylee.* Dublin: Dolmen, 1965.

Herbert, A.P. *Uncommon Law.* London: Bibliophile Books, 1984.

Holmes, Oliver Wendell, Jr. *The Common Law.* Boston: Little Brown, 1881.

Homer. *The Odyssey.* Translated by Robert Fitzgerald. New York: Anchor, 1963.

Homer. *The Odyssey of Homer.* Translated by George Chapman. London: J.R. Smith, 1857.

Howe, Irving, and Greenberg, Eliezer, eds. *A Treasury of Yiddish Stories.* New York: Schocken Books, 1973.

Iliowizi, Henry. *In the Pale: Stories and Legends of the Russian Jews.* New York: Jewish Publication Society of America, 1897.

Jacoby, Susan. *Wild Justice: The Evolution of Revenge.* New York: Harper and Row, 1983.

Jeffares, A. Norman. *The Circus Animals.* New York: Macmillan, 1970.

Jessin v. County of Shasta, 79 Cal. Rprtr. 359 (1969).

Joyce, James. *Ulysses.* New York: Random House, 1934.

Jung, C.G., v. Franz, M.-L. *Man and His Symbols.* New York: Doubleday, 1964.

Kafka, Franz. *The Complete Short Stories.* Translated by Willa and Edwin Muir. New York: Vintage, 2005.

— *The Trial.* Translated by Willa and Edwin Muir. New York: Alfred A. Knopf, 1956.

Kaplan, Aryeh (ed.). *Sefer Yetzirah: The Book of Creation.* San Francisco: Weiser Books, 1997.

Kelman, James. *How Late It Was, How Late.* New York: Vintage, 1998.

Kennedy, Peter (ed.). *Folksongs of Britain and Ireland.* London: Oak, 1975.

King, Jr. Martin Luther. "I've Been to the Mountaintop," www.stanford. edu/group/King/publications/speeches/I%27ve_been_to_the_mountain top.pdf.

Kornstein, Daniel J. *Kill All the Lawyers: Shakespeare's Legal Appeal*. Princeton: Princeton University Press, 1994.

La Bossière, Camille R., "Marcel Aymé and Colin Wilson on the Bourgeois, the Outlaw, and Poetry." *Dalhousie Review* (Spring, 1981): 103–12.

Langbein, John H., Lerner, Renée Lettow, Smith, Bruce P. *History of the Common Law*. New York: Wolters Kluwer-Aspen, 2009.

Lao, Mer. *Sirens: Symbols of Seduction*. Rochester (Vt.): Park Street Press, 1998.

Leach, MacEdward. *The Ballad Book*. New York: Barnes and Company, 1955.

— *MacEdward Leach and the Songs of Atlantic Canada*, "Songs of Newfoundland." Memorial University of Newfoundland Folklore and Language Archive http://www.mun.ca/folklore/leach/songs/NFLD2/6-06_51.htm.

Ledwon, Lenora. *Law and Literature: Text and Theory*. New York: Garland Publishing, 1996, section one (selections of criticism).

Lee, Harper. *To Kill a Mockingbird*. New York: Harper, 2010 (1960).

Lévi-Strauss, Claude. Translated by Claire Jacobson and Brooke Grundfest Schoepf. *Structural Anthropology*. New York: Basic Books, 1963.

Lewis v. Economical Insurance Group, 2010 ONCA 528.

Lubet, Stephen. "Reconstructing Atticus Finch." 97 *Michigan Law Review* (1999): 1344.

Lumbermens Mutual Casualty Co. v. Herbison, [2007] 3 S.C.R. 393.

Mackenzie, W. Roy. *Ballads and Sea Songs from Nova Scotia*. Cambridge: Harvard University Press, 1928.

Madsen, William. "The Fortunate Fall in *Paradise Lost*." *Modern Language Notes* LXXIV (1959): 1185–7.

Malcolm, Janet. *The Journalist and the Murderer*. New York: Vintage, 1990.

Mallais v. D.A. Campbell Amusements Ltd. (2007), 277 D.L.R. (4th) 210 (Ont. C.A.).

Maple, Eric. *Old Wives Tales*. London: Robert Hale, 1981.

Markson, David. *Reader's Block*. Champaign (Ill.): Dalkey Archive, 2010.

Marshall, William H. "*Paradise Lost: Felix Culpa* and the Problem of Structure." *Modern Language Notes* LXXVI (1961): 15.

McNeill, W.K. *Southern Folk Ballads*, Little Rock: August House, 1987.

Megarry, R.A. *Miscellany-at-Law*, London: Stevens, 1955.

– *A Second Miscellany-at-Law*. London: Stevens, 1973.

Melville, Herman. *Billy Budd and Other Tales*. New York: Signet, 1961.

Meyler, Bernadette. "The Myth of Law and Literature." *Legal Ethics* 8 (2005): 318–50.

Meyrink, Gustav. *The Golem*. Translated by E. F. Bleiler. New York: Dover, 1976.

Miller, Jeffrey. *Ardor in the Court: Sex and the Law*. Toronto: ECW Press, 2002.

– *Naked Promises: A Chronicle of Everyday Wheeling and Dealing*. Toronto: Random House Canada, 1991.

– *Where There's Life, There's Lawsuits: Not Altogether Serious Ruminations on Law and Life*. Toronto: ECW Press, 2003.

Milton, John. *Aeropogitica, A speech of Mr. John Milton for the liberty of unlicensed printing to the Parliament of England* (1644).

– *The Complete Poetry*. Edited by John T. Shawcross. New York: Anchor, 1971.

Mortimer, John. *The First Rumpole Omnibus*. London: Penguin, 1983.

Mulisch, Harry. *The Procedure*. New York: Penguin, 1998 (trans. Paul Vincent).

Nash, Ogden, "Kind of an Ode to Duty," *I Wouldn't Have Missed It: Selected Poems of Ogden Nash*. Boston: Little Brown, 1975, 141.

Neugroschel, Joachim, trans. *The Golem*. New York: W.W. Norton and Co., 2006.

Orwell, George. *1984*. London: Penguin, 2008.

Ozick, Cynthia. *The Puttermesser Papers*. New York: Vintage 1998

– *Quarrel and Quandary*. New York: Vintage, 2000.

Patai, Raphael. *The Hebrew Goddess*. Detroit: Wayne State University Press, 1966, 1990.

Petch, Simon. "Law, Literature, and Victorian Studies." *Victorian Literature and Culture* 35 (2007) 361–84.

Plimpton George (ed.). *The Writer's Chapbook*. New York: Penguin Books, 1989.

Posner, Richard A. *Law and Literature*. Cambridge: Harvard University Press, 1988.

Prose, Francine. *The Blue Angel*. New York: Harper, 2000.

Punter, David. "Fictional Representation of the Law in the Eighteenth Century." *Eighteenth-Century Studies* 16 (1982): 47–74.

R. v. Balazsy (1980), 54 C.C.C. (2d) 346.

R. v. Collins, [1973] Q.B. 100.

R. v. Cox (1844), 1 Car. and K., 494, 495.

R. v. Halloway (1823), 1 C & P. 127.

R. v. Lifchus, [1997] 3 S.C.R. 320.

R. v. Pappajohn, [1980] 2 S.C.R. 120.

R. v. Pierce and Goloher (1982), 37 O.R. (2d) 721.

R. v. Walcott (1694), 4 Mod. 395; aff'd (1696), Shaw P.C. 127.

Raffield, Paul and Watt, Gary (eds.). *Shakespeare and the Law*. Oxford: Hart Publishing, 2008.

Rawls, John. *Justice as Fairness: A Restatement*. Cambridge: Belknap/Harvard University Press, 2001.

– *A Theory of Justice*, revised edition. Cambridge: Belknap/Harvard University Press, 1999.

Reich, Charles A. "Towards the Humanistic Study of Law." *Yale Law Journal* 74 (1964): 1402–8.

Reik, Theodor. *Mystery on the Mountain: The Drama of the Sinai Revelation.* New York: Arno Press, 1959.

Re Strum and Cooperators Insurance Assn. (1974), 2 O.R. (2d) 70.

Rembar, Charles. *The End of Obscenity*. New York: Harper Perennial, 1968.

– *The Law of the Land: The Evolution of Our Legal System.* New York: Simon and Schuster, 1980.

Richler, Mordecai. *St. Urbain's Horseman*. New York: Vintage, 1971.

Rilke, Rainer M. *Der Tod Moses* (1915), *Poems 1906–26*. Translated by J.B. Leishman. San Francisco: New Directions, 1957.

Rosen, Lawrence. *Law as Culture: An Invitation*. Princeton: Princeton University Press, 2006.

Rosenberg, Yudl, *The Golem and the Wondrous Deeds of the Maharal of Prague.* Edited and translated by Curt Leviant. New Haven: Yale University Press, 2007.

Roumette, Sylvain. *Nouveau dictionnaire des auteurs*, vol. I. Paris: Robert Laffont, 1994.

Sayles, John. *The Anarchists' Convention*. New York: Harper Perennial, 1992.

Scarry, Elaine. *On Beauty and Being Just*. Princeton: Princeton University Press, 1999.

Scholem, Gershom. *On the Kabbalah and Its Symbolism*. Translated by Ralph Manheim. New York: Schocken Books, 1965.

Sensobaugh v. State, 244 S.W. 379 (C.C.A. Tex., 1922).

– Shakespeare, William. Edited by R.A. Foakes. *King Lear. Arden Shakespeare*, 3d ed. Toronto: Thomson Learning, 1997.

– *Measure for Measure*. Edited by J.W. Lever. *Arden Shakespeare*, 2d ed. Toronto: Cengage Learning, 2008 (1967).

– *The Merchant of Venice*. Edited by John Russell Brown. *Arden Shakespeare*, 2d ed. Toronto: Thomson Learning, 2007.

Shaw, T.E. *The Odyssey*. Oxford: Oxford University Press, 1932.

Slater v. Evans, [1916] 2 K.B. 916.

Smith, J.C., Hogan, Brian. *Criminal Law*, fifth ed. London: Butterworths, 1983.

State v. Bass, 120 S.E.2d (S.C.N.C., 1961).

Steiner, George. *Language and Silence*. New York: Atheneum, 1970.

Stern, Simon. "Law & Literature: Draft Syllabus." Posted on SSRN at *papers.ssrn.com/sol3/papers.cfm?abstract_id=1297690* 2008.

– "Literary Evidence and Legal Aesthetics." Sarat, Austin, et al., *Teaching Law and Literature*. New York: Modern Language Association of America, 2011.

Stone-Peters, Julie. "Law, Literature and the Vanishing Real: On the Future of an Interdisciplinary Illusion," 120.2 PMLA (2005): 442–52.

Suetonius, Gaius. *The Historie of Twelve Caesars* (1606). Translated by Philemon Holland, at 226, as reproduced in Miller, Marion Mills, *The Classics, Greek And Latin; The Most Celebrated Works of Hellenica and Roman Literature, Embracing Poetry, Romance, History, Oratory, Science, And Philosophy*. New York: Parke, 1909.

Talbot v. Gan General Insurance Co., (1999), 44 O.R. (3d) 252 (S.C.J.).

Theroux, Paul. *The Mosquito Coast*. New York: Penguin, 1981.

Tucci v. Pugliese (2009), 98 O.R. (3d) 151 (S.C.J.).

Twain, Mark. *Adventures of Huckleberry Finn*. Edited by Thomas Cooley. New York: Norton, 1998.

Updike, John. *Too Far To Go*. New York: Fawcett, 1979.

U.S. v. Foster, 133 F.3d 704 (1998, USCA ninth circ.).

Victor v. Nebraska, 127 L Ed 2d 583 (1994).

Ward, Ian. *Law and Literature: Possibilities and Perspectives*. Cambridge: Cambridge University Press, 1995.

Weisberg, Richard. *The Failure of the Word: The Protagonist as Lawyer in Modern Fiction*. New Haven: Yale University Press, 1984.

– *Poethics and Other Strategies of Law and Literature*. New York: Columbia University Press, 1992.

West, Robin, *Narrative, Authority, and Law*. Ann Arbor: University of Michigan Press, 1993

– *Caring for Justice*. New York: New York University Press, 1999.

– "Jurisprudence as Narrative: An Aesthetic Analysis of Modern Legal Theory," *NYU Law Review*, vol. 60, no. 2 (May 1985): 145–211.

White, R.S. *Natural Law in Renaissance Literature*. Cambridge: Cambridge University Press, 1996.

Widmer, Pierre. *Unification of Tort Law: Fault*. New York: Wolters Kluwer, 2005.

Wordsworth, William. "Ode to Duty." *The Norton Anthology of English Literature*, vol. II. New York: Norton, 1968 (1962), 154.

Yeats, William Butler. *The Collected Poems*, 2nd ed. London: Macmillan, 1956.

Index